Editor
Mary S. Jones, M.A.

Managing Editor
Karen J. Goldfluss, M.S. Ed.

Cover Artist
Brenda DiAntonis

Art Production Manager
Kevin Barnes

Art Coordinator
Renée Christine Yates

Imaging
James Edward Grace
Ricardo Martinez

Publisher
Mary D. Smith, M.S. Ed.

Author
Sarah Kartchner Clark, M.A.

Teacher Created Resources, Inc.
12621 Western Avenue
Garden Grove, CA 92841
www.teachercreated.com

ISBN: 978-1-4206-3492-1

Reprinted, 2018
Made in U.S.A.

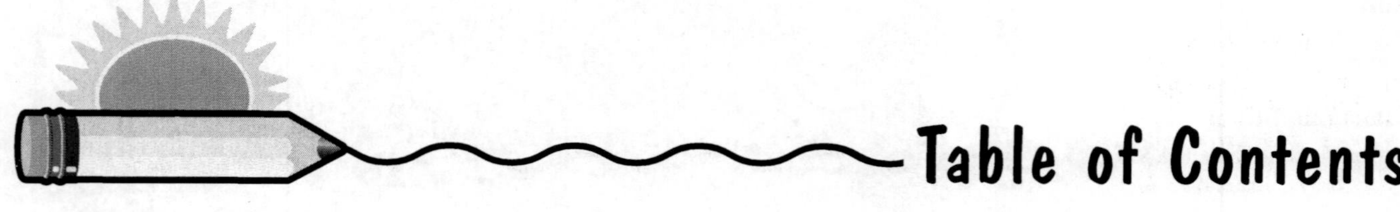

Table of Contents

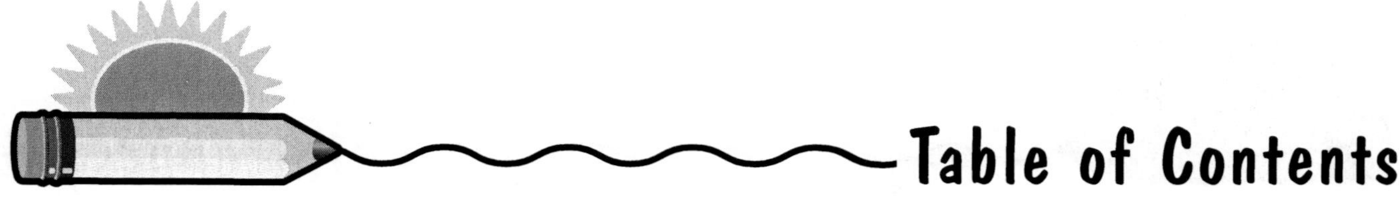
Table of Contents

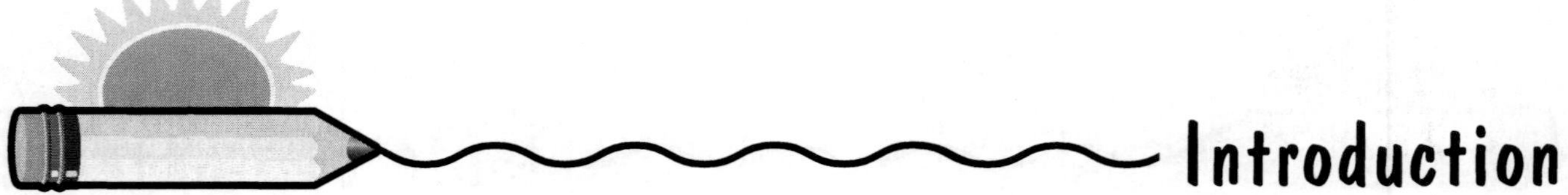

Introduction

The goal of this book is to improve students' reading and comprehension skills. The more experience a child has with reading and comprehending, the better reader and problem solver he or she will be. *Daily Warm-Ups: Reading* contains a variety of passages to be read on a daily basis. Each passage is followed by comprehension questions. The questions that follow the passages are based on Bloom's Taxonomy and allow for higher-level thinking skills. Making this book a part of your daily classroom agenda can help your students' reading and comprehension abilities improve dramatically.

Nonfiction and Fiction

Daily Warm-Ups: Reading is divided into two sections: nonfiction and fiction. It is important for students to be exposed to a variety of reading genres and formats. The nonfiction section is divided into five categories. These categories are animals, biography, American history, science, and current events. By reading these nonfiction passages, your students will be exposed to a variety of nonfiction information, as well as questions to stimulate thinking on these subjects.

The fiction section of the book is also divided into five categories. These categories are fairy tales/folklore, historical fiction, contemporary realistic fiction, mystery/suspense/adventure, and fantasy. Each story is followed by questions to stimulate thinking on the plot, characters, vocabulary, and sequence.

Comprehension Questions

Comprehension is the primary goal of any reading task. Students who comprehend what they read perform better on both tests and in life. The follow-up questions after each passage are written to encourage students to improve in recognizing text structure, visualizing, summarizing, and learning new vocabulary. Each of these skills can be found in scope-and-sequence charts as well as standards for reading comprehension. The different types of questions in *Daily Warm-Ups: Reading* are geared to help students with the following skills:

- Recognize the main idea
- Identify details
- Recall details
- Summarize
- Describe characters and character traits
- Classify and sort into categories
- Compare and contrast
- Make generalizations
- Draw conclusions
- Recognize fact
- Apply information to new situations
- Recognize sequence
- Understand vocabulary

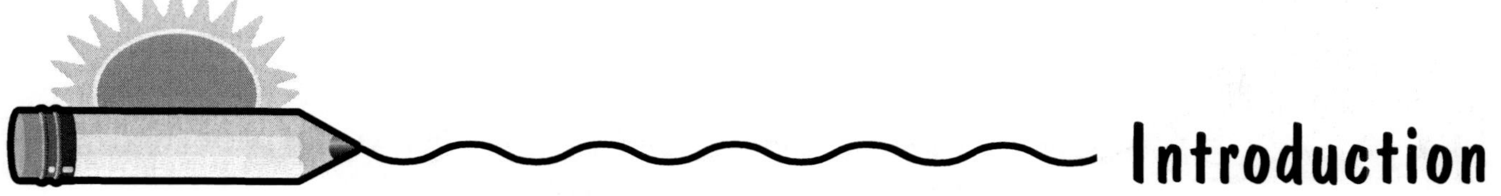

Readability

Each of the reading passages in *Daily Warm-Ups: Reading* varies in difficulty to meet the various reading levels of your students. The passages have been categorized as follows: below grade level, at grade level, and above grade level. (See Leveling Chart on page 175.)

Record Keeping

Use the tracking sheet on page 6 to record which warm-up exercises you have given to your students. Or, distribute copies of the sheet for students to keep their own records. Use the certificate on page 176 as you see fit. You can use the certificate as a reward for students completing a certain number of warm-up exercises. Or, you may choose to distribute the certificates to students who complete the warm-up exercises with 100% accuracy.

How to Make the Most of This Book

Here are some simple tips, which you may have already thought of, already implemented, or may be new to you. They are only suggestions to help you make your students as successful in reading as possible.

- Read through the book ahead of time so you are familiar with each portion. The better you understand how the book works, the easier it will be to answer students' questions.
- Set aside a regular time each day to incorporate *Daily Warm-Ups* into your routine. Once the routine is established, students will look forward to and expect to work on reading strategies at that particular time.
- Make sure that any amount of time spent on *Daily Warm-Ups* is positive and constructive. This should be a time of practicing for success and recognizing it as it is achieved.
- Allot only about 10 minutes to *Daily Warm-Ups.* Too much time will not be useful; too little time will create additional stress.
- Be sure to model the reading and question-answering process at the beginning of the year. Model pre-reading questions, reading the passage, highlighting information that refers to the questions, and eliminating answers that are obviously wrong. Finally, refer back to the text once again, to make sure the answers chosen are the best ones.
- Create and store overheads of each lesson so that you can review student work, concepts, and strategies as quickly as possible.
- Utilize peer tutors who have strong skills for peer interaction to assist with struggling students.
- Offer small group time to students who need extra enrichment or opportunities for questions regarding the text. Small groups will allow many of these students, once they are comfortable with the format, to achieve success independently.
- Adjust the procedures, as you see fit, to meet the needs of all your students.

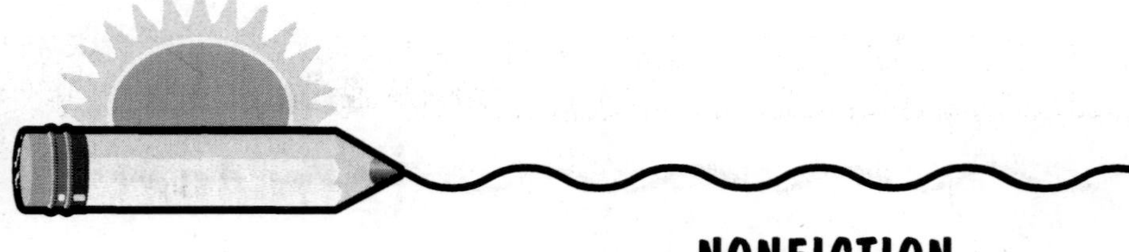

Tracking Sheet

NONFICTION

Animals		Biography		American History		Science		Currents Events	
Page 9		Page 26		Page 42		Page 57		Page 72	
Page 10		Page 27		Page 43		Page 58		Page 73	
Page 11		Page 28		Page 44		Page 59		Page 74	
Page 12		Page 29		Page 45		Page 60		Page 75	
Page 13		Page 30		Page 46		Page 61		Page 76	
Page 14		Page 31		Page 47		Page 62		Page 77	
Page 15		Page 32		Page 48		Page 63		Page 78	
Page 16		Page 33		Page 49		Page 64		Page 79	
Page 17		Page 34		Page 50		Page 65		Page 80	
Page 18		Page 35		Page 51		Page 66		Page 81	
Page 19		Page 36		Page 52		Page 67		Page 82	
Page 20		Page 37		Page 53		Page 68		Page 83	
Page 21		Page 38		Page 54		Page 69		Page 84	
Page 22		Page 39		Page 55		Page 70		Page 85	
Page 23		Page 40		Page 56		Page 71		Page 86	
Page 24									
Page 25									

FICTION

Fairy Tales/ Folklore		Historical Fiction		Contemporary Realistic Fiction		Mystery/Suspense/ Adventure		Fantasy	
Page 89		Page 105		Page 120		Page 136		Page 152	
Page 90		Page 106		Page 121		Page 137		Page 153	
Page 91		Page 107		Page 122		Page 138		Page 154	
Page 92		Page 108		Page 123		Page 139		Page 155	
Page 93		Page 109		Page 124		Page 140		Page 156	
Page 94		Page 110		Page 125		Page 141		Page 157	
Page 95		Page 111		Page 126		Page 142		Page 158	
Page 96		Page 112		Page 127		Page 143		Page 159	
Page 97		Page 118		Page 128		Page 144		Page 160	
Page 98		Page 114		Page 129		Page 145		Page 161	
Page 99		Page 115		Page 130		Page 146		Page 162	
Page 100		Page 116		Page 131		Page 147		Page 163	
Page 101		Page 117		Page 132		Page 148		Page 164	
Page 102		Page 118		Page 133		Page 149		Page 165	
Page 103		Page 119		Page 134		Page 150		Page 166	
Page 104				Page 135		Page 151			

NONFICTION

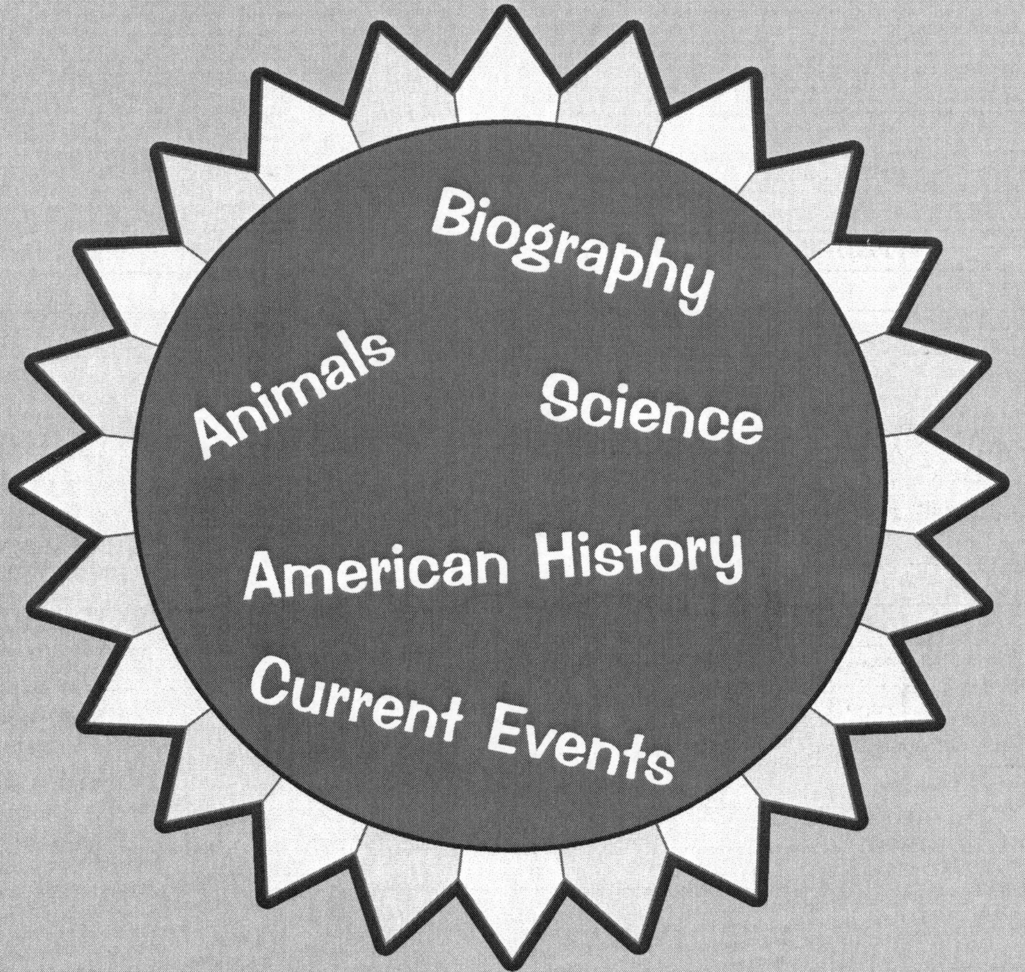
Biography
Animals
Science
American History
Current Events

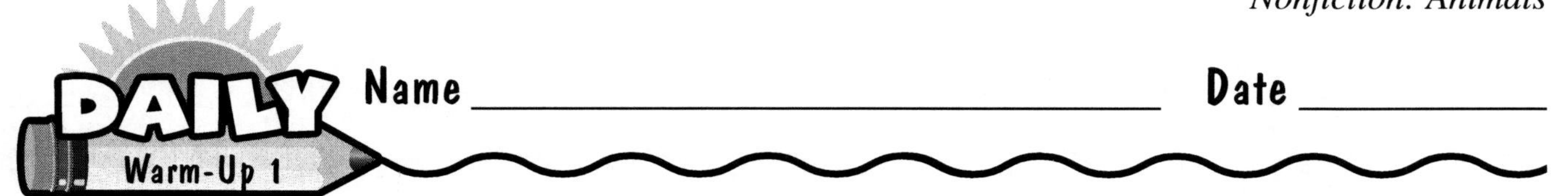

THE OCTOPUS

The word *octopus* means eight feet. That is how the octopus got its name. The octopus is an animal that has eight arms that extend from the center. It eats small crabs and scallops along with fish, turtles, and crustaceans. It is even known to eat other octopuses. The octopus is able to catch its prey with its long arms. It then bites the prey and poisons it with a nerve poison. This poison softens the flesh and the octopus is then able to suck the flesh of the animal out of its shell or outer covering.

The octopus can mostly be found hunting during nighttime. Some people fear the octopus, but there is only one octopus that has been known to have a poison that is strong enough to kill a person. This is the Australian blue-ringed octopus.

Along with its eight arms, the octopus has a head with two eyes on either side. It has very good eyesight. The octopus does not have hearing. Each arm has suction cups in two rows. These suction cups help the octopus hold things. It is true that if the octopus loses an arm it will grow back. The octopus also has blue blood.

The octopus lives in dens and crevices of the ocean floor. This protects the octopus from its main predator, the moray eel. It also provides a place for the octopus to lay its eggs. The octopus can squirt black ink as a defense against its enemies.

STORY QUESTIONS

1. What is one feature that the octopus does **not** have?
   a. good eyesight
   b. excellent hearing
   c. blue blood
   d. the ability to squirt ink
2. This passage is mostly about . . .
   a. the description of and eating practices of the octopus.
   b. how an octopus eats.
   c. anatomy of the octopus.
   d. how the octopus defends itself.
3. What is the meaning of the word *extend* as used in the passage?
   a. ingest
   b. spread
   c. ignore
   d. arrange

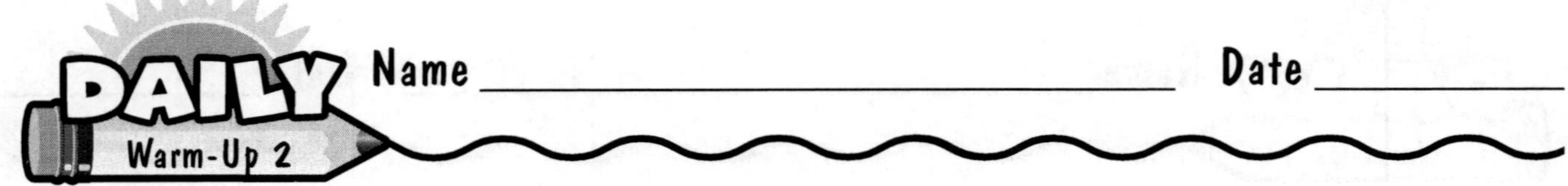

TOUCAN

What do you know about the colorful bird called the toucan? Did you know that this bird comes from South America? It is found living in small flocks in the rain forest. This bird does not fly very well. It manages to get around by hopping from tree to tree. The toucan lives in holes in the tree. It makes a croaking sound.

The toucan has brightly colored feathers that are very light. The toucan has four toes on its feet. Two of the toes face frontward, and two of the toes face backwards. This helps the toucan grasp the branch of the tree easily and hold on. A large bill protrudes from the front of the toucan. The bill is larger than the toucan's head and is a third of the size of the toucan. The average toucan reaches 20 inches in length. The male toucan is a little bit larger than the female, but unlike many other birds, they have very similar coloration.

Living in the rain forest, the toucan eats mostly fruit but it also eats insects, bird eggs, and tree frogs. The fruit is eaten whole and then the toucan will regurgitate the seeds back up. This allows the seeds to continue growing in the rain forest.

The female toucan lays up to four eggs at a time. These eggs are laid in the holes of the trees where the toucans live. The male and female work together to incubate the eggs and care for the chicks.

STORY QUESTIONS

1. A good title for this reading passage would be . . .
   a. "Toucan Paradise."
   b. "The Rain Forest's Bird."
   c. "All You Want to Know About the Toucan."
   d. "Illegal Killing of the Toucan."
2. The author wrote this passage to . . .
   a. justify keeping the toucan in captivity.
   b. inform the reader of how toucans are mistreated.
   c. share general information about the toucan.
   d. raise awareness of the shrinking numbers of toucans in the rain forest.
3. What can you infer about toucans from this passage?
   a. that toucans have many predators
   b. that toucans spend a lot of time in trees
   c. what toucan chicks look like
   d. what the colors of the toucan's feathers are

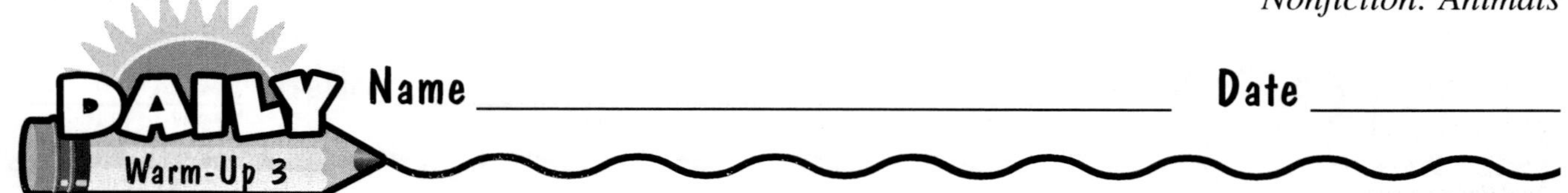

THE OCEAN FOOD CHAIN

Seafood is the term used to describe the food that humans eat, but what does the seafood eat? Just like all animal groups, ocean creatures follow a food chain. The food chain in the ocean begins with tiny floating plants. These plants are known as phytoplankton. These plants float around in the ocean water near the surface. You can't see these plants with the naked eye because they are so small.

Next in the ocean food chain is zooplankton. Zooplankton are very small animals. They are microscopic as well. Small fish, which travel in groups, eat the zooplankton. These fish swim together and eat zooplankton as they go.

Larger fish then eat these smaller fish. The tuna fish is an example of these larger fish. The tuna will eat the fish that swim in schools, or shoals. Humans then eat these larger fish. By eating seafood, you are actually part of the ocean food chain.

Humans aren't the only ones that eat these larger fish. Sharks and sea lions along with other sea creatures eat these fish. The killer whale is the top predator in the sea. It is the top predator because it is not eaten by anything. The baleen whale bypasses the food chain by feeding on the zooplankton directly. The scavengers of the sea also play a role in eating the leftovers and parts of fish and animals left on the sea floor. Crustaceans are examples of scavengers.

STORY QUESTIONS

1. In the last paragraph, what does the word *scavengers* mean?
   a. meat eating
   b. foragers
   c. plant eating
   d. predators
2. What does the third paragraph explain?
   a. how to catch a tuna fish
   b. why fish swim in schools
   c. the names of all of the fish that are at the top of the food chain
   d. how humans are a part of the ocean food chain
3. Based on information in the passage, how do baleen whales bypass the food chain?
   a. They hunt in groups.
   b. They eat the zooplankton directly.
   c. They smaller than most whales
   d. They are the top predator of the ocean.

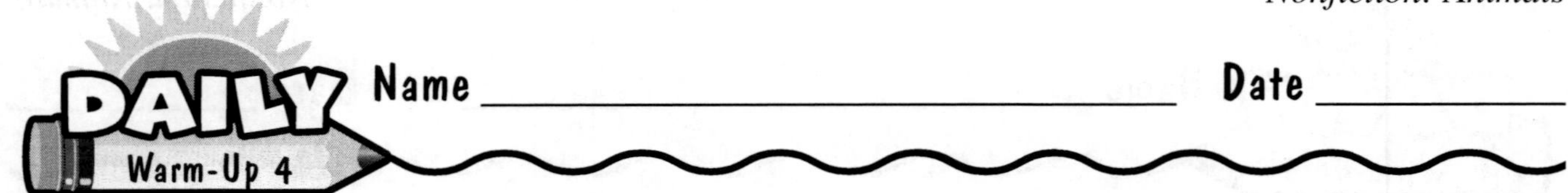

MOUNTAIN ANIMALS

Animals live in many different places. Some live in high places and some live in low places with a variety of terrain. Animals that live high on the mountaintop have learned to adapt in order to survive the harsh weather conditions. Temperatures in the high mountains can get very cold and the terrain is rugged with sparse plants and trees.

Many mountain animals have thick, furry coats and extra layers of fat to keep them warm. During the cold winter months, many of these animals hibernate. Hibernation is when the body temperature drops, the heartbeat slows down, and the body's fat reserves are slowly used up. Due to the low oxygen levels, many of these animals have larger hearts and lungs.

Animals that live in the mountaintops also have very thin blood. This allows them to breathe the thin mountain air and to breathe at very high altitudes.

Examples of high mountain dwellers are the llama and the vicuna found in the mountains of South America. Yaks use their long fur coat to keep them warm in the Himalayan Mountains. Cougars and bobcats can be found in the mountains of North America. Goats are quick-footed animals able to handle the rugged mountainous terrain. Scientists have found over 200 different types of animals that make their homes in the mountains.

STORY QUESTIONS

1. In order for an animal to live in the high mountains it needs . . .
   a. courage.
   b. to be the right size.
   c. curved claws.
   d. to learn to adapt.
2. Why did the author include the first paragraph?
   a. to introduce the common characteristics of mountain dwellers
   b. to clear up misconceptions about animals that live on the mountain
   c. to generate questions about mountain animals
   d. to mention the terrain that exists high on the mountaintops
3. A good way to find the answer to the question just above this one is to . . .
   a. reread the entire passage.
   b. reread the first paragraph and determine the main idea.
   c. guess.
   d. skim the passage and look for clues.

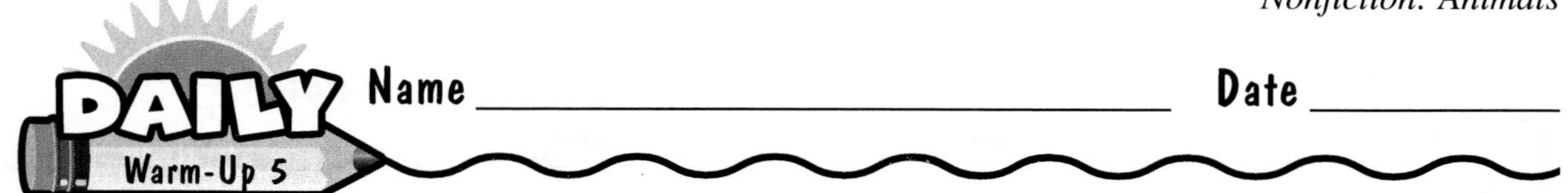

THE FLYING SQUIRREL

Have you ever heard of the squirrel that can fly? Actually the flying squirrel can't really fly, and it doesn't have wings. It actually glides from one place to another. Between the wrists and the legs, flying squirrels have membranes of skin that stretch out giving it the ability to glide pretty far distances. Their long flat tails also help guide where they are gliding or going.

The flying squirrel also has very thick, dense, soft fur. Flying squirrels are brown and white in color. Brown is on the back and the white is underneath.

These squirrels feed on fruit, nuts, insects, as well as the buds on trees. These squirrels store nuts and foods for consumption during the winter. Flying squirrels are nocturnal animals. They have big eyes which help them see at night. They build their homes in trees, deserted buildings, and birdhouses. Flying squirrels are sometimes mistaken for bats.

Flying squirrels are typically found in the forests of Canada. This social animal has strong maternal instincts. The principal enemies of the flying squirrel are the owl, the hawk, and the domestic cat. Flying squirrels seldom go down to the ground. Being on the ground makes them vulnerable to predators. Many times, the flying squirrel has been adopted as a pet. These pets are easy to care for and have cute, intelligent-looking faces. When the squirrel is made a pet at a young age, it is easy for the squirrel to form a strong attraction with humans.

STORY QUESTIONS

1. How does the author feel about the flying squirrel?
   a. The author thinks the flying squirrel has been given a bad name.
   b. The author has been bitten by a flying squirrel.
   c. The author is afraid of flying squirrels.
   d. The author shares a matter of fact passage about the flying squirrel.

2. The second paragraph will instruct the reader on what . . .
   a. to do if they see a flying squirrel.
   b. to do if bitten by a flying squirrel.
   c. a flying squirrel looks like.
   d. a flying squirrel preys on.

3. Where might this information about flying squirrels most likely be found?
   a. on a website about flying squirrels
   b. on a cereal box
   c. in a book about rodents
   d. in a book about nocturnal animals

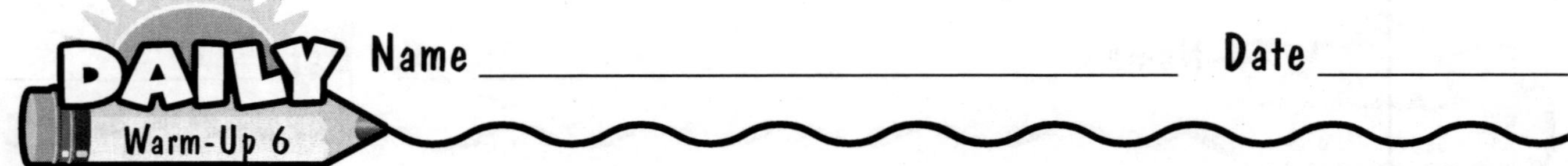

Name ______________________________ Date ____________

TARANTULAS

There are at least 800 species of tarantulas. The most common types of tarantulas are found in the southwestern United States and Mexico. The legs of the tarantula get as long as three to four inches. The body gets to be about two inches long.

Tarantulas are the biggest known spiders. There are some species of tarantulas that can span 10 inches. They weigh from one to three ounces. The tarantula lives from 25 to 40 years. Most tarantulas are black and brown, but some species come in very striking colors, such as bright red and blue. Tarantulas can be trained as pets and are harmless to humans. They do not spin webs but rather hunt for their prey.

The tarantula has eight hairy legs and a hairy body. There is a bald spot on the abdomen. When being pursued by an enemy, the tarantula will rub its legs on the abdomen brushing hairs off in the direction of the enemy. These hairs are irritating to the enemy. The tarantula can make a hissing sound by rubbing its jaws or front legs together. This spider has eight eyes, as well as two large fangs.

The typical diet of a tarantula is insects. It feeds specifically on grasshoppers, crickets, beetles, sow bugs, other spiders, and even small lizards. It is a nocturnal animal that lives in small burrows. The tarantula lines this hole with silk webbing to prevent the dust from getting inside.

STORY QUESTIONS

1. Where would you read to determine the color of the tarantula?
   a. first paragraph
   b. second paragraph
   c. third paragraph
   d. the title

2. What does the tarantula throw at its predators for protection?
   a. claw-like arms
   b. poison
   c. hair
   d. strong scent

3. The author probably wrote this passage to . . .
   a. warn humans of the tarantula.
   b. enlighten scientists to the benefits of the tarantula.
   c. to determine the genealogy of the tarantula.
   d. inform the reader about the tarantula.

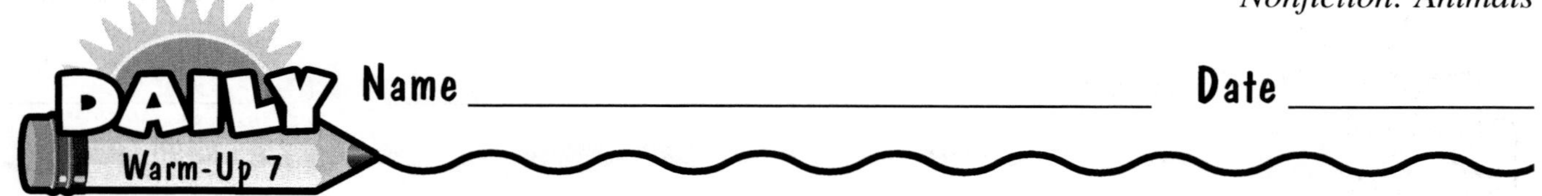

THE PEACOCK

The peacock is known as a beautiful bird that fans its feathers in colorful display. Did you know that the male peacock is the only one with these beautiful feathers? The female peahen has very dull colored feathers such as dull green, brown, and gray. The male is known as the peacock and the female is known as the peahen. Both males and females are commonly called peacocks.

The peacock is omnivorous, which means that it eats both plants and animals. Peacocks typically consume plant parts, seeds, and flower petals. They also eat small reptiles, small snakes, arthropods, and amphibians. The peacock has spurs on its feet that help protect it from predators.

The feathers on the "tail" of the male peacock are iridescent blue-green and green. It is striking to see the full plumage of the male peacock. When not in use, the train of the peacock trails on the ground behind the body. The peacock displays its feathers when it is startled or in danger.

The peacock is native to India and Sri Lanka. It builds a shallow nest made of sticks, leaves, and branches. These nests are often found in the undergrowth. The peahen will lay anywhere from one to four eggs. These beautiful birds do not migrate.

STORY QUESTIONS

1. What can you infer about the peacock after reading this passage?
   a. Peacocks are shy animals.
   b. Peacocks can reach speeds up to 35 mph.
   c. Peacocks keep moving, as they are nomadic animals.
   d. Peacocks are worth looking at when at a zoo.
2. Which of the following can be verified after reading the passage?
   a. The peacock can run very quickly.
   b. The peacock is an extinct animal.
   c. The peacock engages in social activity.
   d. The peacock is an interesting animal and has an interesting history.
3. Peacocks are native to which of the following places?
   a. farms and ranches
   b. zoos and animal parks
   c. India and Sri Lanka
   d. none of the above

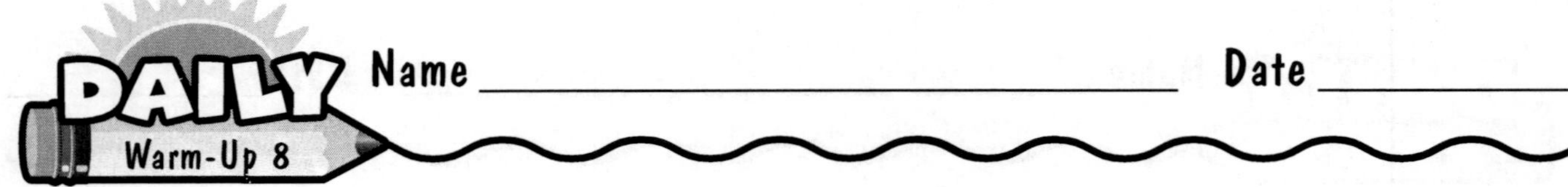

LEOPARDS

Leopards are wild cats that live in many different places throughout the world. Leopards are found living in the rainforests, woodlands, plains, and deserts. Leopards live in China, India, Africa, Siberia, as well as Southeast Asia. Leopards are a threatened species because they are hunted, they do not have enough food, and because their habitats are being destroyed.

An adult leopard can weigh from 65 to almost 180 pounds. They are long and lean wild cats. The female leopard is smaller than the male leopard. The tail of a leopard is long and can get up to three feet long.

When a leopard cub is born, it is the color gray. As the leopard grows, its fur will become darker. Some leopards have dark rosettes on a background. This makes them look black. These are called black leopards. On other leopards, there are dark rosettes but a lighter background.

Leopards are nocturnal animals, which means they typically hunt at night. They are also carnivores, which mean they eat meat. They hunt mammals, reptiles, fish, and birds. The leopard will also eat carrion. These are opportunistic animals that actively hunt their prey.

The leopard is capable of running as fast as 40 miles per hour for brief periods. It is also an adept swimmer. The leopard is very agile and can jump up to 20 feet long horizontally or 10 feet high vertically. The leopard is very powerful and has strong limbs with a heavy torso and thick neck.

STORY QUESTIONS

1. Based on the information in the passage, what can be inferred about the leopard?
   a. The leopard is an extinct animal.
   b. The diet of the leopard is being extinguished.
   c. The leopard is a very strong animal.
   d. The leopard enjoys fighting humans.
2. What is the main idea of the first paragraph?
   a. to introduce the main points of a leopard
   b. to clear up misconceptions about the leopard
   c. to generate questions about the leopard
   d. to identify the habitat of the leopard
3. A good way to find the answer to the question just above this one is to . . .
   a. reread the entire passage.
   b. reread the first paragraph and determine the main idea.
   c. look for the words "leopard" and "habitat."
   d. skim the passage and look for clues.

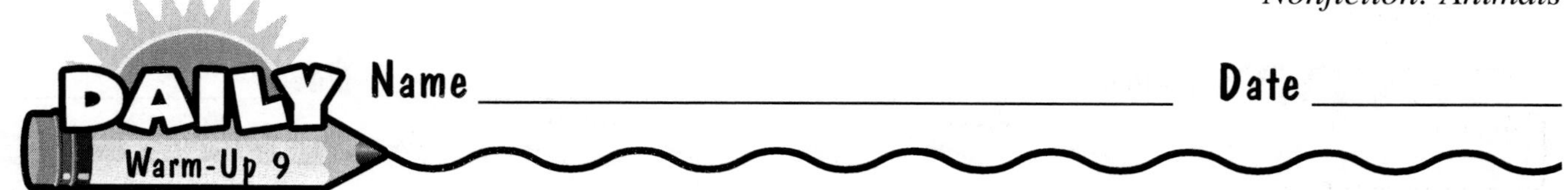

THE ANT COLONY

Have you ever been on a picnic that was interrupted by ants? Ants are insects. The parts of an ant include the head, thorax, abdomen, antennae, and six legs. There are thousands of species of ants, and they are found living all over the world. Did you know that there is a science of studying ants that is called myrmecology?

Ants are social animals. That means they live and work together in groups. Each group of ants is called a colony. Each ant that lives in the colony has a specific role to play. There are four main roles in the ant colony. The first is the queen. The queen ant will mate with male ants and then fly to set up her colony. Once she has arrived at her nesting place, she will lose her wings and spend the rest of her life laying eggs.

The male ants have wings. They use these wings to fly and mate with the queen. Once the male ant has mated, it will die. The worker ants are non-reproducing female ants. These ants collect food and feed members of the colony. They are also responsible for defending the colony. If you see a group of ants, most of these are worker ants.

The last group of ants is called soldier ants. They are also non-reproducing ants that are bigger in size. Their main job is to defend the colony and to raid and attack other colonies.

STORY QUESTIONS

1. Where would you read to find out the role of the worker ant?
   - a. end of the first paragraph
   - b. middle of the second paragraph
   - c. in the third paragraph
   - d. from the title
2. What is the meaning of the word *social* as used in this passage?
   - a. claw-like
   - b. has wings
   - c. communal
   - d. has a strong scent
3. The writer probably wrote this passage to . . .
   - a. warn humans of the ant.
   - b. enlighten farmers to the benefits of the ant.
   - c. to determine the genealogy of the ant.
   - d. inform the reader about the ant colony.
4. Which of these is <u>not</u> a fact about the ant?
   - a. The ant is a meat-eating insect.
   - b. The ant lives in a colony.
   - c. The male ant has wings.
   - d. The ant is on average a small insect.

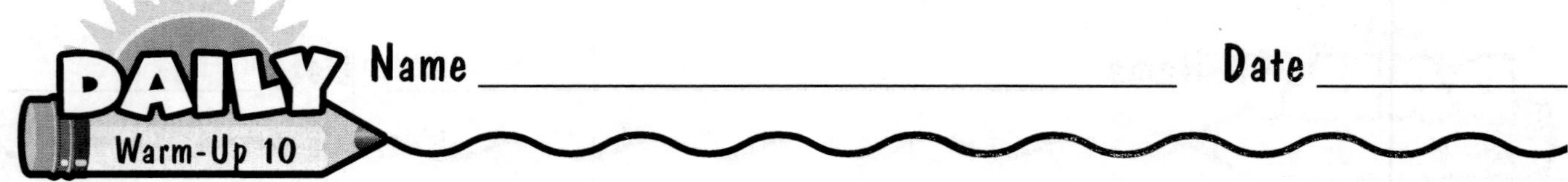

BATS

Did you know that the bat is the only flying mammal? Just like other mammals, bats give birth to live young and nourish them with milk. Another unusual fact about the bat is that it lives most of its life upside down. Most species of bats are nocturnal, which means they are active at night. A misconception about bats is that they suck blood. In actuality, there are only a few bats that feed on animals this way. Most bat species are harmless.

There are at least 900 different species of bats. Bats can be found all over the world except in the two polar regions. During the winter, many bats migrate to warmer areas. Other bats hibernate through the winter.

There are two main types of diets for bats. Some bats send out high-pitched sounds to locate insects and small animals to eat. This technique is known as echolocation. Other bats use their sense of smell to locate and eat fruit and nectar.

The bat's wings are made up of long fingers covered in skin. The bat has a furry body and no tail. It has weak legs and doesn't walk very well. Its main form of movement is flying. Bats "roost" in caves hanging upside down. The roost is generally located in a very high place. This along with the hanging upside down allows the bat to leave quickly at a moment's notice. Unlike a bird, a bat cannot launch itself from the ground.

STORY QUESTIONS

1. What is the purpose of the skin covering the bat's fingers?
   a. to stabilize the bat from falling over
   b. to identify the difference between bat species
   c. to help the bat protect itself
   d. to aid the bat in flying

2. Identify a supporting detail that explains the statement, "The roost is generally located in a very high place."
   a. This technique is known as echolocation.
   b. Unlike a bird, a bat cannot launch itself from the ground.
   c. Other bats use their sense of smell to locate and eat fruit and nectar.
   d. During the winter, many bats migrate to warmer areas.

3. After reading the passage, which question could you answer about the bat?
   a. How does the bat protect itself?
   b. How many different species of bats are there?
   c. How does the bat get its color?
   d. When do bats learn to fly?

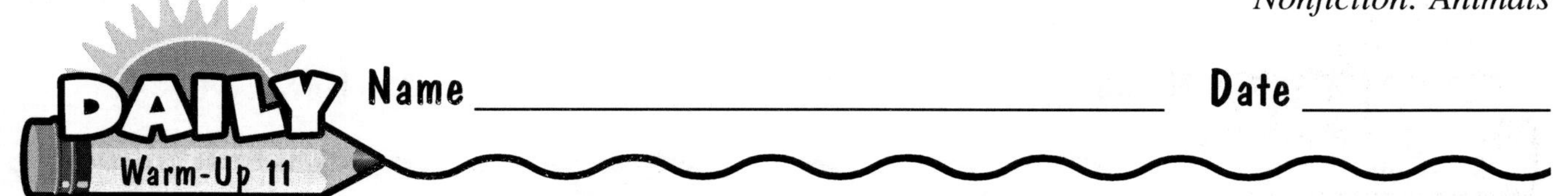

SALAMANDERS

Salamanders are slender amphibians with short legs and long tails. Because of their moist skin, salamanders need to live near water or in moist ground. Most salamanders live in a forest habitat. Different species of salamanders need different amounts of water. Some spend their entire time in the water, while others will visit water intermittently.

Salamanders look a lot like lizards except they do not have scales. Most salamanders are small, but some rare species of salamanders can get up to five feet in length. The salamander has a very long tail. If the salamander loses its tail or leg, it will grow back. As the salamander matures, it will shed its skin.

A salamander begins its life as an egg in the water. The egg hatches to form a larva. The larva breathes with gills and swims. As the larva continues to mature, it will form lungs and begin to breathe air. This allows the salamander to live on the land. The salamander never travels far from where it is born because it is so dependent on the water to survive. The salamander is a predator and eats insects, snails, slugs, small fish, and worms.

Because of their moist skin, salamanders must live near water to avoid drying out. Most salamanders are active in the nighttime. This means they are nocturnal animals. On sunny days they will generally hide under logs or other hiding places to avoid the sun. Salamanders are harmless to people. They do not bite, nor do they have poison.

STORY QUESTIONS

1. What is the meaning of the word *intermittently* as used in this passage?
    a. too much
    b. regularly
    c. sporadically
    d. often
2. According to this passage, salamanders need water because of their . . .
    a. weight.
    b. habitat.
    c. mating instincts.
    d. moist skin.
3. You can conclude that a salamander would probably do well living in . . .
    a. the Sonoran Desert.
    b. the high mountain tops.
    c. dry land with plenty of bushes.
    d. moist forest land.

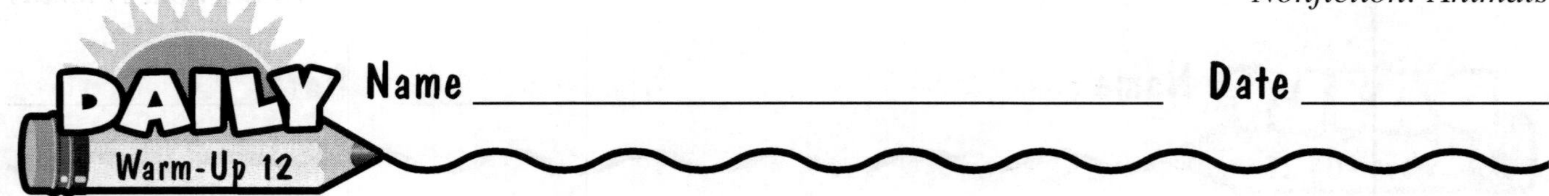

PUFFER FISH

There are over 120 different species of puffer fish. These fish are found typically in tropical and subtropical waters. They are found in the Atlantic, Pacific, and Indian Oceans. Another name for the puffer fish is the blowfish or the globefish. The puffer fish inflates itself with either water or air as a form of protection. When inflated, it is difficult for predators to swallow them. They can puff themselves up because they have elastic skin and no ribs.

The teeth of the puffer fish are so sharp that they could sever a finger. The upper and lower jaws of the puffer fish are fused together. The puffer fish uses its beak-like teeth to prey on coral and hard-shelled animals. They blend in with the coral and like to live on the bottom of the ocean. They feed on mollusks and crustaceans. The puffer fish grows to be about 50 cm long.

The puffer fish is fatally poisonous. This is unusual because humans actually eat puffer fish. In Japan they are considered a delicacy. Even though the poison is removed, some people still die after eating them.

Puffer fish are some of the few fish known to close and blink their eyes. Scientists have observed dolphins using puffer fish as a sort of toy in the wild. The dolphin irritates the puffer fish so that it will inflate. Some species of puffer fish are territorial and aggressive.

STORY QUESTIONS

1. In this passage, the word *territorial* means . . .
   a. to mock.
   b. to imitate.
   c. patronizing.
   d. protective.
2. Which statement is false?
   a. The puffer fish is poisonous.
   b. The puffer fish can blink its eyes.
   c. The puffer fish mimics a blown up ball.
   d. The puffer fish is a good aquarium fish.
3. The puffer fish is also known as the . . .
   a. blow fish.
   b. globe fish.
   c. blowfish or globefish.
   d. ballfish

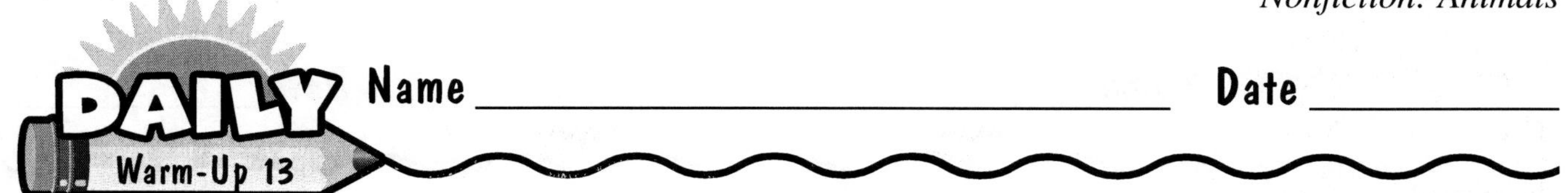

Name ______________________________ Date ____________

THE SILKWORM

The silkworm is actually the larva of a moth. This interesting creature changed the way fabric was used and clothes were made. The silkworm received its name because it literally produces silk. As it spins its cocoon, it weaves a long piece of raw silk. This single continuous piece of silk can be as long as 900 meters. The fibers of this piece of silk are very fine.

The silkworm was discovered in China and Persia over 4,000 ago. Today, over 70 million pounds of silk are produced each year. The silkworm's diet consists of only mulberry leaves. The silkworm is a voracious eater, eating mulberry leaves day and night. This causes the silkworm to grow very quickly.

A silkworm spins a cocoon of silk threads around itself. Before the moth hatches from the cocoon, the cocoon is thrown into boiling water. If the moth comes out of the cocoon on its own, it will break the silk and it will be deemed useless. Each cocoon holds between 500 and 1200 yards of silk. That is a lot of silk from one cocoon!

The story of how silk was discovered tells of a Chinese empress who was drinking tea under a mulberry tree. One of the cocoons fell into the tea. She noticed the uncoiling of the cocoon. This silk thread was soon used in weaving and fabrics. Silk became a huge part of the Chinese economy as a result of this. The Chinese would trade fine silk with the rest of the world. How the silk was produced remained a secret for many years.

STORY QUESTIONS

1. Which of the following statements is an opinion?
   a. The silkworm produces a long strand of silk.
   b. The silk from the silkworm was discovered in China.
   c. A Chinese empress is credited with discovering silk.
   d. It was smart of the Chinese to keep the silk a secret.

2. Which paragraph provides information about when silk was discovered?
   a. first paragraph
   b. second paragraph
   c. third paragraph
   d. fourth paragraph

3. A synonym for the word *literally* in the first paragraph is . . .
   a. factually.
   b. insistently.
   c. encouragingly.
   d. ordinarily.

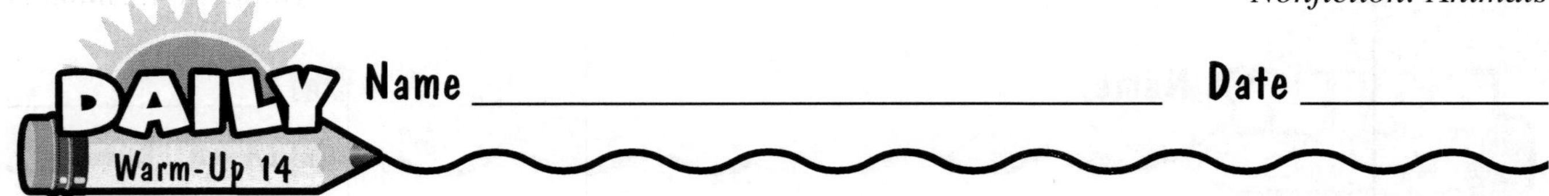

BLACK WIDOWS

One of the most feared spiders is the black widow. It is not only the unusual name but also the fear of being bitten by a black widow. There is good reason for this fear. The black widow spider is the most venomous spider in the United States. The black widow's venom is much more toxic than that of the rattlesnake. The black widow, however, is not usually deadly to adults because it only inserts a small amount of venom.

The black widow gets its name from the fact that after the male and female spiders mate, the female will eat the male spider. The black widow is found mainly in warm areas of the world. This spider is a shiny black color with a red hourglass shape on its abdomen. The black widow hangs upside down in her web and seldom leaves. She feeds on other insects such as flies, cockroaches, and beetles. Once caught in the web, the black widow will make small holes in the insects and suck out all of the juices.

The bite of a black widow spider is not necessarily painful, and it may go unnoticed. But the resulting abdominal pains and pain in the soles of the feet will soon follow. Other signs of being bitten by a black widow are sore muscles, swollen eyelids, and extreme sweating. Those with heart conditions may have to spend time in a hospital. You can see that playing around with this spider is not wise.

STORY QUESTIONS

1. Which statement explains how the black widow eats its prey?
   a. She feeds on other insects such as flies, cockroaches, and beetles.
   b. The black widow spider is the most venomous spider in the United States.
   c. The black widow will stalk its prey.
   d. Once caught in the web, the black widow will make small holes in the insects and suck out all of the juices.

2. Which statement is true?
   a. The black widow eats her babies.
   b. The black widow must be careful once she has mated.
   c. The black widow's poison is more venomous than the rattlesnake.
   d. The black widow is an endangered spider.

3. In this passage, the word *toxic* means . . .
   a. unchanged.
   b. unharmed.
   c. lethal.
   d. unchallenged.

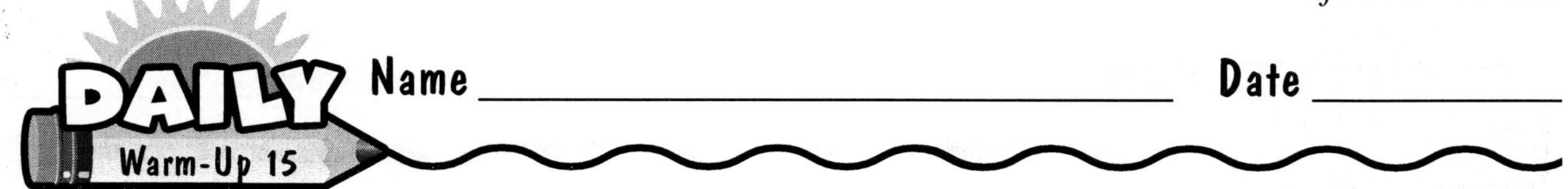

Name ______________________ **Date** __________

THE DOVE

The white dove is a symbol of peace throughout the world. The dove is actually a pigeon. Doves live together in small colonies. Its main predator is the Peregrine falcon. The white dove ranges in size from 12 to 14 inches long. It has white feathers, pink feet and legs, a pink bill, and red eyes. The dove has good eyesight and can see in color.

The dove will build a small shallow nest made of twigs and sticks. The nests are usually found on ledges. They are found along the seaside cliffs or even in the city on buildings and skyscrapers. The dove lays its eggs in the nest and both parents incubate the eggs. Only one to two eggs, called a clutch, are laid at a time.

Like most pigeons, the dove eats mostly seeds but will eat just about anything. The pigeon has only 37 taste buds, while humans have over 9,000. This means that pigeons are not picky eaters. When the dove drinks water, it actually sucks it up, which is unlike any other bird. The pigeon can fly up to 50 mph. Most doves stay pretty close to home and never go farther than 12 miles from their home. However, the dove has very strong wings and can fly much farther if necessary. The dove has a life expectancy of five years in the wild.

STORY QUESTIONS

1. A likely reason people are fascinated with the dove is because it . . .
   a. is a fearless bird.
   b. can get as heavy as 150 pounds.
   c. is called by a variety of names.
   d. has all white feathers.
2. Another word for *predator* is . . .
   a. hunter.
   b. characteristic.
   c. victim.
   d. diet.
3. After reading the passage, which of the following statements could be inferred?
   a. The dove is a peacemaker with other animals.
   b. The dove is a messy eater.
   c. The dove is a great flyer.
   d. The dove prefers the city to the seaside.

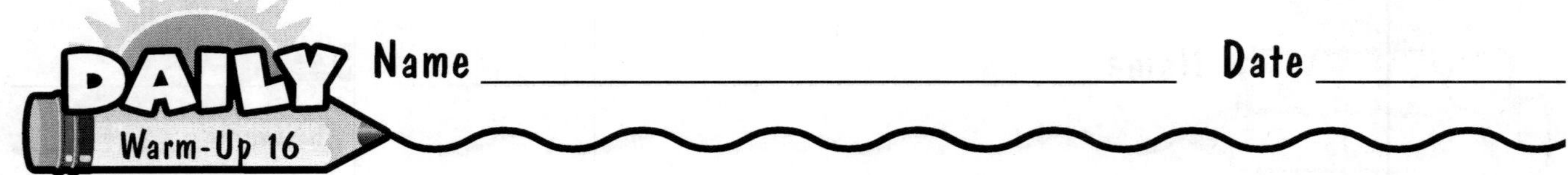

HOLSTEIN COWS

Have you ever seen a black and white cow? It is a Holstein cow. It originated in Europe and was developed specifically in the Netherlands. This cow comes from two breeds. The Batavians and the Friesians, who were migrant European tribes, first bred these cows. Dairy breeders throughout the world began searching for a good milk cow. A Massachusetts dairy breeder purchased one of these cows from a Dutch sailor who was bringing cargo to Boston in 1852. The cow gave such good production of milk that the breeder purchased more cows. Holsteins soon became an established cow breed in the Americas.

The Holstein breed is easily identified with its black and white markings. It is known for its great milk production. This is very important to dairy farmers. These cows are big animals. The Holstein calf weighs about 90 pounds at birth. An adult female Holstein weighs somewhere around 1,500 pounds. It stands as tall as 58 inches from the shoulder.

A normal Holstein is productive for about six years. Once the cow is no longer productive, the cow is typically sent to the slaughterhouse. The Holstein cow can be bred as early as 15 months. The gestation of a Holstein cow is typically nine months. Most Holstein cows are able to deliver their calves with little assistance. Once the baby is born, it is kept in a calf stall where it is bottle-fed. The mother is able to produce gallons of milk.

STORY QUESTIONS

1. What could be another good title for this reading passage?
   a. "The Holstein's Diet"
   b. "The Holstein's Habitat"
   c. "The Life of a Holstein Cow"
   d. "Indigenous Animals of the Netherlands"

2. Which paragraph explains the history of the Holstein?
   a. first paragraph
   b. second paragraph
   c. third paragraph
   d. none of the above

3. Locate the statement below that is a fact from the passage.
   a. The Holstein cow is an adorable animal.
   b. The Holstein cow is a nocturnal animal.
   c. The Holstein cow is productive approximately six years.
   d. The Holstein's life cycle is short.

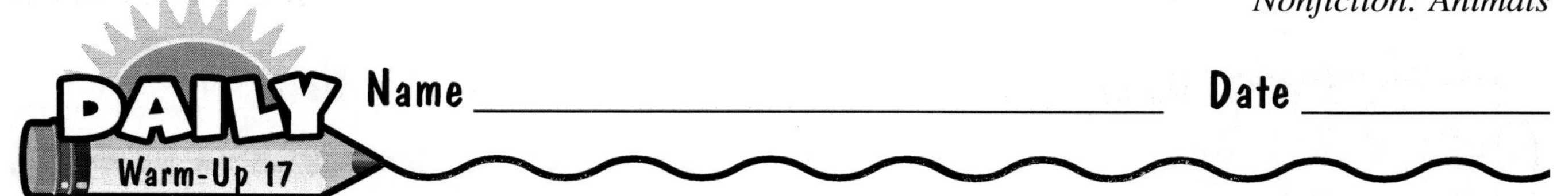

THE SEA HORSE

The sea horse is found living in tropical and temperate waters all around the world. This unusual-looking fish resembles a horse, which is how it got its name. This sea animal is truly a fish. It has a dorsal fin on the lower body and a pectoral fin on its head. It also has gills. This intriguing fish is endangered because it is overly hunted. The sea horse is used as medicine in Asian countries. Over 20 million sea horses are used each year for this purpose. The sea horse can also be kept in an aquarium under the right conditions. But outside of their natural environment, most sea horses are not able to survive.

The sea horse is known for its peculiar looks, but it is also different in how it reproduces. The male sea horse is the one that becomes pregnant. It takes anywhere from ten days to six weeks for the baby sea horses to develop. At least a hundred babies are born at this time but only a few will mature to adulthood. One of the best ways the sea horse is able to survive is by hiding. A sea horse uses camouflage as a form of protection.

There are at least 30 different types of sea horses. They range in size from about an inch to a foot long. There are a variety of colors and patterns found on sea horses. Some are beige and brown while others are bright orange or purple. The sea horse's diet consists of krill, zooplankton, and other tiny animals.

STORY QUESTIONS

1. Why does the author say that sea horses are interesting animals?
   a. They eat krill.
   b. They are related to the sea dragoon.
   c. They have interesting looks and the males reproduce.
   d. They are made up of mostly water.
2. What is the main idea of the second paragraph?
   a. the diet of the sea horse
   b. the enemies of the sea horse
   c. the color of the sea horse
   d. the reproduction of the sea horse
3. What is the meaning of the word *temperate* in the first paragraph?
   a. settled
   b. unconcerned
   c. bothered
   d. moderate

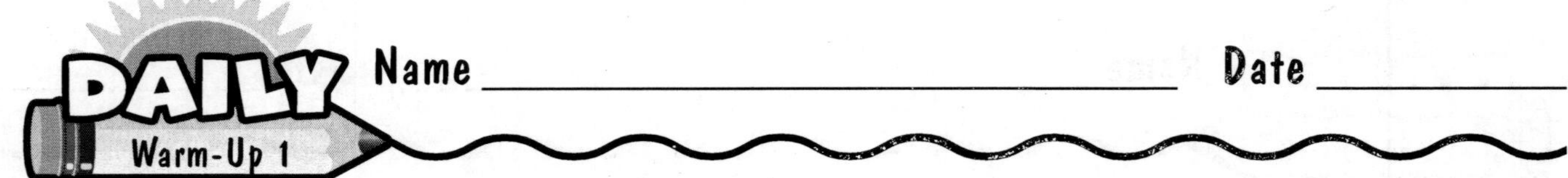

NELSON MANDELA

Nelson Mandela was born in Transkei, South Africa, on July 18, 1918. He was the first member of his family to attend school. A Methodist teacher gave him the name "Nelson" at school. He continued in school and later attended the University of South Africa in Johannesburg. He became a lawyer representing those who would otherwise go without legal assistance.

Mandela was first involved in nonviolent protests but was eventually arrested for treason and placed in prison. He was fighting against the apartheid and the treatment of his people. Apartheid was the practice of keeping the races separated in South Africa. Locked in his cell for years on end, Nelson's spirit was not broken. Nelson Mandela spent 27 years in prison. Most of this time was spent in a tiny cell on Robben Island. His captivity became widely publicized. He was considered a terrorist when he was imprisoned, but as time wore on, it became apparent that he was treated unjustly in his fight to end apartheid.

Once released from prison, Nelson Mandela went on to receive hundreds of awards. He received the Nobel Peace Prize which many felt was also a tribute to the people of South Africa as much as to him. On April 27, 1994, Nelson Mandela was elected President of South Africa. He served until 1999. He continues to work today pushing for peace throughout the world. In South Africa, he is known as Madiba, which is an honorary title. Nelson Mandela continues to inspire many.

STORY QUESTIONS

1. What can you infer about why Nelson was so successful in life?
   a. People felt sorry for him and took pity on him.
   b. He eventually got the vision of his life.
   c. He learned great lessons and was able to overcome obstacles and work hard.
   d. He was able to become president.
2. What is the meaning of the word *treason* as used in the passage?
   a. disloyalty
   b. selfishness
   c. violence
   d. protest
3. Which of the following statements is true after reading the passage?
   a. Nelson Mandela spent his life seeking restitution for his treatment.
   b. Nelson Mandela was a perfect person.
   c. Nelson Mandela went on to inspire millions because of his experiences.
   d. Apartheid no longer exists on the African continent.

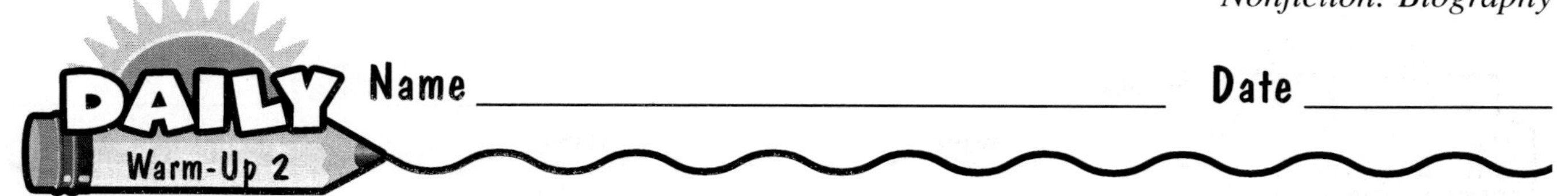

CATHERINE BERTINI

Catherine Bertini is a voice of inspiration to many people who are starving in the world. Catherine was the head of the World Food Programme (WFP) and served to prevent hunger and starvation across the world. She has worked with countries around the world that have starving people. She believes strongly that if you get the food to women, then children and all others will be fed. Her goal is to end hunger.

Catherine wasn't always helping the poor and hungry. At one time she wanted to be a music teacher. She was raised in Cortland, New York. Later her interests turned to government service. She felt that she could make more of a difference helping others this way. And what a difference she has made! She has seen 25 countries go from receiving emergency money to being able to provide food for people in their countries.

Catherine Bertini has very high goals. She works to see that 80% of the food goes to women. She knows that women will feed the people. In the past, most of the food has gone to men. She has another goal, and that is to help girls go to school. She sees to it that there are meals available for the girls at school. This has encouraged families to send their girls to school. Catherine Bertini is making a difference in the lives of millions.

STORY QUESTIONS

1. What position did Catherine Bertini hold?
   a. She was delegate to the U.N.
   b. She was volunteer.
   c. She was Ambassador to Africa.
   d. She was head of the World Food Programme.
2. What can be inferred about Catherine Bertini's beliefs of women and their care of children?
   a. She believes women will feed children and others.
   b. She believes that women are dying.
   c. She believes that men aren't as hungry as women.
   d. She believes that women are stronger.
3. What does the passage say about how Catherine Bertini's encourages girls to attend school?
   a. She teaches them the importance of learning to read.
   b. She makes sure that meals are provided for girls at school.
   c. She sets a good example by sharing her own school experiences.
   d. She gives presentations on the importance of getting an education.

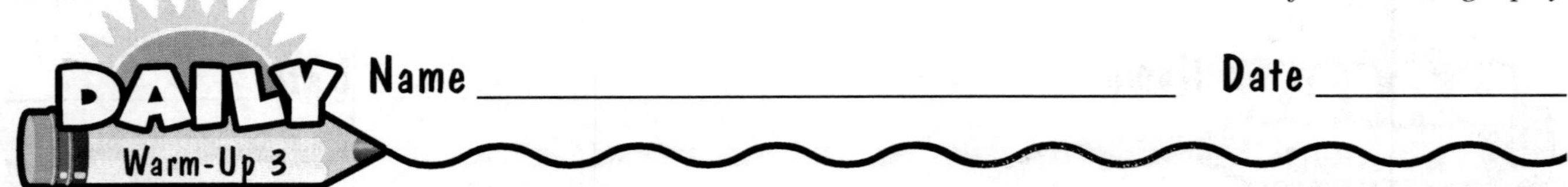

MOTHER TERESA

For most people, the name Mother Teresa symbolizes unconditional love and support. She was a symbol of hope to many dying and sick people around the world. Mother Teresa was born Agnes Gonxha Bojaxhiu in Macedonia. She was the youngest of three children. She went on to become a nun in the Catholic Church. One of her first assignments was work at a mission in India. The mission ran the schools. This is where Agnes took on the name Sister Teresa. A year later, Sister Teresa arrived in Calcutta to teach at St. Mary's High School.

She would eventually move to the slums of Calcutta to live and set up a school. She gave every cent she ever earned to the hungry and poor. She opened an orphanage to house children who had no parents and were dying. She won many prizes for her great work, and each time she would use the money from the prizes to house or feed people. In 1979, she won the Nobel Peace Prize.

Through the years, her name changed to Mother Teresa. She was indeed a mother to many. But life was not easy for her. She would struggle with heart problems and other illnesses, but her efforts to help those in need continued until the day she died. Mother Teresa's examples and words of wisdom continue to inspire millions.

STORY QUESTIONS

1. What Mother Teresa's original name?
   a. Sister Teresa
   b. Agnes Teresa Bojaxhiu
   c. Mother of Calcutta
   d. Agnes Gonxha Bojaxhiu
2. What can be inferred about Mother Teresa since she was the winner of the Nobel Peace Price?
   a. She was a U.S. citizen.
   b. She worked for peace in the world.
   c. She received the highest honor awarded to Catholic nuns.
   d. She would go on to win the Medal of Freedom.
3. After reading the passage, which of the following words could be used to describe Mother Teresa?
   a. studious
   b. notorious
   c. rugged
   d. empathetic

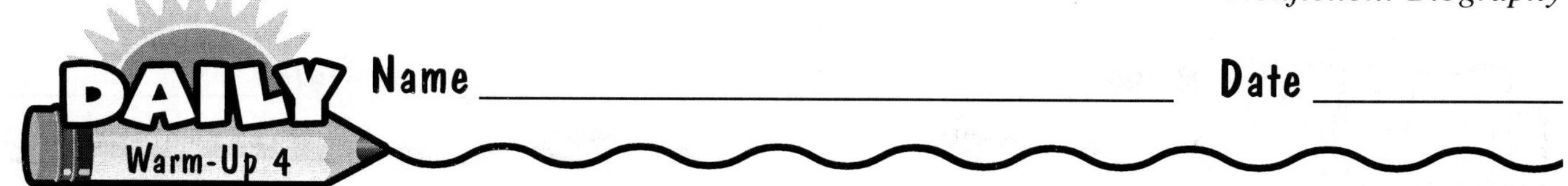

MADAME CURIE

Madame Curie was a great scientist who made many great discoveries. Her story is one of inspiration and determination. She was born Maria Sklodowska on November 7, 1867, in Warsaw, Poland. Poland was in turmoil and her family struggled to make ends meet. Maria's parents were teachers, and they taught their children the importance of school. Maria went on to graduate with honors from high school at 16. She lost her mother and her oldest sister to disease, and Maria struggled with a nervous illness. She went to the countryside to live with cousins.

Maria returned to Warsaw where she and her sister attended a "floating university." The classes were held at night, and they had to avoid being caught by the police. They eventually left for Paris where she received a degree in physics and math. It took many years as she had to put her sister through school and then she put herself through school.

Marie eventually married Pierre Curie. Madame Curie, along with her husband, discovered two radioactive elements. This work laid the foundation for future discoveries in nuclear physics and chemistry. She and her husband received the Nobel Prize for Physics. Madame Curie would go on to receive another Nobel Prize for Chemistry eight years later. Madame Curie's work was credited with making great strides in science.

STORY QUESTIONS

1. Based on the reading passage, what interests did Marie have?
   a. how to win the Nobel prize
   b. how to run an experiment
   c. math and chemistry
   d. physics, chemistry, and math

2. Marie worked so that she could . . .
   a. be trained in how to run experiments.
   b. go to school.
   c. graduate from school.
   d. put her sister through school and then herself.

3. What is the meaning of the word *credited* as used in the last paragraph?
   a. added to
   b. known for
   c. increasing debt
   d. disregarded

4. What is the main idea of paragraph three?
   a. Curie's discoveries and contributions to science
   b. Curie's family background
   c. Curie's love of science
   d. Curie's choice of partner and husband

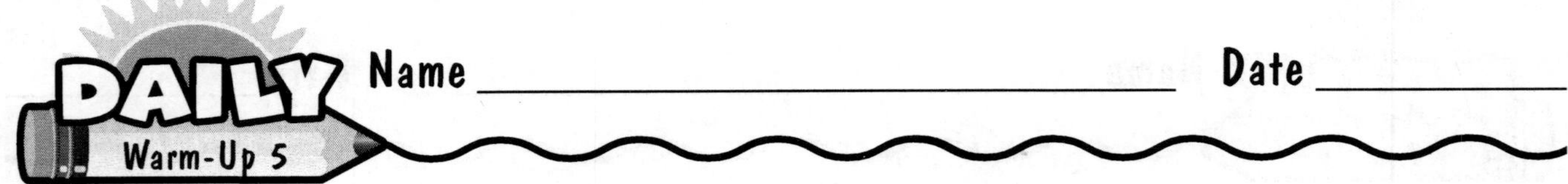

FLORENCE NIGHTINGALE

Florence Nightingale is best remembered as the "lady with the lamp," but her efforts in nursing made a lasting impact. She was the pioneer of nursing as we know it today, and she also set the standard for hospital sanitation methods.

Because of her efforts, hospitals were cleaned and sanitized. This helped prevent endless deaths due to filth and disease. These changes saved many lives.

Florence was born on May 12, 1820, in Florence, Italy. She was named after this city. She was born to a wealthy family. They were surprised when Florence announced that she wanted to become a nurse, turning down many invitations to marry. At this time, nurses were usually working class women. Her desire to be a nurse was reinforced when she met Elizabeth Blackwell, the first female doctor in the United States. They were crusaders for changes in health care.

During the Crimean War, Nightingale volunteered her services to care for the wounded soldiers. Nightingale was appalled with the conditions she found in the army hospital. Diseases such as dysentery, typhus, and cholera were killing more soldiers than the war wounds.

Nightingale worked to change the cleanliness and sanitary conditions at the hospital. One of her greatest achievements was to set up a nursing school and to bring nursing to a level of respect.

STORY QUESTIONS

1. What conclusions can be drawn about Florence's family?
   a. They were religious and dedicated to missionary work.
   b. They were wealthy and lived a life of luxury.
   c. They were hard working and persevering.
   d. They were lazy and undetermined.

2. Which statement explains why Florence's changes in hospital conditions and procedures were so effective?
   a. They were cutting edge procedures on cleanliness.
   b. People had the same experiences that Florence had in the hospitals.
   c. Books were written about Florence Nightingale.
   d. none of the above

3. What is the meaning of the phrase "crusaders for changes in health care" that is used in the passage?
   a. They were connected and couldn't get apart.
   b. They were willing to sacrifice and get sick together.
   c. They didn't like the male doctors so they spent time together.
   d. They paved a new path in the health care profession and for women.

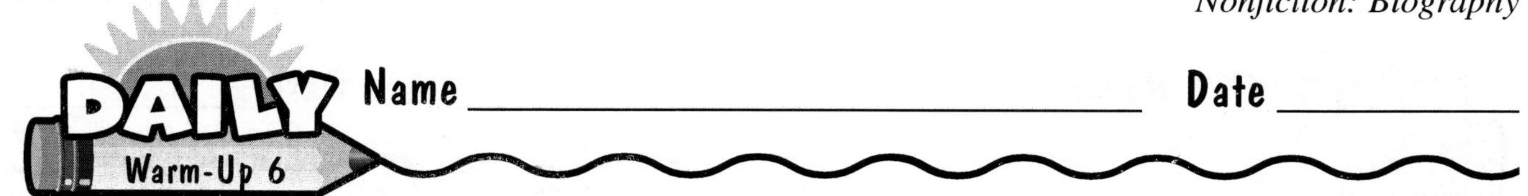

JIM THORPE

Jim Thorpe was one of the greatest athletes to ever live. In fact, Sweden's King Gustav V called Thorpe the "greatest athlete in the world." Thorpe did not have a life of luxury, but he was able to accomplish many things. James Francis Thorpe was born in 1887 in a one-room cabin in Oklahoma. He was a Potawatomi Indian and a descendent of the great Sauk and Fox Chief Black Hawk. He was born a twin, but his brother died at the age of nine.

Jim participated in the 1912 Olympics for the United States, even though he did not become a U.S. citizen until 1919. At the Olympic Games, Jim won the gold in both the pentathlon and the decathlon events. He came back from Sweden with $50,000 worth of trophies.

A month later, the Amateur Athletic Union filed charges against Thorpe. They said he had played summer baseball with the Rocky Mountain Club for money, which discredited his amateur status. Jim had played for a small amount of money, but he was stripped of his medals and trophies. The same year after the Olympics were over, Jim led his team to the national collegiate football championship. From there, Jim went on to play six years with major league baseball.

Jim was the only American to excel as an amateur and professional in three major sports. Jim Thorpe's Olympic medals were returned posthumously on October 13, 1982. After his death, a town in Pennsylvania was renamed "Jim Thorpe" in his memory.

STORY QUESTIONS

1. Why was Jim Thorpe named the greatest athlete of the year?
   a. He was able to win a medal at the Olympics.
   b. He was highly talented in many sports.
   c. He was injured and was still able to run in the Olympic finals.
   d. He was the favorite to win the Heisman trophy.

2. After reading the passage, what can you infer about Thorpe's upbringing?
   a. He was born in very humble circumstances.
   b. Not much is known about Thorpe's upbringing.
   c. He was given the best athletic training.
   d. He was born into an average family.

3. Which statement does <u>not</u> explain Thorpe's experience with the Amateur Athletics Union?
   a. Thorpe was happy to be recognized by the union.
   b. Thorpe was treated strictly by the union.
   c. Thorpe was stripped of his medals by the union.

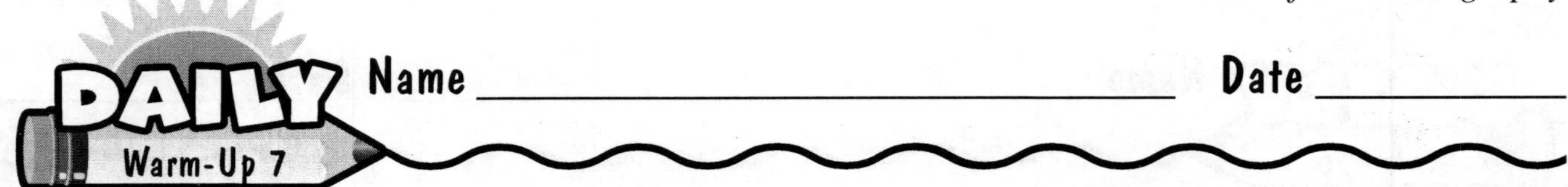

CLARA BARTON

There are many famous faces of the Civil War, but one that stands out as a source of comfort and strength is Clara Barton. The Civil War was a horrible war. There were so many killed or wounded on both sides. To be wounded during the Civil War would often mean death. There were not very many hospitals, doctors, and no trained nurses that could help care for the wounded soldiers. There was also a lack of medical supplies, medicines, and sanitary conditions.

Clara Barton was 40 years old when the Civil War started. She was working in Washington, D.C. She began hearing of all the wounded soldiers and quit her job working in the Patent Office. She traveled to the battlefields to care for the wounded soldiers. She was a hard worker with skill and dedication. She was appointed to be the superintendent of nurses for one of the Union armies. After the Civil War had ended, her work was not finished. She began searching for soldiers that were missing.

Clara's life became a mission to help others. She established the American branch of the Red Cross in 1881. She was the first president and held this position for 22 years. Clara saw to it that the Red Cross was available to help in other wars as well as in disasters throughout the world. Clara's legacy at the Red Cross is still felt. She made a major impact, and her example is one to be followed today.

STORY QUESTIONS

1. Another good title for this reading passage could be . . .
   a. "The Red Cross."
   b. "Honoring a Nurse."
   c. "Clara Barton: The Amazing Nurse."
   d. "Clara Barton and Her Patients."
2. Which of the following is a similarity between Florence Nightingale and Clara Barton?
   a. They both graduated from nursing school together.
   b. They both worked hard to make a difference in caring for others.
   c. They both were reprimanded by male doctors.
   d. They both helped during the Civil War.
3. In the last paragraph, what does the word *impact* mean?
   a. targeted
   b. hit
   c. insight
   d. influence

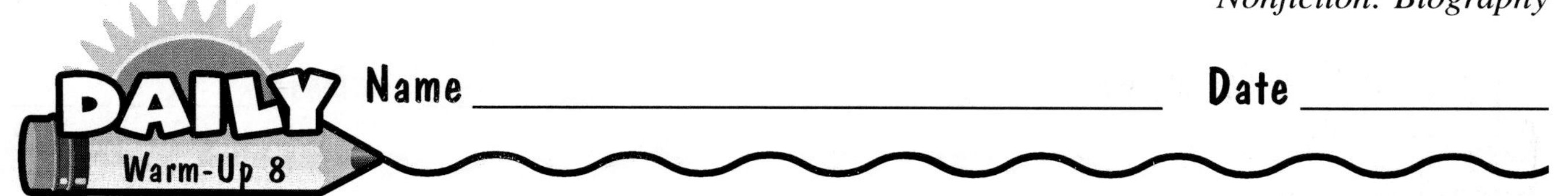

RUDOLPH GIULIANI

Rudolph Giuliani was born in Brooklyn, New York in 1944. He was a natural leader. He went to college and then law school. He became a lawyer working for the U.S. Justice Department. He led a successful fight against organized crime. In 1989, Giuliani ran for mayor of New York City. He lost to David Dinkins. He came back to run for mayor in 1993, and this time he won. He worked to reduce the crime in New York City and to improve its economy. He wanted to make New York City a better place for people to live. He served as mayor for two terms. Many New Yorkers were very happy with his efforts.

Others weren't as happy. Some people felt that he didn't do enough to help the minorities and the poor people. They also felt that he was unkind and harsh. Giuliani still had a lot to give, so he decided to run for the U.S. Senate. Not long after this decision, he was diagnosed with cancer. He decided to continue serving as mayor.

When terrorist attacks on New York City took place on September 11, 2001, Giuliani was a helpful and dedicated mayor. Many people felt his support and encouragement as they worked to put their lives back together. For his efforts, Giuliani was made an Honorary Knight by Queen Elizabeth II. Many people felt that Giuliani's leadership helped the country find peace and courage in the turmoil of that time.

STORY QUESTIONS

1. What is the meaning of the word *turmoil* as it was used in the passage?
   a. mayhem
   b. excitement
   c. annoyance
   d. organization

2. After reading the article, what assumptions can be made about the role that Giuliani played during the time following the attacks on New York?
   a. He was a rescuer who managed to save hundreds of people.
   b. He played the role of scapegoat for what happened.
   c. He was helpful, supportive, and encouraging.
   d. He was tough on crime and anxious to punish the offenders.

3. Many people did not agree with how Giuliani worked as mayor of New York City, but what fact from the passage indicates that many people must have liked him?
   a. He was a lawyer at the Justice Department.
   b. He was made an Honorary Knight by the Queen of England.
   c. He was elected to serve at the United Nations.
   d. He was elected to serve two terms as mayor.

DAILY Warm-Up 9 **Name** ______________________ **Date** __________

ADOLF HITLER

Adolf Hitler was born in 1889 in the small town of Branau Am Inn, Austria. Adolf and his younger sister, Paula, were the only children of six to live to adulthood. Young Hitler attended church regularly and attended school, as well. He was not as diligent in his schooling and later dropped out to become an artist or an architect. Hitler was said to be a shy and quiet young boy, yet he was quick to anger with those who disagreed with him.

Hitler moved to Vienna in 1909 to attend the Academy of Arts, but he was not admitted. He lived in homeless shelters. He was able to sell a few paintings on which to live. He read pamphlets that were unfavorable towards the Jews and began to develop a slow hatred for them. When World War I began, Hitler volunteered for service in the army in Munich, Germany. After the war, Hitler became leader of the Nazi party. Hitler gained acceptance for his anti-Jewish remarks, and his power in the Nazi party allowed him to act on his beliefs.

Hitler would soon lead Germany into a war that wiped out millions of Jews and terrorized millions of people and countries around the world. Hitler began taking over most of Europe in a swift advance. The United States eventually joined the world war and put a stop to the war and Hitler. Hitler died, but not before killing about six million Jews and several million others. This tragedy is known as the Holocaust.

STORY QUESTIONS

1. What inferences can be made about how Hitler was able to convince so many people to follow him?
   a. He was elected the leader of Germany.
   b. He had already had experience of dealing with war.
   c. He was fit and in good health.
   d. He was an influential leader and speaker.

2. What is the main idea of the third paragraph?
   a. It introduces the main idea of the passage.
   b. It discusses some of Hitler's actions during World War II.
   c. It discusses Hitler's experience as a politician.
   d. It explains the treatment the Jews received in the Holocaust.

3. A good way to answer the previous question is to . . .
   a. reread the entire passage.
   b. reread the first paragraph.
   c. look for the words *Holocaust* and *Hitler*.
   d. reread the third paragraph and determine the main idea.

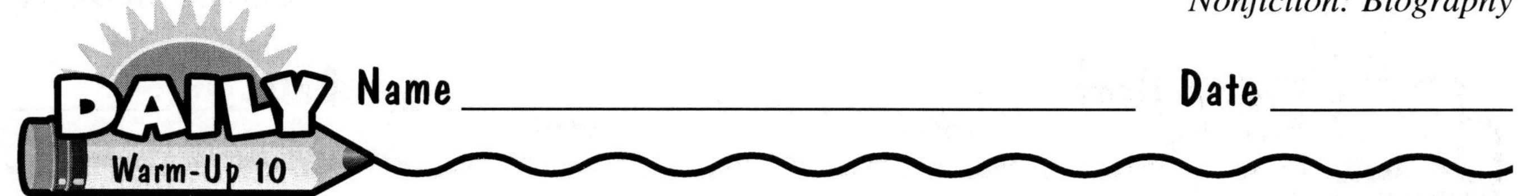

HARRIET TUBMAN

Harriet Tubman was born a slave in Maryland's Dorchester County around 1820. Harriet saw firsthand what slavery was like. In her early teens, Harriet stood in the doorway to protect a slave from an angry overseer. In the process she was hit in the head with a large weight. She never fully recovered from the blow, but her desire to help other slaves grew stronger.

By the time Harriet was 29, she heard rumors that the slaves where she worked were about to be sold and sent further south. Harriet did not want that to happen, so late one night she went to the home of a white woman who promised to help her escape. She went from home to home. She eventually made her way to the North, hiding by day and traveling by night. She finally crossed the border of Pennsylvania where slavery was not allowed.

The people who helped Harriet Tubman escape were members of the Underground Railroad. It wasn't a real railroad but a network of people willing to hide slaves and help them escape. The slaves escaped to either free northern states or Canada. Harriet joined the Underground Railroad helping more slaves including her family escape. She made over 19 trips and helped over 300 slaves escape. At one point there was a reward of $12,000 offered for her capture. Harriet Tubman was happy to say that not one slave had been lost on her watch. She was an influence to so many.

STORY QUESTIONS

1. What prompted Harriet Tubman to escape in the first place?
   a. She heard that a new overseer was coming.
   b. She heard that she was definitely going to be sold further south.
   c. She heard that there were more jobs available in the South.
   d. none of the above
2. How does the author feel about Harriet Tubman?
   a. The author thinks Harriet was powerless.
   b. The author admires Harriet and thinks she was brave.
   c. The author didn't have the chance to free all the slaves.
   d. The author admired how she fought for independence from slave masters.
3. Which statement hints at the author's opinion of Harriet Tubman?
   a. She eventually made her way to the North, hiding by day and traveling by night.
   b. She was an influence to so many.
   c. Harriet Tubman was happy to say that not one slave had been lost on her watch.
   d. She never fully recovered from the blow, but her desire to help other slaves grew stronger.

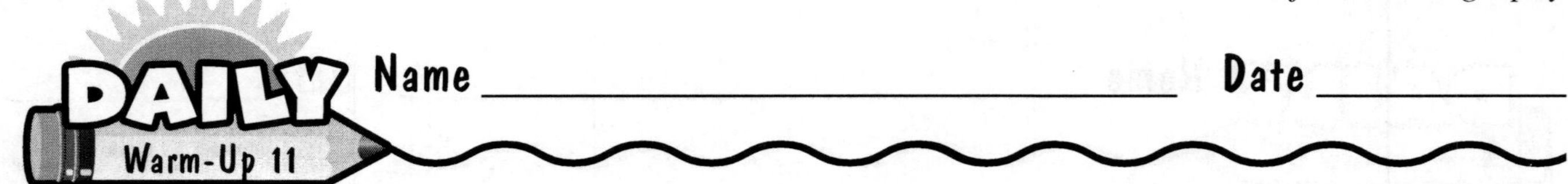

SUSAN B. ANTHONY

Susan B. Anthony was a great leader in Women's Rights. Born in 1820 in Adams, Massachusetts, Susan was the second of eight children in a Quaker family. Her father was said to be a strict man who enforced principled convictions and self-discipline. Susan learned to read and write at the age of three. She received more schooling and eventually became a teacher at the female academy, Eunice Kenyon's Quaker Boarding School.

In 1849, Susan gave her first public speech for the Daughters of Temperance and went on to found the Woman's State Temperance Society of New York. The temperance movement was to aid women and children dealing with the abuse of alcoholic husbands.

In 1872, Susan demanded that women be given the same civil and political rights as black men had been given with the 14th and 15th amendments. She led marches and demonstrations campaigning for women's rights. During this time, Susan met Elizabeth Cady Stanton. The two became great friends and went on to fight for women's suffrage and higher pay.

STORY QUESTIONS

1. What is the meaning of the word *public* as used in the passage?
   a. organized
   b. community
   c. oral
   d. female

2. Where would you read to find out when Susan met Elizabeth Cady Stanton?
   a. first paragraph
   b. second paragraph
   c. third paragraph
   d. not in the passage

3. The author probably wrote this passage to . . .
   a. warn listeners of Susan's background.
   b. inform the reader about Susan's weaknesses.
   c. inform the reader of Susan's history and background.
   d. inform the reader or of Susan's love for women.

4. Which of the following statements is <u>not</u> a fact about Susan B. Anthony?
   a. Susan B. Anthony thought that women were smarter than men.
   b. Susan led marches and demonstrations for women to receive the right to vote.
   c. Susan made her first public speech to the Daughters of Temperance.
   d. The temperance movement was set up to help women and children. Susan worked for this cause.

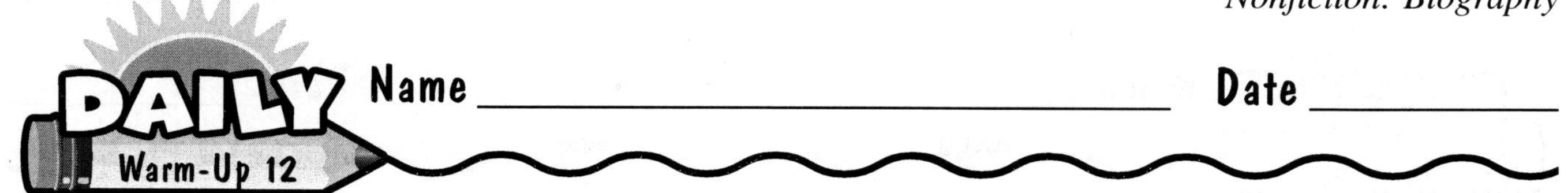

THOMAS EDISON

Thomas Edison is credited with doing more to shape our modern-day civilization than any other person. He was a creative, hard working, and dedicated person. He was also a very interesting person. Being the youngest in his family of seven children, he didn't learn to walk until he was four years old. He began asking questions at a very young age.

Edison was born in 1847 to middle-class parents in Milan, Ohio. Tom's inquiring mind was too much for his schoolteacher. She felt he was self-centered and asked too many questions. His mother eventually taught Tom at home. His father encouraged him to read the classics and would pay him for each one he finished. Edison grew to love reading and writing—especially poetry. Edison soon grew to love the sciences and could not be turned away. His parents found it hard to keep up with their son's quest for knowledge.

Edison put all of his knowledge to great use. He went on to become an inventor who held at least 1,093 patents. Many of these patents were improvements on earlier patents. Edison's greatest innovation was Menlo Park. Menlo Park was a research laboratory built in New Jersey. It was here that Edison created many inventions. One of his greatest inventions was the electric lamp.

STORY QUESTIONS

1. Where would you read to find out about Edison's work at Menlo Park?
   a. end of the first paragraph
   b. in the second paragraph
   c. end of the third paragraph
   d. in the third paragraph
2. The author probably wrote this passage to . . .
   a. inform the reader of Edison's background and life.
   b. inform the reader about all of Edison's patents.
   c. portray the support that Edison received from his mother.
   d. portray Edison's commitment to helping and serving others throughout his life.
3. What does the term *self-centered* mean as used in the passage?
   a. egotistical
   b. unselfish
   c. amorous
   d. anxious

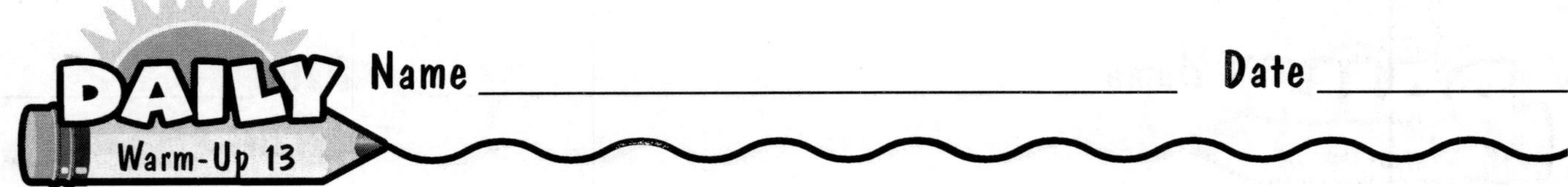

CHIEF JOSEPH

Chief Joseph was a great leader for his people. He was the chief of the Nez Pierce Indians. This nation was located in Idaho and parts of Northern Washington. They were a peaceful nation and maintained good relations with the whites after Lewis and Clark came through on their expeditions. Much of his childhood was spent at a mission run by Christian missionaries.

In 1855, Chief Joseph's father signed a treaty with the United States government. The treaty said that the Nez Pierce were allowed to keep much of their traditional lands. But by 1863, another treaty greatly reduced the amount of land they would own. When Chief Joseph assumed his role as chief in 1877, he challenged the U.S. government on the second treaty. It was stated that the Nez Pierce people never agreed to this treaty.

Months and months of fierce fighting took place before the Nez Pierce people were forced to leave for a reservation in what is now known as Oklahoma. Many of the Nez Pierce people died of malaria and starvation. Chief Joseph tried every possible means to change the minds of the U.S. government, but to no avail. Joseph was eventually sent to a reservation in Washington, where legend says that he died of a broken heart.

STORY QUESTIONS

1. Where did the Nez Pierce live in the beginning?
   a. parts of Northern Idaho and Utah
   b. parts of Idaho and Washington
   c. parts of Oklahoma
   d. parts of Idaho and Oklahoma

2. According to the passage, how did Chief Joseph serve his people?
   a. He waited the official 10 years to set up a reservation.
   b. He worked hard to support the rights of his people by leaving.
   c. He represented his people against the United States government.
   d. He signed a treaty for them.

3. What is the main idea of the passage?
   a. to explain how through hard work and dedication, Chief Joseph was able to accomplish great things
   b. to explain the problems between the Nez Pierce and the U.S.
   c. to explain the role Chief Joseph played and where the Nez Pierce people ended up
   d. to explain how difficult it is to negotiate with the Federal Government

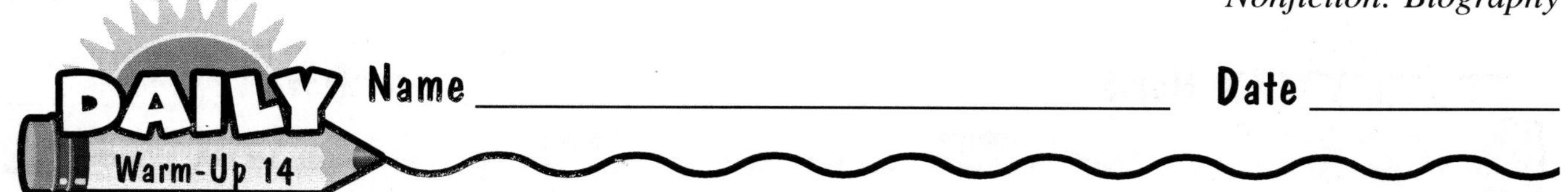

HARRIET BEECHER STOWE

Have you ever heard of the book *Uncle Tom's Cabin*? Harriet Beecher Stowe was born into a family of abolitionists. An abolitionist is a person who does not believe in slavery. She grew up in New England. Stowe was angry when the Fugitive Slave Act was passed in 1850. The Fugitive Slave Act made it easier for slave owners to get back slaves who had escaped. She decided to write a story about just how awful slavery was. She called her book *Uncle Tom's Cabin*.

The book came out in 1852 and was a huge sensation. Over 300,000 copies of the book were sold in that first year. The book was translated into over 20 languages. This book was read by millions of people worldwide. The story was against slavery. It told the story of Eliza, a young slave and mother. Eliza finds out that her baby son has been sold to a slave owner and the baby will be taken from her the next day. Eliza is able to escape with the help of the Underground Railroad.

The characters and the story line became familiar to millions of Americans. Stowe's book was an inspiration to many Northerners who did not feel they had a voice. On the other hand, many Southerners felt that the book gave a false picture of slavery. The divide between the two sides of slavery grew even wider. Eventually, this division would lead to the Civil War.

STORY QUESTIONS

1. Which of the following words could be used to describe Harriet Beecher Stowe?
   a. author, slave owner, mother
   b. author, conductor on the Underground Railroad
   c. mother, Southerner
   d. author and abolitionist

2. What is the meaning of the word *abolitionist* as used in the passage?
   a. a slave owner
   b. a person opposed to slavery
   c. member of the Underground Railroad
   d. a person supportive of slavery

3. Which of the following items would not be on Harriet Beecher Stowe's resume?
   a. fought in the Civil War
   b. worked to make slaves free
   c. tried to educate people on the cruelty of slavery
   d. used writing as a tool to influence many people

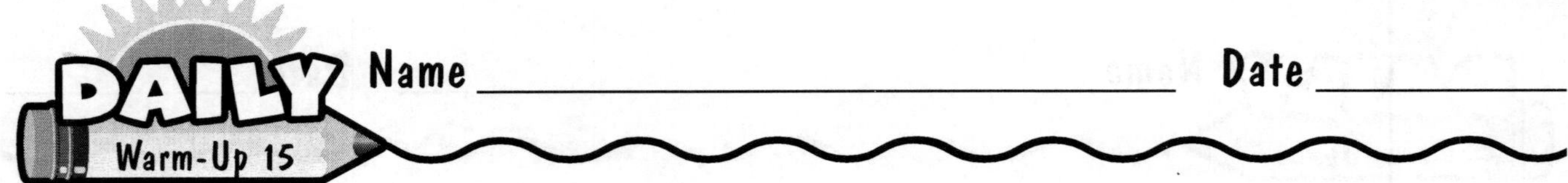

Name ______________________ Date __________

GEORGE WASHINGTON

George Washington is known as the father of our country. This great leader was born in Westmoreland County, Virginia. He studied military science with his brother and then joined the Virginia militia. He was a natural leader and went on to become the chief of the Continental Army. He was able to lead the American troops against the British army to victory in the Revolutionary War.

He married Martha Dandridge Custis on January 6, 1759. She was a young and wealthy widow with two children. George and Martha did not have children of their own, but George adopted Martha's two children.

In 1789, Washington was unanimously voted president. Upon learning of the news that he was elected president, he traveled to New York, which was the temporary capital of the United States. As Washington's coach traveled from town to town on the way to New York, the crowds cheered their new president on.

Thomas Jefferson, Alexander Hamilton, and Henry Knox were some of the members of Washington's cabinet. Washington served two terms as president. Washington quickly tired of the clashes between the two forming parties and retired from politics.

STORY QUESTIONS

1. Why was George Washington considered the father of this country?
   a. He was a good counselor to many.
   b. He was a father figure to many people.
   c. He adopted two children.
   d. He was a great leader in a beginning nation.
2. Which statement best explains the success of George Washington?
   a. Washington grew up in a wealthy family.
   b. Washington learned at an early age how to fight in a war.
   c. Washington had the talent, support, and courage to lead a nation to war.
   d. Washington was motivated to earn a lot of money and respect.
3. Which paragraph explains what happened when George Washington was elected president?
   a. first paragraph
   b. fourth paragraph
   c. second paragraph
   d. third paragraph

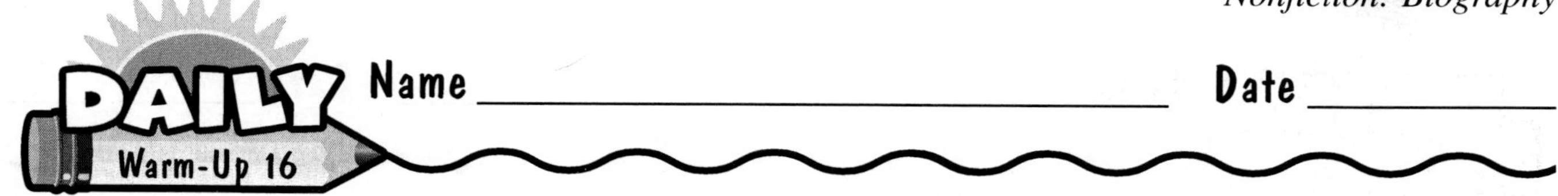

LEWIS AND CLARK

In 1803, the United States bought a large piece of land known as the Louisiana Purchase. Little was known about this land. Was the land good for farming? What kind of animals lived there? What was the climate like? President Jefferson had many questions. He called upon Meriwether Lewis to lead an expedition to explore this new frontier. Lewis asked a friend from his army days to join him. This friend was William Clark. He was an experienced Indian fighter.

Fifty men were hired to accompany Lewis and Clark, and the crew left in May 1804. They paddled up the Missouri River. They traveled for two years, meeting Indians along the way. One such Indian was Sacajawea, the wife of a French fur trapper. She served as an interpreter and guide. They made it to the Continental Divide, the line from which rivers flow to the east on one side and the west on the other.

Lewis and Clark continued with their crew on the dangerous and rocky trail until they reached the Pacific Ocean. In 1806, Lewis and Clark returned to share the information they had gathered. They kept meticulous notes on their findings and discoveries. Together, they had traveled 7,000 miles in 28 months.

STORY QUESTIONS

1. Who asked Lewis and Clark to explore the Louisiana Purchase?
   a. President Washington
   b. Sacajawea
   c. The French Government
   d. President Jefferson
2. What is the meaning of the word *expedition* as used in the passage?
   a. recruitment
   b. danger
   c. journey
   d. endowment
3. Sacagawea is known for . . .
   a. her hard work in impoverished areas.
   b. her interest in literacy and helping others.
   c. being an interpreter and guide.
   d. representing her people.

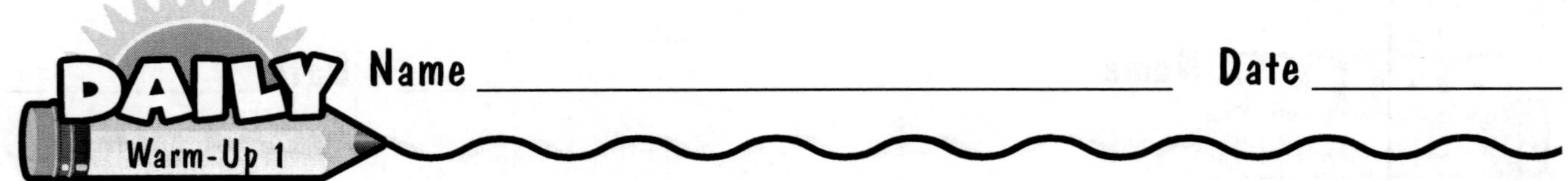

YANKEE DOODLE

Have you sung the song "Yankee Doodle" and wondered what it was talking about? Did you know that "Yankee Doodle" was sung by the British soldiers during the Revolutionary War? They sang this song to make fun of the American soldiers and troops. The British soldiers had fancy uniforms to wear while the Americans didn't have any uniforms to wear. Some of the American soldiers wore buckskin and furs.

Many of the words in the song have different meanings than the ones we use today. *Yankees* was the name the British soldiers called the American soldiers. *Doodle* was another name for hicks or country bumpkins. *Macaroni* in the song didn't refer to pasta, but rather to a fancy style of dress used in England.

Surprisingly enough, the American troops liked the tune of the song. They made up their own words to the song and sang it as they went into battle. They created many verses to the song. Some say there have been 190 verses of the song. It's been said that when Commander Cornwallis of the British surrendered, an American band played, "Yankee Doodle."

STORY QUESTIONS

1. In this reading passage, what does the word "doodle" refer to?
   a. a type of noodle
   b. to scribble or draw
   c. someone who is a hick
   d. sophisticated person

2. Macaroni was a style of . . .
   a. government.
   b. pasta.
   c. military strategy.
   d. dress.

3. What was the purpose of the British soldiers singing the song "Yankee Doodle"?
   a. to scare the American soldiers
   b. to make fun of the American soldiers
   c. to challenge the American soldiers
   d. to inspire the American soldiers

4. What would be another title for this passage?
   a. "The Making of Macaroni"
   b. "The Revolutionary War"
   c. "The British vs. the Americans"
   d. "The History of Yankee Doodle"

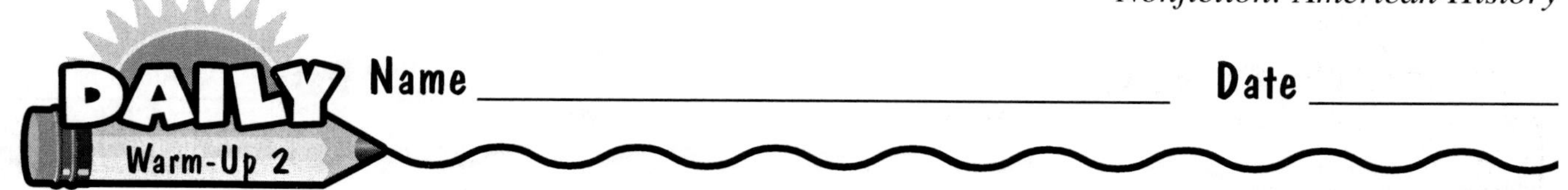

THE GOLD RUSH

Can you imagine finding gold? This was the quest of many people who arrived in California in 1849. They were searching for gold. Gold had been found and so everyone wanted a piece of it. This was called the Gold Rush. People came from all over the world to find gold. Villages sprang up overnight. Tents formed these temporary villages that were set up wherever gold was discovered. These villages would be abandoned as soon as gold was found elsewhere.

Many gold prospectors were able to strike it rich. Some found thousands of dollars worth of gold nuggets or gold dust. Not everyone was so lucky. With so much gold around, the price for items went up and up. People had to spend a lot of money to buy food and supplies. They spent all of their money trying to find the gold that was never to be found. Most went home broke.

Years later, gold was found in 1896 near the Klondike River in Canada's Yukon Territory. This sparked another gold rush. Within a year over 100,000 men and women arrived in Canada. It was a long trip and many would never complete it because of the cold weather and the raging rivers. People died along the way. Most of the people that did make it to the Yukon were not able to find gold in Canada, and soon the Gold Rush was over.

STORY QUESTIONS

1. What brought so many people to California in 1849?
   a. They were seeking gold.
   b. They were starting a new territory.
   c. They were sent by the federal government.
   d. They were fighting in the Mexican War.
2. The author wrote this passage to . . .
   a. justify the reasons people went to California.
   b. inform the reader of how gold miners were not mistreated.
   c. share general information about the Gold Rushes in North America.
   d. raise awareness of mistreatment of immigrants to California.
3. Which of the following statements is a fact about the results of the Gold Rush?
   a. Many had their land taken away from them.
   b. Gold Rushers spent all of their money in land.
   c. With gold around, prices for food and supplies went up.
   d. With so much gold around, people were robbed.

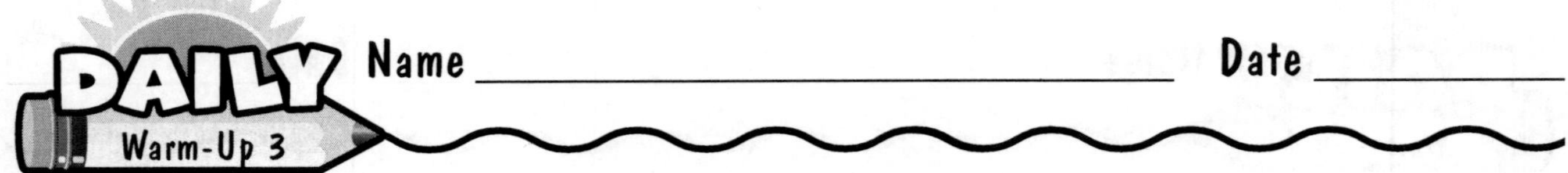

THE FIRST AMERICANS

North America is a large and varied land with great resources and beauty. No one knows for sure when the first people inhabited this land, but scientists believe it was thousands of years before Columbus and any explorers came along. It has been determined that many groups of Native Americans lived in North America. These groups of people lived in tribes. They developed their own ways to meet their needs for food, shelter, and clothing.

North American tribes did not leave written records. Archaeologists have had to depend on the items they left behind. These items are called artifacts. Artifacts can share clues as to how these early settlers lived. Some of these tribes lived near water while others lived in the desert. Each group of people had to learn different skills to survive.

Each of these tribes or groups of people had their own name. There were four main North American Indian groups. These groups were the Pacific Northwest Indians, the Southwest Indians, the Plains Indians, and the Eastern Woodland Indians. These groups of Native Americans had rich cultures and traditions that were passed on through the generations.

STORY QUESTIONS

1. Who were some of the first people to live on the American continent?
   a. Columbus and his crew
   b. Eastern Europeans
   c. Native Americans
   d. British Soldiers

2. The scientists who study these early cultures are called . . .
   a. biologists.
   b. archaeologists.
   c. geologists.
   d. sociologists.

3. After reading the passage, what can you infer about how scientists are able to learn about these early cultures?
   a. by studying the foods and traditions of each group
   b. by studying the systems of government
   c. by reading the written history
   d. by studying the artifacts

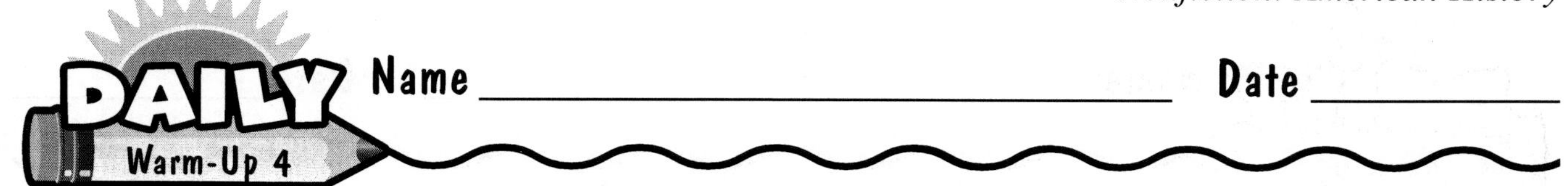

SPANISH EXPLORATIONS

Explorers are people who search for new places and new things. Some of the early explorers discovered great things about the world. Some of these fearless explorers were Columbus, Cabot, Magellan, Verrazano, and Cartier. But none of these men actually had much interest in the Americas. They were all trying to find the route to the East Indies and Asia. They found gold and other precious items in Asia. America was just a stop along the way.

The Spanish soon realized that America might have even greater riches than the Indies. Conquistadors, another name for conquerors, set out to discover what America had in store. One of these great Conquistadors was Ponce de Leon. He had sailed with Columbus on his second voyage. He was also a soldier on Hispaniola. He went to Puerto Rico to look for gold. He found some and he also found some native Indians. He conquered the land and set up Spanish rule.

In the year 1513, he set off again in search of gold, but some say he was searching for the fountain of youth. He never found the fountain of youth, but he traveled to a beautiful peninsula filled with flowers. Ponce de Leon named this peninsula "Florida." Years later, the first European colony was established in what is now known as the United States at St. Augustine.

STORY QUESTIONS

1. What is a conquistador?
   - a. a sailor
   - b. a Native American
   - c. a ruler of a peninsula
   - d. another name for conqueror
2. After reading the passage, what characteristics do explorers have?
   - a. fear and trepidation
   - b. courage and calmness
   - c. adventuring spirit and a will to try
   - d. a large support army
3. Ponce de Leon was in search of . . .
   - a. silver.
   - b. gold and a fountain of youth.
   - c. Columbus.
   - d. a new country.
4. Which of the following explorers was <u>not</u> mentioned in the passage?
   - a. Cartier
   - b. Cortez
   - c. Cabot
   - d. Magellan

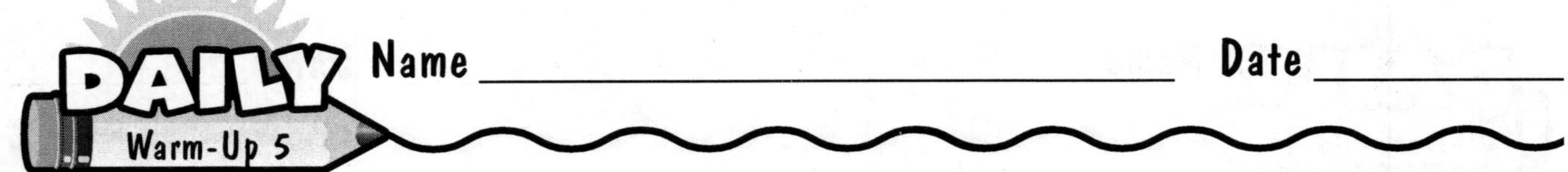

EARLY EUROPEAN SETTLEMENTS

France and England explored and settled in the New World. These countries claimed portions of land in North America. English colonies began to grow quickly. Many of these countries saw Spain's treasury filling with gold, and they were jealous. They wanted some of this gold for themselves. One of these people was Sir Walter Raleigh. He was a friend of the Queen in England and he was also very wealthy. He received permission to set up a colony in North America.

In 1585, Raleigh sent 100 colonists with food and supplies to Roanoke Island, off the coast of what is now North Carolina. The colonists thought that they would receive help and aid from the Native Americans, so they didn't plant their own crops. The Native Americans did help the colonists for a while but that didn't last very long. The settlers began to starve. Fortunately, Francis Drake, another explorer, stopped on one of his voyages. He brought the colonists back to England.

Raleigh lost a fortune trying to start the colony on Roanoke Island. He learned that it was too expensive for one person to start a colony. He got a group of merchants to join him in starting a colony by forming a joint-stock company. This was called the Virginia Company of London. The stockholders made plans to send colonists back. The colonists were to send furs, lumber, as well as other products back to London. These were some of the first settlers of Jamestown in Virginia off the Chesapeake Bay.

STORY QUESTIONS

1. What motivated England and France to set up American colonies?
   a. They were ready to leave their own countries.
   b. They saw Spain getting wealthy.
   c. They were trying to learn from the Native Americans.
   d. none of the above
2. What conclusions can be drawn about the people who were early settlers in the American colonies?
   a. They were corrupt and dishonest.
   b. They were hard workers that believed in making changes.
   c. They were inexperienced and naive.
   d. They weren't very organized.
3. After reading the passage, which of the following statements is false?
   a. Raleigh didn't lose a fortune trying to start the colony on Roanoke Island.
   b. The colonists were to send furs, lumber, as well as other products back to London.
   c. The colonists thought that they would receive help and aid from the Native Americans, so they didn't plant their own crops.
   d. France and England explored and settled in the New World.

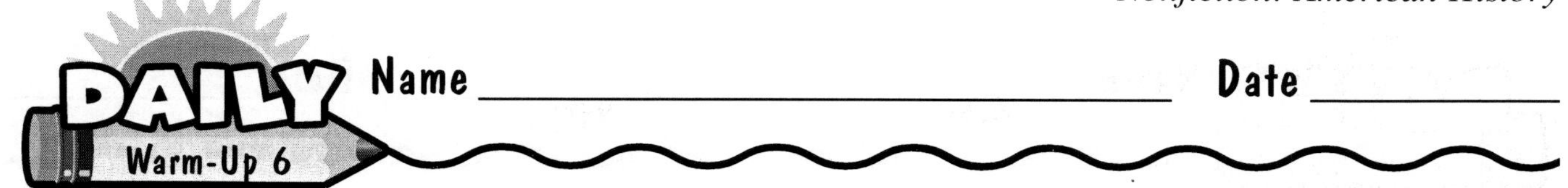

THE FEDERAL GOVERNMENT

There are three main branches of the federal government. These branches are the judicial branch, the executive branch, and the legislative branch. Each of these branches plays an important role in the federal government. Do you know what role each branch performs?

The judicial branch is made up of the court system. The Supreme Court is the highest court in the land. The Supreme Court decides whether a law is constitutional or not. The courts decide arguments about the meaning of laws, how they are applied, and whether they break the Constitution or not.

The executive branch of the federal government makes sure that the laws are obeyed. The president is part of the executive branch. The president needs a lot of help from the vice president, the cabinet, departments, as well as independent agencies to enforce the law.

The legislative branch is made up of Congress and government agencies. Congress has two parts. They are the Senate and the House of Representatives. This branch of government creates and passes the laws of the land. Congress also makes laws about taxes and borrowing money, and it approves the making of money. Congress can also declare war on other countries.

Each branch has its own functions that help our government run smoothly. Each branch can also limit the power of the other two branches. This is called Checks and Balances.

STORY QUESTIONS

1. Which branch of government passes new laws in this country?
   a. Library of Congress
   b. judicial
   c. executive
   d. legislative

2. Which paragraph explains which branch of the federal government the Senate and the House of Representatives belong to?
   a. first paragraph
   b. second paragraph
   c. third paragraph
   d. fourth paragraph

3. After reading the passage, who assists the president in enforcing the law?
   a. vice president and the cabinet
   b. The Supreme Court
   c. constituents
   d. Congress

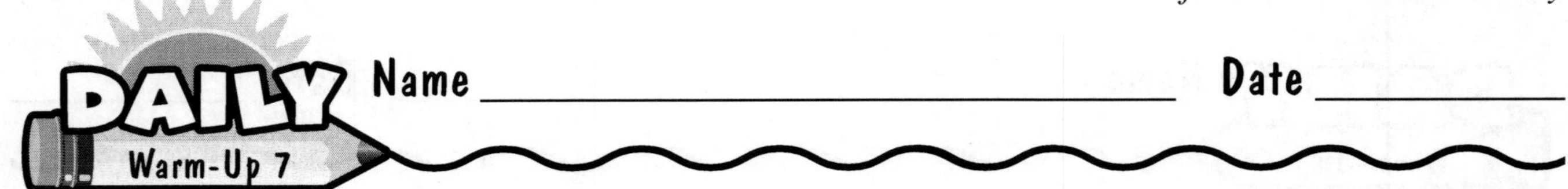

NORTH VS. SOUTH

The Civil War was a war in which Americans fought against Americans. It was the deadliest war of all the wars fought by Americans. The country had been split into two divisions known as the North and South. Many southern states had formed a confederacy. This was essentially a new country. The southern states no longer wanted to be a part of the United States of America. There were many reasons for this action, but one of the main issues was slavery. The southern states wanted to be able to have slaves.

In April of 1861, the Confederate soldiers bombarded Fort Sumter. This was the last of the southern forts still in the hands of the United States government. This event began the Civil War. Both the North and the South had advantages during the Civil War. The North had a larger population. The North also had most of the factories and mills. They could produce more supplies and guns than the South. The South had to depend on help from European countries. The North also had railroads to move troops and supplies.

The South had advantages as well. The biggest advantage was that the South was fighting a defensive war. This meant that they were fighting to defend their country and their beliefs, and their way of life. In order for the North to win, they would have to conquer the South. The South also had better generals than the North at the beginning of the war. These generals had experience fighting the Mexican War.

STORY QUESTIONS

1. What happened in April 1861 that initiated the Civil War?
   a. United States declared victory.
   b. Abraham Lincoln was elected president.
   c. Fort Sumter was fired upon.
   d. General Lee joined the Confederacy.
2. The Southern generals had experience fighting in the . . .
   a. Civil War.
   b. Battle of Bull Run.
   c. war against slavery.
   d. Mexican War.
3. Which of the following would make another good title for this passage?
   a. "Between the North and South"
   b. "Sweeping Changes for Confederacy"
   c. "Women's Assistance in the Civil War"
   d. "The Civil War Soldiers"

DAILY Warm-Up 8 **Name** ______________________________ **Date** ____________

THE COTTON GIN

Since the mid-1700s, Southern plantation owners had been growing cotton. This cotton was used to make cloth. As a result of the Industrial Revolution in the United States, the demand for cotton increased. The problem came from the fact that cotton was filled with green, sticky seeds. It was a tedious task to remove all the sticky seeds so that the cotton could be used. It took most workers an entire day to clean one pound of the cotton. This made the cotton very expensive.

In 1793, Eli Whitney made a visit to a plantation in Georgia. Eli was known for tinkering with machines and solving problems. Eli was encouraged by a plantation owner to see if he could create a machine that could remove the sticky seeds from the cotton. Eli was able to do just that. He was able to do it in just 10 days! This new machine was called the cotton gin. In a short amount of time, Eli was able to build a large cotton gin. This new gin was able to clean 50 pounds of cotton in one day.

As a result of this new invention, cotton could be sold at a cheaper price. Plantation owners began selling their cotton to factories in the North as well as in Great Britain. They were able to grow larger and larger crops. Soon cotton became the south's biggest crop. As a result, the need for slaves was even greater. The South's economy depended on this slave labor. This would eventually lead to a debate about the legality and morality of owning slaves. This debate fueled a division that would lead to the Civil War.

STORY QUESTIONS

1. After reading the passage, what can be inferred about why Eli Whitney invented the cotton gin?
   a. to eliminate slavery
   b. to remove the sticky seeds from the cotton
   c. to satisfy southern slave owners
   d. to fulfill an order

2. What can be implied about why the invention of the cotton gin made the need for slavery even greater?
   a. Cotton could be sold at a cheaper price.
   b. The cotton gin made cleaning the cotton easier, leading to more cotton needing to be picked.
   c. This new gin was able to clean 50 pounds of cotton in one day.
   d. Eli was encouraged by a plantation owner to see if he could create a machine that could remove the sticky seeds from the cotton.

3. What skills did Eli Whitney have that helped him invent the cotton gin?
   a. He had been well trained in his profession.
   b. He was personally in need of a new cotton machine.
   c. He was a natural at tinkering with machines and learning how they work.
   d. He was good friends with many plantation owners.

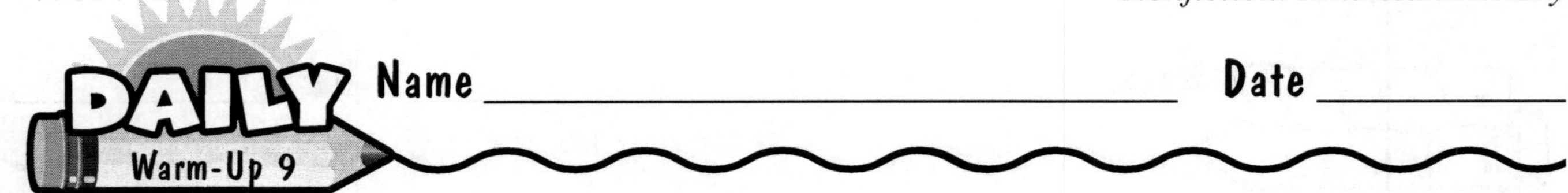

THE MEXICAN WAR

By the 1840s, territory in the United States was spreading in all directions. Some people felt that the country should not spread from the Atlantic to the Pacific Oceans and from Canada to the Rio Grande. But because of its economic and political superiority and growing population, many felt that it was the destiny of America to rule North America. This was known as the Manifest Destiny.

The president at the time was James Polk. He believed very strongly in the Manifest Destiny. He offered to buy the Mexican territory, which consisted of the California and New Mexico areas, which also included Arizona. Mexico refused. President Polk sent troops into a territory near the Rio Grande that both countries claimed as their own. American soldiers as well as Mexican soldiers were killed in the small conflict. President Polk claimed that American blood had been shed. He asked Congress to declare war on Mexico. Congress did so.

In 1848, Mexico and the United States signed a peace treaty. The treaty stated that the United States received all the land that today makes up California, Nevada, and Utah. It also received most of what is now the state of Arizona, parts of Wyoming, New Mexico, and Colorado. In return, the United States paid Mexico 15 million dollars. This is known as the Mexican Cession.

STORY QUESTIONS

1. What land did the United States want to buy from Mexico?
   - a. Texas and the surrounding areas
   - b. The Southwest
   - c. San Diego
   - d. California and New Mexico areas
2. Which paragraph helps you answer the previous question?
   - a. first paragraph
   - b. second paragraph
   - c. last paragraph
   - d. none of the above
3. Which of the sentences below explains the outcome of the Mexican War?
   - a. It also received most of what is now the state of Arizona, parts of Wyoming, New Mexico, and Colorado.
   - b. In return, the United States paid Mexico 15 million dollars. This is known as the Mexican Cession.
   - c. In 1848, Mexico and the United States signed a peace treaty.
   - d. The treaty stated that the United States received all the land that makes up California, Nevada, and Utah today.

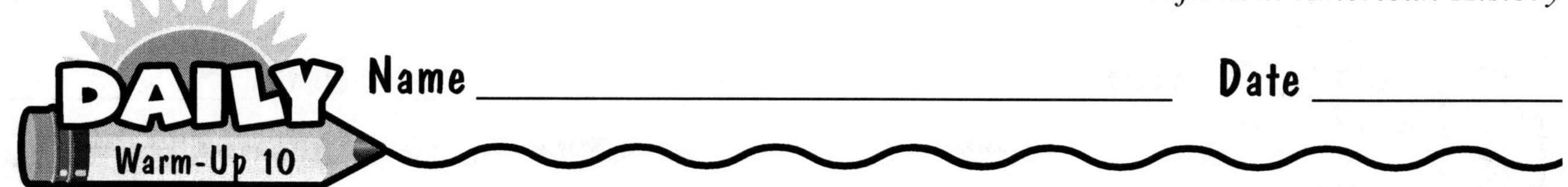

FREE BLACKS JOIN UNION ARMY

At the beginning of the Civil War, there were many African Americans who volunteered to fight for the Union. However, the navy and the army denied these Americans the opportunity to fight in the Civil War. They were hired to drive wagons, cook meals, and work with shovels and other tools, but they were not soldiers.

But as the Civil War went on, more and more soldiers were needed. In 1863, the Emancipation Proclamation was passed and the army and navy decided to allow African Americans to join. These African Americans were encouraged to join the army in an effort to free the millions of slaves in the South. It was believed that if these Americans helped to fight, they would not be denied the right to citizenship.

By the end of the Civil War, there were approximately 185,000 African Americans fighting in the army and the navy. Some of them were free from the North, but the rest of them were men who had escaped the slave states. Black soldiers were not treated the same as other soldiers. In the beginning they only received half their pay. By the end they all received the same amount. Most white soldiers would not fight alongside them. But the fighting record of black soldiers was honorable. The country's highest award, the Congressional Medal of Honor, was given to 21 black soldiers.

STORY QUESTIONS

1. What jobs were black soldiers given at the beginning of the war?
   a. They fought alongside white soldiers.
   b. They served on ships in the navy.
   c. They were able to fight but without weapons.
   d. They were allowed to drive wagons, cook meals, and work with shovels.
2. What is the primary purpose of this reading passage?
   a. to inform the reader about the Civil War
   b. to explain the prejudice that people had during the Civil War
   c. to explain the role that blacks played in the Civil War
   d. to look for a better way of life
3. What is the meaning of the word *emancipation* as used in this passage?
   a. initiation
   b. freedom
   c. registration
   d. coronation

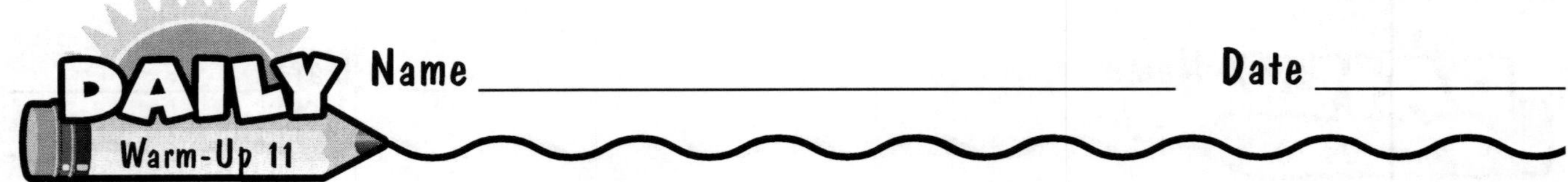

THE STATUE OF LIBERTY

The United States is a nation of immigrants. Since the beginning, immigrants have come to America looking for a better way of life. In the late 1800s they came in large numbers. There had never been so many immigrants at one time. It was faster and easier to cross the Atlantic Ocean than ever before. It took just five days to cross the ocean from England.

Those who came after 1886 were greeted with the sight of the Statue of Liberty. The Statue of Liberty is 15 stories high. In one hand she holds the torch. In the other hand she holds the tablet bearing the date of the Declaration of Independence. The people of France presented this statue as a gift to the United States. It was meant to celebrate the friendship between the two countries.

Some immigrants became farmers in the West, but most immigrants moved to cities such as New York, Chicago, Philadelphia, Cleveland, and Boston. Here they looked for work to support their families. Members of the same immigrant groups often lived together in the same neighborhoods. This made it easier to communicate with one another and share similar customs and traditions.

These immigrants were often poor. They did not speak English and they were unskilled workers. They would usually take any jobs they could get. They had to work hard with very low pay. Often the entire family, including the children, were required to work to make ends meet.

STORY QUESTIONS

1. What is the main idea of paragraph three?
   a. to inform the reader about the Statue of Liberty
   b. to explain the struggles immigrants had getting into the United States
   c. to explain the role that the government played in donating the statue
   d. to explain where immigrants went for work once they arrived
2. Which country presented the United States with the Statue of Liberty?
   a. Russia
   b. France
   c. Germany
   d. Ellis Island
3. Which of the following statements is an opinion?
   a. These immigrants were often poor.
   b. Here they looked for work to support their families.
   c. The Statue of Liberty is a beautiful reminder of the purpose of this country.
   d. Those who came after 1886 were greeted with the sight of the Statue of Liberty.

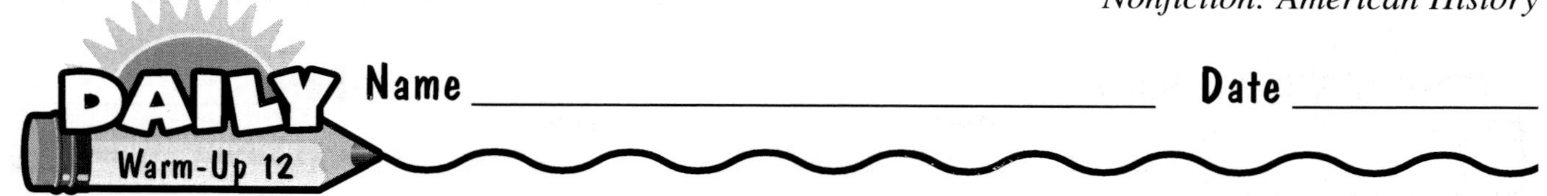

HAWAII BECOMES A STATE

Hawaii is a group of islands west of the Pacific Coast of the United States. These islands are about 2,000 miles from the continental United States. In the early 1800s, American ships began arriving in Hawaii to stop for supplies on their way to and from Asia.

Before long, missionaries arrived in Hawaii to teach religion and to try to convert people. Some of these missionaries became business people. They began purchasing land for sugar plantations. These Americans soon took over and began running the islands. In 1891, Liliuokalani was named the new queen of Hawaii. She made the decision that a foreigner could not rule Hawaii. The plantation owners were concerned. The queen was overthrown by the people who then asked the United States government to take over Hawaii.

President Grover Cleveland was president of the United States at the time. He didn't think it was right to overthrow the queen and take over another country. But as time went on, William McKinley became president of the United States. He felt differently about Hawaii. President McKinley and Congress agreed to make Hawaii a territory of the United States. Many years later, in 1959, Hawaii became a state. In fact, Hawaii became the 50th state of the United States.

STORY QUESTIONS

1. Originally, why did people stop in Hawaii?
   a. They were helping the native people there.
   b. They used Hawaii as a summer residence.
   c. They bought land and set up sugar plantations.
   d. They stopped for supplies on their way to and from Asia.

2. Why did President Cleveland refuse to take over Hawaii?
   a. He believed that Hawaii had economic as well as political superiority.
   b. He felt like it was a poor business deal.
   c. He didn't feel it was right to overthrow the queen.
   d. He believed that Hawaii belonged to Asia.

3. What is the meaning of the word *overthrown* as used in the passage?
   a. thrown overboard
   b. arraigned
   c. removed from power
   d. none of the above

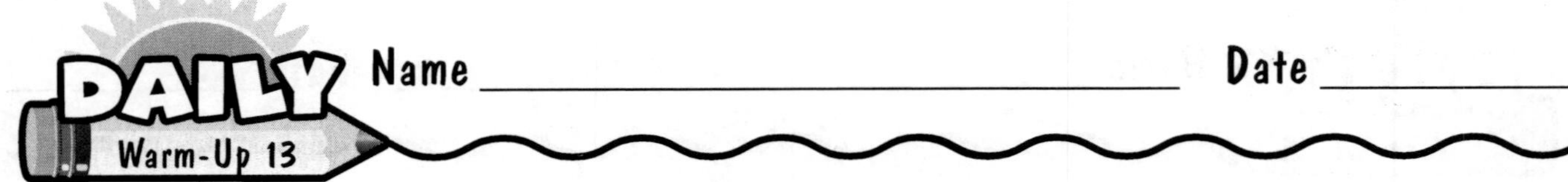

THE GREAT WAR

In 1914, war broke out in Europe. The countries of Europe were divided against each other. The two main sides during World War I were the Allied Powers and the Central Powers. The Allied Powers consisted of Great Britain, France, and Russia. The Central Powers consisted of Germany, Turkey, and Austria-Hungary. The colonies of these nations in Asia, Africa, the Middle East, and the Pacific were soon drawn into the war as well.

World War I was known as the Great War because this conflict was the first war that involved so many countries worldwide. Many felt that this would be the war to end all other wars. History shows that this would not be the case. This war was also different in that the weapons used were new and more deadly. Armies had never used tanks, airplanes, or gas grenades. Losses in each battle were greater than ever. Another effective weapon was the submarine. Submarines could sink large ships carrying troops and supplies.

Trench warfare was a new concept introduced during World War I. Soldiers dug long, deep trenches, or ditches in the ground, and lived in them for long periods of time. These trenches were used as a place to stay and also as a form of protection.

The war finally ended after the German leader Kaiser Wilhelm resigned. On November 11, 1918, an armistice haulted the fighting and a peace treaty followed.

STORY QUESTIONS

1. Which countries formed the Central Powers?
   a. Germany, Russia, Great Britain
   b. Germany, Turkey, and Austria-Hungary
   c. Germany, Turkey, and France
   d. Germany and France
2. How were trenches used during World War I?
   a. Soldiers used them to store their weapons.
   b. Trenches were dug to capture the enemy and for protection.
   c. Trenches were used to store supplies and for protection.
   d. Soldiers dug trenches to live in them and use them as a means of protection.
3. Based on the reading passage, why was this called the Great War?
   a. It was the first war to ever divide Europe.
   b. It was a great war for both sides.
   c. It was the largest war that had ever been fought in the world.
   d. It would be the last war ever fought.

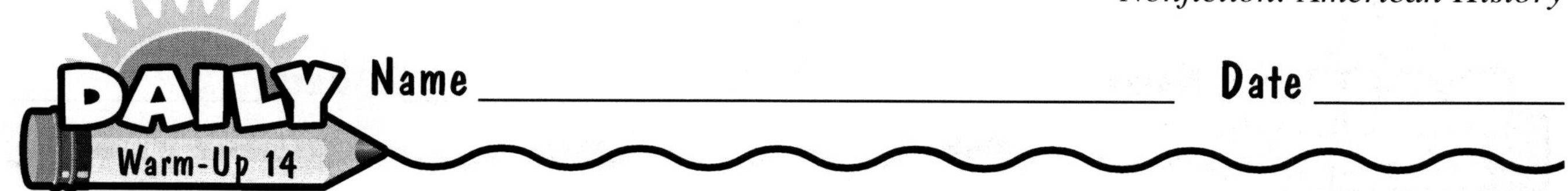

THE ASSEMBLY LINE

When the first "horseless carriages" were introduced, few people were interested. Many people thought they were unsafe, too expensive, and too noisy. These horseless carriages were actually the beginnings of the car as we know it. The invention of cars changed transportation in the United States forever. Henry Ford is credited with changing the way that people looked at cars. He was one of the early automobile makers, and his techniques changed the way cars were made. His ideas made the car cheaper and accessible not only to rich people, but also to farmers and ordinary workers.

In the beginning cars were made by a group of mechanics working to put the entire car together. Henry Ford had different ideas on how to build an automobile. Henry Ford divided up the tasks into a process of steps. Each worker was assigned a different step in the process. That meant that each worker was only responsible for one job and he or she did this job over and over on each automobile. This meant that the workers became specialists. This also meant that cars would be produced much faster. This also meant the car was less expensive, so that it could be sold more cheaply.

Ford improved upon his system even more by introducing the assembly line. The assembly line was a large moving belt that brought the cars to the workers. The worker would continue to perform each step in the process, but bringing the cars to the workers saved even more time.

STORY QUESTIONS

1. What was the first reaction to the "horseless carriage"?
   a. People loved the new invention.
   b. People were nervous about driving the new car.
   c. People thought they were cheap and inexpensive.
   d. People thought they were dangerous and noisy.

2. What is the definition of an assembly line?
   a. a group of workers standing in a line
   b. a large moving belt
   c. the line where buyers purchased their cars
   d. the place where the nuts and bolts are held

3. Based on reading the passage, what effect did the cost of making the car have on the purchasing price of the car?
   a. The price of the car went down.
   b. The price of the car went up.
   c. The price of the car stayed the same.
   d. none of the above

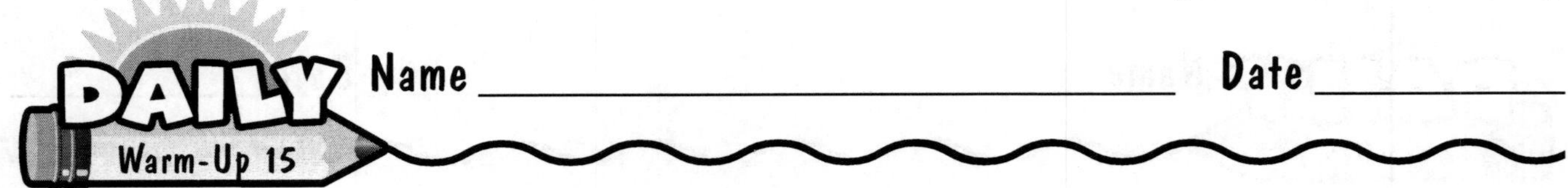

CIVIL RIGHTS

Martin Luther King, Jr. was born in Atlanta, Georgia. He went on to graduate and become a Baptist minister. His greatest accomplishments were his civil rights efforts from the middle of the 1950s until he was assassinated in the 1960s. His civil rights crusade was different. It was one that called for peace and nonviolence. In 1963, King led a march on Washington, D.C. He delivered his famous "I Have a Dream" speech at the Lincoln Memorial. He was demanding equal justice for all Americans. He was challenging the government to help all Americans regardless of their race or religion.

His famous speech would go on to inspire many people for many years to come. In 1964, he won a Nobel Peace Prize for his work. Much of his work and efforts resulted in the passage of the Civil Rights Act of 1964 and the Voting Rights Act of 1965.

Dr. King was hated by many white southern segregationists. On April 4, 1968, King was preparing to lead a local march. He was shot in the throat on the balcony of a hotel in Memphis, Tennessee. He died a few hours later. President Lyndon Johnson declared a day of mourning for the slain civil rights leader. And yet, Dr. Martin Luther King's legacy lives on. He is honored on Martin Luther King Day, which is a national holiday. It is held on the third Monday of January around King's birthday on January 15. His great legacy continues to inspire many.

STORY QUESTIONS

1. Who was Martin Luther King, Jr.?
   a. He was the first black president of the United States.
   b. He was a civil rights leader.
   c. He worked for the federal government
   d. He was a member of Congress.
2. What is the meaning of the word *justice* as used in the passage?
   a. impartiality
   b. apartheid
   c. emancipation
   d. realignment
3. What was Dr. King seeking to secure for many Americans?
   a. emancipation from slavery
   b. a black president of the United States
   c. a job with the F.B.I.
   d. civil rights and voting rights for all Americans

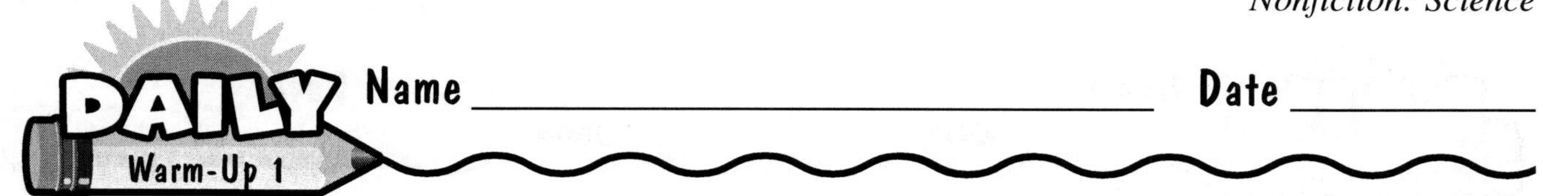

THE SUN

How much do you know about the sun? Did you know that it is the closest star to the planet Earth? The sun is actually just like billions of other stars in the sky. It just looks different because it is so close. It is also the center of the solar system. The sun is a huge ball of gas. The temperature of the sun is over 27,000,000 degrees Fahrenheit.

From Earth, the sun doesn't look that big, but the sun is so large that more than a million Earths could fit inside of it. The sun is by far the largest object in the solar system. It is even bigger than the planet Jupiter.

Astronomers say that the sun has layers. These layers are called the photosphere, chromosphere, and the corona. Astronomers have also discovered that the sun spins just like the Earth except more slowly. The sun has quiet periods and active periods. During active periods, there are solar flares and sunspots. Sunspots are dark spots that often appear on the surface of the sun. What makes these sunspots? Scientists think that they are cool spots. Solar flares are bursts of hot gases. These bursts shoot far into the solar system.

STORY QUESTIONS

1. What would be another good title for this passage?
   a. "The Sun: The Closest Star"
   b. "Solar Flares"
   c. "Sun Spots"
   d. "Stars in the Universe"

2. Which of the following is a fact about the sun?
   a. The sun is the largest planet.
   b. The sun is the central planet.
   c. The sun has a great red spot.
   d. The sun has quiet and active periods.

3. What was meant by the term *solar flares*?
   a. sun spots on the sun
   b. indications of being the largest object in the solar system
   c. bursts of hot gases
   d. a way to track the sun's movement

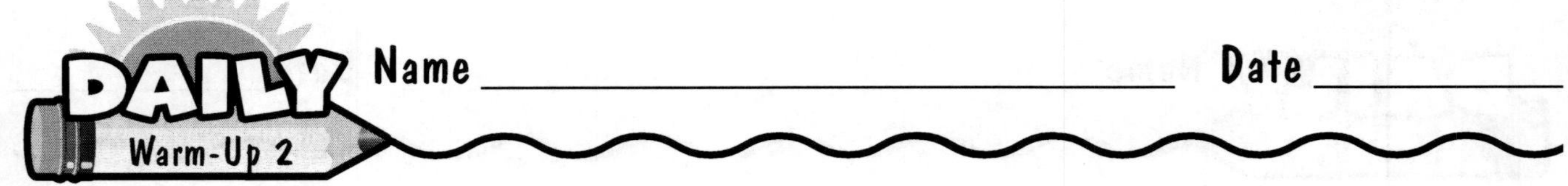

MATTER

What is matter? Everything is made up of matter. Matter is made up of tiny particles called atoms, molecules, or ions. Matter is ordinarily found in three states. These states are liquid, gas, or solid. There are two forces at work regardless of the state of matter. These two forces are energy and attraction. Energy makes the matter move. Attraction pulls and keeps the particles together.

Solids are packed together. Examples of solids are wood, plastic, stone, and iron. You can hold solids in your hand. Liquids are a state between gases and solids. Liquids flow and change shape. The best example of a liquid is water. Gases are floating around you and inside bubbles. Gases don't have any particular shape, but they are fluid. They can also be compressed. Vapor and gas mean the same thing.

Matter can change from one state to another. For example, a liquid can change to a solid or gas. Solids can change to a liquid. Temperature influences the changes in matter from one state to another. For example, heating a liquid can turn it into a gas. Cooling or freezing a liquid can turn it into a solid. Scientists continue to study matter, molecules, and ions to better understand our world.

STORY QUESTIONS

1. After reading the passage, what do you think would happen if a liquid was boiled?
   a. It would immediately double in size.
   b. It would turn into a gas.
   c. It would turn into a solid.
   d. Scientists have not yet determined what happens in this case.
2. The main idea of this passage is . . .
   a. to inform the reader about what happens when it is raining.
   b. to inform the reader about the definition of matter.
   c. to inform the reader about how important it is to see ice, rain, and condensation.
   d. to share general information about the universe and how it is organized.
3. Where can you find information about the three types of matter?
   a. second paragraph
   b. all three paragraphs
   c. third paragraph
   d. first paragraph

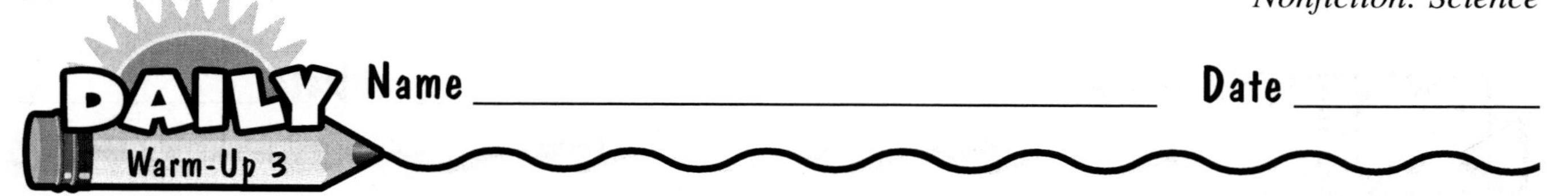

THE HEIMLICH MANEUVER

Have you ever seen a person choking on his or her food? Perhaps he or she needed the Heimlich maneuver. What is the Heimlich maneuver? It is a maneuver that can save a person from choking to death. Henry Heimlich was a doctor who in 1974 published information on the Heimlich maneuver. His methods of how to help someone from choking have saved over 50,000 people from dying.

The Heimlich maneuver is a simple method, but it must be followed correctly. It should only be attempted after appropriate training. People can sometimes cause more harm to a victim if they perform this maneuver without training. When a piece of food gets lodged in the windpipe, it keeps you from breathing. This means that oxygen can't get to the brain. The brain can go no longer than four to six minutes without oxygen. That's why it is important to get the food out of the windpipe as quickly as possible.

You can use the Heimlich maneuver to help other people. If you see a person choking, stand behind him or her and put both arms around the person's waist. Have the person lead forward just a little bit. Place one hand between the person's belly button and the rib cage. Make a fist with this hand. Be sure that your thumb is facing the stomach. Place your other hand over the fist. Press your open hand onto the hand in a fist in a sharp upward movement. This should force air out from the body to push out the blocked food.

STORY QUESTIONS

1. Who was the Heimlich maneuver named after?
   a. Jonathon Heimlich, Ph.D.
   b. Jason Heimlich
   c. Frederick Heimlich III
   d. Henry Heimlich, M.D.
2. Based on reading the passage, where does the food get lodged?
   a. in the windpipe
   b. in the stomach
   c. in the liver
   d. in the intestine
3. Which paragraph would help you answer the previous question?
   a. second paragraph
   b. first paragraph
   c. fourth paragraph
   d. third paragraph
4. Without air, what happens to the brain?
   a. It can't get the oxygen it needs to be healthy.
   b. It will not be able to perform certain functions.
   c. It will go into a coma.
   d. The brain begins to override the intake of air.

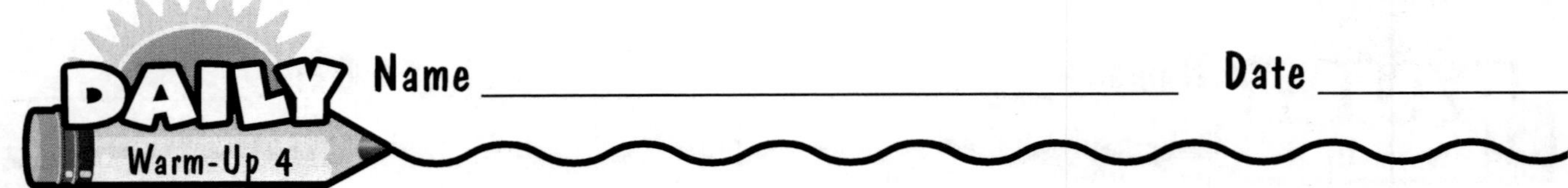

Name ______________________________ Date ____________

HURRICANES

Have you ever been in a hurricane? Hurricanes are serious weather storms. They can do a lot of damage. But what is a hurricane? Another name for a hurricane is a tropical cyclone. A hurricane consists of thunderstorms, torrential rains, and waves with winds up to 75 mph or higher. A hurricane is a tropical storm that starts out in the ocean and gathers speed and strength as it travels.

When the winds inside these storms reach 39 mph, they are given names. An international committee developed the list of names. Hurricanes alternate back and forth between male and female names. Giving the hurricanes names makes it easier for meteorologists to identify and track certain storms. This makes it easier to announce hurricane warnings, as well.

The best place to be during a hurricane is indoors and away from windows and doors. If the hurricane is very bad, you will probably be asked to evacuate and move to safer ground. It's important to keep a kit ready that contains fresh water, non-perishable food, first aid kit, flashlight, rain gear, and other items that would be useful if you had to leave your home for a few days.

STORY QUESTIONS

1. How fast does a tropical storm need to be moving in order to receive a name?
   a. 25 mph
   b. over 39 mph
   c. 100 mph
   d. over 76 mph
2. Where would you find the answer to the previous question?
   a. second paragraph
   b. third paragraph
   c. in the title
   d. none of the above
3. What is the definition of the word *non-perishable* as used in the passage?
   a. long-lasting
   b. freeze-dried
   c. emergency
   d. fresh

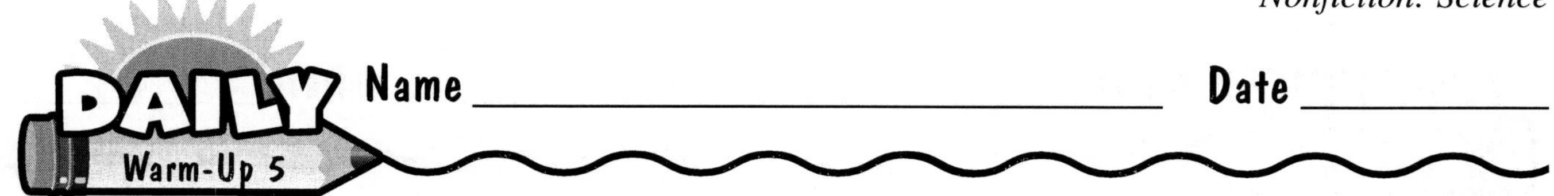

Name ______________________ Date __________

THE DIGESTIVE SYSTEM

Each time you take a bite of food, your digestive system begins its work. In fact, your digestive system begins working long before you take your first bite. Any time you smell or taste or even think about something good, your body begins to form saliva, or spit. The saliva helps break down the food as you chew it in your mouth.

Your tongue helps by pushing the food back, and your teeth go to work breaking the food up into tiny pieces. The tongue sends the food back to your esophagus. The esophagus is a pipe about 10 inches long. It is a stretchy pipe that brings the food to your stomach.

Your stomach is a sack shaped in the form of the letter J. It is responsible for breaking down the food you have eaten, storing the food, and slowly emptying the liquified food into the small intestine. The stomach churns and mashes all the food together, kind of like a washing machine. The gastric juices in the stomach help break the food down. The food is then sent to the intestines.

The small intestine breaks the food down even more so that your body can absorb the nutrients and vitamins. The food then passes through the large intestine, the colon, and on through the body. Some things you can do to help your digestive system is to drink plenty of water and high fiber foods. Is all of this making you hungry?

STORY QUESTIONS

1. Why is the stomach likened to a letter of the alphabet?
   a. It is easier to learn about the stomach this way.
   b. It explains the relationship between eating and the alphabet.
   c. It is a mnemonic device used to memorize parts of the stomach.
   d. It is shaped like the letter "J."
2. What is the purpose of the third paragraph?
   a. to explain how the digestive system is measured
   b. to explain how the body receives its nutrients
   c. to explain how the small intestine, large intestine, and colon help digest food
   d. to explain how the stomach works
3. Where would you read to find out about the role of saliva?
   a. first paragraph
   b. end of the third paragraph
   c. second paragraph
   d. end of the first paragraph

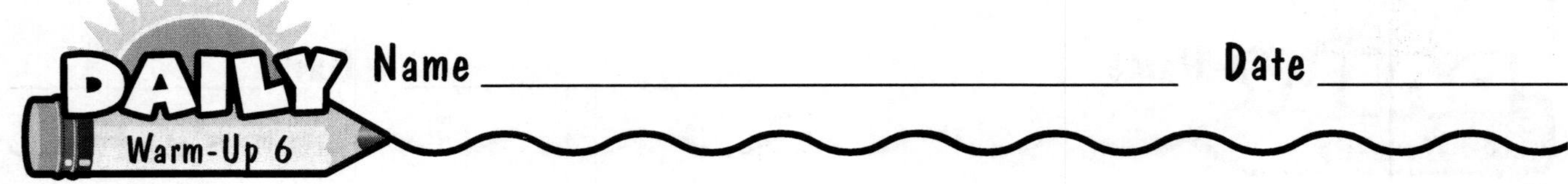

THE MOON

Many of the planets in our solar systems have satellites. Satellites are objects or items that rotate around a planet. These can be manmade or they can be natural satellites. Did you know the moon is a natural satellite of the Earth? There are moons in this solar system that are larger, but it is still very big. On the other hand, the moon is smaller than the Earth. That is why objects weigh less on the moon than they do on Earth. When the astronauts traveled to the moon, they could float and bounce around because they weighed less on the moon.

The moon does not have any liquid water on it. The moon, however, does have craters, mountain ranges, and lava plains as well as other special features. The inside of the moon is made up of layers. Some of these layers are rock solid while others are molten like lava.

One thing that scientists have learned is that there is no wind on the moon. That is because there is no atmosphere on the moon. Because there is no atmosphere, there is no protection from the sun. The moon can get very hot during the day and very cold at night.

Humans have been able to see the moon since the beginning, but Galileo was the first person to look at the moon close up. He used a telescope to let him see things more closely. Galileo learned a lot of amazing things about the moon.

STORY QUESTIONS

1. Which paragraph explains the physical features of the moon?
   a. first paragraph
   b. second paragraph
   c. third paragraph
   d. fourth paragraph

2. What inferences can you make about the moon after reading this passage?
   a. Unaided, humans cannot live on the moon.
   b. The moon used to be considered one of the planets.
   c. The moon has living organisms on it.
   d. The moon rotates around the sun more quickly than the Earth.

3. Which statement shows the author's opinion about the moon?
   a. Galileo learned a lot of amazing things about the moon.
   b. Scientists have been studying the moon and its surface for years.
   c. On the other hand, the moon is smaller than the Earth.
   d. He used a telescope to let him see things more closely.

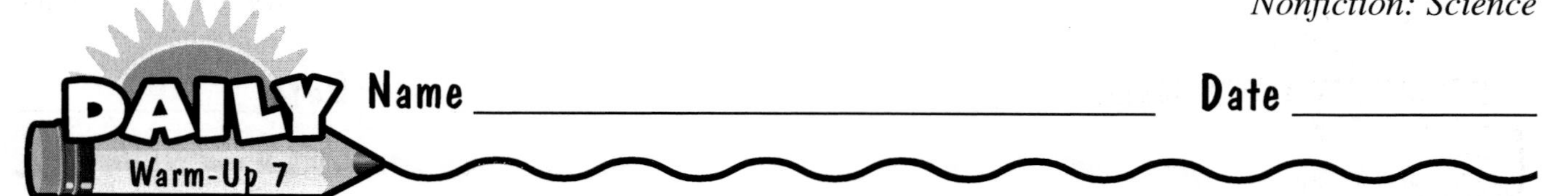

Name ______________________ Date __________

WATER CYCLE

What is the water cycle? How does it affect us? The water cycle is very important to our existence. A *cycle* is another word for circle. The water cycle is like one continuous circle. Water can be found in the form of liquid (drinking water), gas (vapor or steam), or a solid (ice or snow) at any given part of the water cycle. There are three phases that make up the water cycle. These phases are condensation, precipitation, and evaporation.

Condensation is when water vapor in the air turns to liquid. Temperature and air pressure have a lot to do with condensation. Warm air can hold more water than cool air, and therefore the water vapor condenses into small droplets as the temperature falls.

Precipitation is what happens when the water vapor condenses into large droplets. Gravity pulls on the liquid droplets and causes them to fall to the ground. Precipitation can be in the form of snow, sleet, rain, or hail. Air temperature and wind patterns determine the type of precipitation.

Evaporation is when liquid water changes to a gas. This happens with an increase in temperature or a dry wind blowing across the water. Gas rises into the air and forms clouds. Sometimes it even forms fog.

STORY QUESTIONS

1. After reading the passage, which statement is <u>not</u> accurate?
   a. Air temperature and wind patterns determine the type of precipitation.
   b. Precipitation is what happens when the water vapor evaporates.
   c. A *cycle* is another word for circle. The water cycle is like one continuous circle.
   d. Gas rises into the air and forms clouds.

2. The main idea of this passage is . . .
   a. to inform the reader about what happens when it rains.
   b. to inform the reader about the connection between the Earth's orbiting the sun and the water cycle.
   c. to inform the reader about how important condensation is to the Earth.
   d. to share general information about the water cycle and its role.

3. Where can you find information about how water changes to a gas?
   a. second paragraph
   b. not in the passage
   c. fourth paragraph
   d. third paragraph

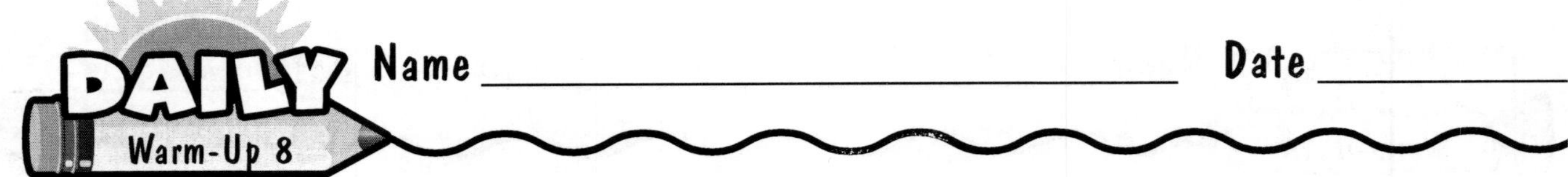

LIFE CYCLE OF A FROG

Have you ever wondered how a frog is formed? It is an interesting process. In early spring, adult frogs make their way to the breeding pools. Once they arrive, the male frogs croak very loudly. They are trying to attract the females so they can breed. The female releases her eggs into the water so the male can fertilize them. Once fertilized, these groups of eggs are called frogspawn. It is a jelly-like substance that absorbs water. It floats up to the surface of the pond so that the sun can warm it. One clump of frogspawn can hold thousands of eggs inside.

After 10 days, tadpoles will wiggle free from the eggs and begin swimming around. A tadpole is more like a fish than a frog at this point. It uses its tail and gills to breathe and swim. It takes five weeks for the tadpole to develop lungs and breathe air. Once the lungs are developed, the tadpole needs to go to the surface of the water for air. By seven weeks, miniature teeth are formed so that the tadpole can eat other insects and sometimes other tadpoles.

By eight weeks, the tadpole begins to grow back legs. It takes 10 or more weeks for the front legs to grow. At around 14 weeks, the tadpole begins to lose its tail and look like a real frog. In three years, the frog will have reached maturity and the whole cycle begins again.

STORY QUESTIONS

1. What is frogspawn?
   a. the frog's habitat
   b. food for the frog to eat
   c. a jelly-like substance
   d. the frog's territory
2. Which of the following statements can you infer after reading the passage?
   a. Frogs go through many changes before they are mature.
   b. Frogspawn is very dangerous when humans touch it.
   c. Scientists still do not know a lot about how the frog develops.
   d. Only some tadpoles turn into frogs.
3. The purpose of the third paragraph is to . . .
   a. inform the reader about frogspawn.
   b. inform the reader about how the female frog fertilizes the eggs.
   c. inform the reader about how the lungs of the frog develop.
   d. none of the above

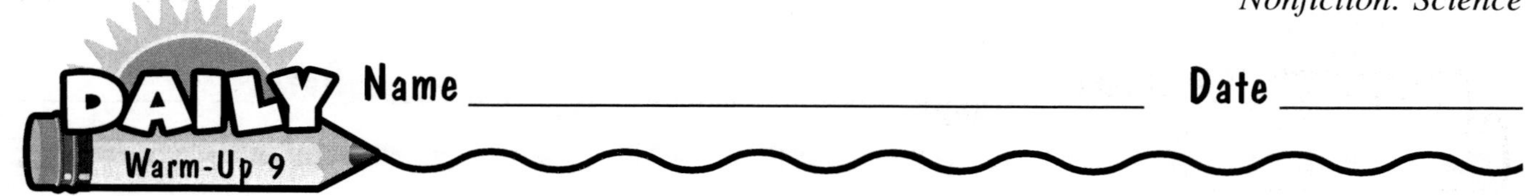

CELLS

The cell is the smallest unit of living matter. Many living things are made up of millions and millions of cells. Cells come in all different sizes, shapes, and forms. They each have different jobs to perform as well. There are three main parts to a cell. Each cell has a cell membrane, a nucleus, and cytoplasm.

The cell membrane is found along the outer edge of the cell. It works like a filter or a sieve. It lets the good things like nutrients in, and it gets rid of all the bad stuff. It serves as a protection to the cell.

The nucleus of a cell is like the brain of the cell. It is dark and is usually located in the center of the cell. It controls all the actions of the cell. The nucleus also contains the DNA. The DNA is a like a blueprint or a plan that the cell will use to reproduce.

The cytoplasm is located inside the cell membrane and around the nucleus. It is a jelly-like substance. This is where all the action takes place. The cytoplasm responds to the nucleus. This is where the cell uses the nutrients. It is made of water and other chemicals. Cells can live for different amounts of time. Cells are constantly reproducing.

STORY QUESTIONS

1. What are the three parts of a cell?
   - a. cell membrane, shell, cytoplasm
   - b. cell membrane, brain, cytoplasm
   - c. cell membrane, nutrients, cytoplasm
   - d. cell membrane, nucleus, cytoplasm
2. What does the word *sieve* mean as used in the passage?
   - a. strainer
   - b. proof
   - c. instruction
   - d. plan
3. What role does DNA play in the cell?
   - a. It depends on the amount of cytoplasm in the cell.
   - b. It carries the information to the brain.
   - c. It carries the overall plan or blueprint of the cell's reproduction.
   - d. It depends on how many years it has been a cell.
4. Which paragraph helps answer the previous question?
   - a. first paragraph
   - b. fifth paragraph
   - c. third paragraph
   - d. fourth paragraph

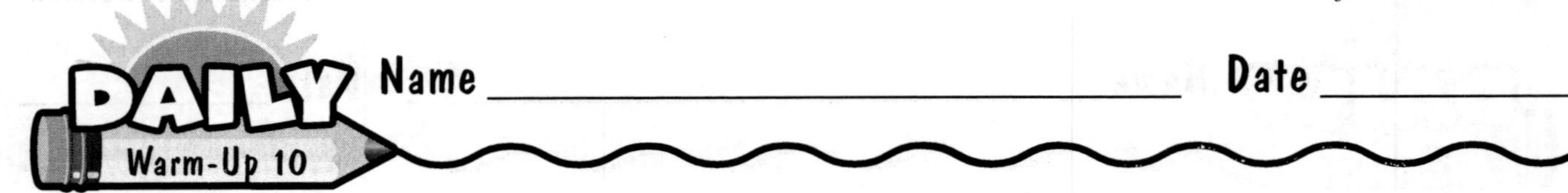

Name ______________________ Date __________

GERMS

Our world is filled with viruses, bacteria, and fungi. Even the healthiest body can be attacked by one of these microscopic creatures. Millions of these microbes can be found in a spoonful of dust. But not all of these microbes are bad. Some of them are very good. The good ones help us digest our food. The bad ones are called germs.

Germs enter our body through our mouth, nose, other openings, or even a cut on the skin. It is important that we get enough sleep and eat healthy foods so that our bodies can withstand the attack of these bad germs. The less healthy we are, the easier it is for these germs to mount an attack.

These germs are spread by someone sneezing, coughing, or by touching door handles or other surfaces. We can also get some of these germs from some of the food we eat. These germs can be found in the water we drink. The older we get, the more experienced our body becomes at recognizing these germs and fighting them. The system that recognizes these germs is called our immune system. The cells in our immune system help us fight off these germs.

STORY QUESTIONS

1. What are the names of microbes mentioned in this article?
   a. viruses, illness, fungi
   b. viruses, germs, and colds
   c. antibiotics
   d. viruses, bacteria, fungi
2. Which of the following statements is listed in the passage about germs?
   a. Germs enter our body through our mouth, nose, other openings, or even a cut on the skin.
   b. Billions of these microbes can be found in our bodies.
   c. Money has been raised to research more about how the immune system works.
   d. The cells in our immune system learn to decode bad germs.
3. Which paragraph helps you answer the previous question?
   a. second paragraph
   b. first paragraph
   c. fourth paragraph
   d. third paragraph
4. Without the immune system, what would happen?
   a. Our bodies could filter all the germs inside.
   b. There would be no predictable patterns.
   c. Another organ of the body would have to take over its role.
   d. The human body could not survive.

DAILY Warm-Up 11 Name ______________________ Date __________

MISSION TO MARS

For years, there has been speculation about whether or not there is life on Mars. Mars has always been an intriguing planet to humans. For centuries, stories have been told and retold about Martians invading the earth. Does life really exist on Mars? A group of scientists have been working to find out.

One of the latest space probes to travel to Mars was the *Odyssey* sent by NASA, the U.S. space agency. The *Odyssey* traveled through space for about seven months before it reached the orbit of Mars. It orbited about 200 miles from Mars' surface. The most important task for the *Odyssey* is to identify signs of water. Water means that there are possible signs of life.

There are many important instruments on the *Odyssey*. The Gamma ray spectrometer is an instrument that is used to detect oxygen and carbon on the surface of Mars. The solar array collects energy from the sun. This is how the *Odyssey* gets its power. The cameras are used to orient the *Odyssey*. Communication to earth is possible through the antenna. The Martian radiation environment experiment tests levels of radiation. And finally, the imaging system locates minerals on Mars' surface.

Because of the *Odyssey*, scientists have gained valuable information about the planet Mars.

STORY QUESTIONS

1. Which instrument allows the *Odyssey* able to communicate with earth?
   - a. radiation environment experiment
   - b. gamma ray spectrometer
   - c. imaging system
   - d. antenna
2. What is the meaning of the word *orient* as used in this passage?
   - a. arrange
   - b. adjust
   - c. modify
   - d. opposite
3. What is the purpose of the third paragraph?
   - a. to explain how the *Odyssey* was developed
   - b. to explain how the animals survive on other planets
   - c. to explain how scientists designed the *Odyssey*
   - d. to explain the instruments on the *Odyssey*
4. Where would you read to find out about the travels and tasks of the *Odyssey*?
   - a. first paragraph
   - b. end of the third paragraph
   - c. second paragraph
   - d. end of the second paragraph

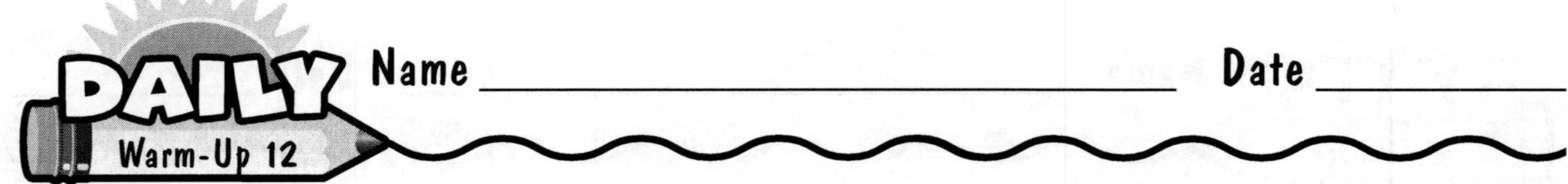

THE CORAL REEF

A coral reef is a beautiful underwater community filled with many different types of species. You can find fish, coral, sea plants, and much more. These coral reefs have been around for millions and millions of years. Recently, some scientists believe that coral reefs may be in danger. Scientists believe that pollution and human error has destroyed more than a quarter of the world's coral reefs.

Some of the living animals that make up the coral reefs are struggling to survive. For example, coral looks and feels like rock. This causes people to treat coral like rocks. But coral is actually made up of tiny, clear animals. These animals are called coral polyps. The coral stick together to form large colonies. When the coral polyps die, they leave a hard shell of limestone behind. Coral gets its color from tiny sea plants called algae. There is a delicate balance between the algae and the coral. Coral reefs provide homes and shelter for many sea animals and plants.

Pollution and bad fishing practices have caused harm to the coral and algae. Another problem is the warming of the water. The algae cannot live in warmer waters and therefore, the coral loses its source of food and color. This process has been named coral bleaching.

Scientists are working hard to find solutions to the problems in coral reefs. Their goal is to protect and preserve this natural resource.

STORY QUESTIONS

1. What is coral made up of?
   a. sea anemone
   b. tiny, clear animals
   c. seaweed and moss
   d. rocks and crevices
2. When coral reefs die, they leave a hard shell of . . .
   a. calcium.
   b. helium.
   c. carbon dioxide
   d. limestone.
3. What does the word *error* mean as used in the passage?
   a. extraordinary
   b. fault
   c. inhibited
   d. progressive
4. What is the main idea of this reading passage?
   a. to inform the reader about the coral reefs and their uniqueness
   b. to inform the reader about how coral bleaching occurs
   c. to explain the difference between the two different types of corals
   d. to explain the life of marine biologists

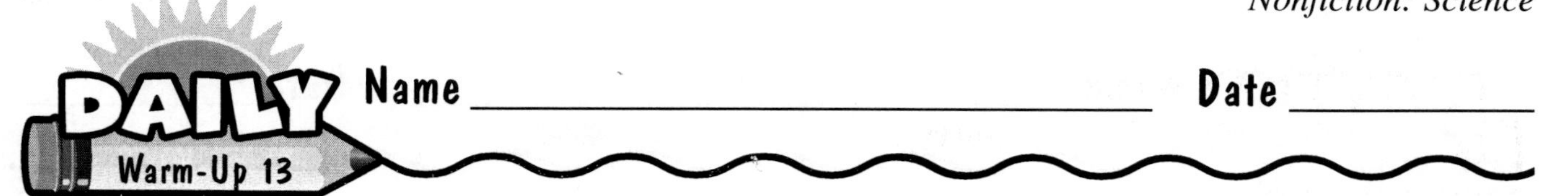

NOCTURNAL ANIMALS

Nocturnal animals are simply animals that are more active at night. Nocturnal animals typically sleep during the day. They also live in a den or a burrow so they are hidden from the sun and the sounds of activity. Many nocturnal animals live in the desert. They prefer to come out at night so they can avoid the extreme temperatures of the daytime.

You may wonder how nocturnal animals can see in the darkness. Most nocturnal animals have special eyes that help them see at night. Owls, cats, and lemurs all have eyes that see better at night. Bats, on the other hand, use sound as a way for them to find their way around. This is called *echolocation*.

Some scientists are finding that nocturnal animals that live close to housing developments or other commercial buildings are having a difficult time. This is because these buildings have lights on all night, lighting up the surrounding area. For example, the sea turtle in Florida lays her eggs at night. When the babies hatch at night and head for the ocean, they can be taken off course by the bright lights. Scientists are studying this problem to find a solution.

STORY QUESTIONS

1. What is unique about nocturnal animals?
   a. These animals are without the sense of smell.
   b. These animals feed their young.
   c. These animals are active at night instead of day.
   d. These animals have evolved significantly through the years.

2. Which paragraph does <u>not</u> explain the definition of or types of nocturnal animals?
   a. first paragraph   b. second paragraph   c. third paragraph

3. Which of the following statements explains *echolocation*?
   a. Bats, on the other hand, use sound as a way for them to find their way around.
   b. Nocturnal animals are simply animals that are more active at night instead of the day.
   c. This is because these buildings have lights on all night, lighting up the surrounding area.
   d. When the babies hatch at night and head for the ocean, they can be taken off course by the bright lights.

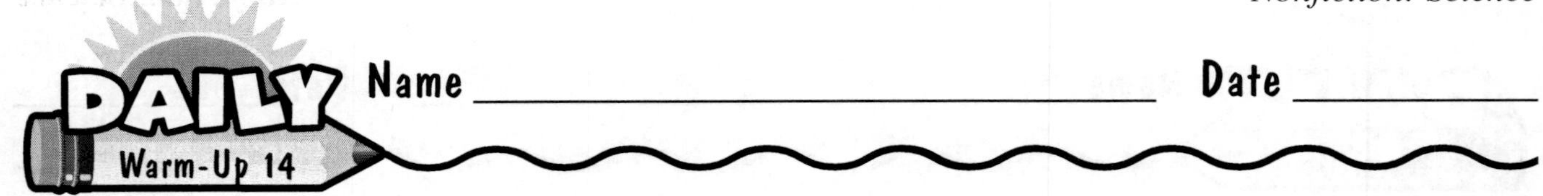

THE EYE

Have you ever wondered how the eye works? The human eye is about as big as a ping pong ball. It sits in the eye socket inside the skull. The eyelid protects the front part of the eye. The eyelid is a piece of skin that is movable so that it can open and close. The eyelid also helps keep the eye moist. It does this by blinking. Blinking is a voluntary and involuntary action. The eye blinks involuntarily several times a minute.

The eyelid also has great reflexes. This is a form of protection for the eye. If a ball or other object is coming towards the eye, the eyelid will quickly close to protect the eye. The eyelid will also close or squint when there is bright sunlight. The eyelashes are another important protection for the eye. Eyelashes keep dirt and other particles from getting into the eyes.

The white part of the eyeball is called the sclera. The sclera is the outside coating of the eyeball. Tiny blood vessels line the sclera. The cornea rests directly on top of the colored part of the eye. The cornea is completely transparent so that light can filter through. Behind the cornea are the iris and the pupil. The iris is the colorful part of the eye. The pupil determines how much light is allowed into the eye. The eye is an amazing part of the body.

STORY QUESTIONS

1. What is the purpose of the eyelashes?
   a. to keep the eye moist
   b. to allow light to filter into the eye
   c. to allow movement in the eye
   d. to keep dirt and other particles out of the eye

2. What part of the eye is the colorful part?
   a. cornea
   b. pupil
   c. iris
   d. sclera

3. Which paragraph helps you answer the previous question?
   a. third paragraph
   b. fourth paragraph
   c. second paragraph
   d. none of the above

4. Name the different ways in which the eyelid protects the eye.

____

____

____

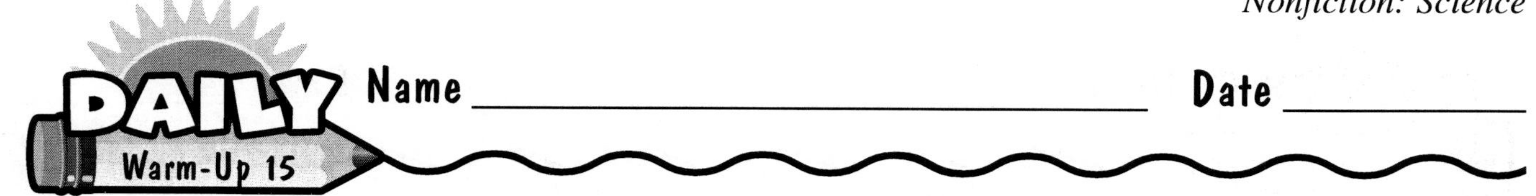

SNOWFLAKES

A snowflake is essentially a piece of ice falling to the ground. A snowflake is a crystalline form of ice. Snowflakes come in many different forms and shapes. It is said that no two snowflakes are ever alike. So while each snowflake is unique, snowflakes do have characteristics in common. They are all hexagonal. This means that they all have six sides or branches. Snowflakes are also symmetrical.

There are many different types of snowflakes. One of the forms is called the stellar dendrites. This form looks like six trees extending from the center. Another form is the sector plate. These snowflakes have plate-like arms that extend from the center. These are made from flat, slender pieces of ice.

Spatial dendrites are another form of snowflake. These snowflakes are not flat and slender pieces of ice. These snowflakes are made from individual snowflakes all jumbled up together. Branches of these crystals extend from the center.

STORY QUESTIONS

1. What do sector plate snowflakes look like?
   a. six trees extending from the center
   b. crystalline form of water ice
   c. individual snowflakes all jumbled together
   d. six plate-like arms that extend from center
2. What do all snowflakes have in common?

   ____

3. What is the meaning of the word *extend* as used in the passage?
   a. scared
   b. steady
   c. excitable
   d. lengthen
4. Where would you read to find out about stellar dendrites?
   a. first paragraph
   b. beginning of the second paragraph
   c. end of the third paragraph
   d. second paragraph

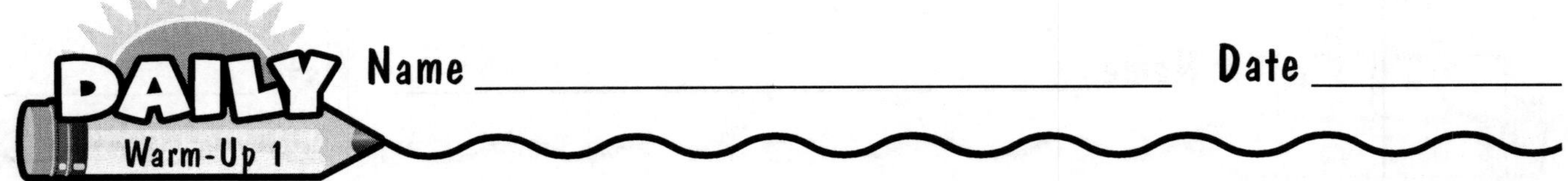

SEPARATE SCHOOLS

There has been a lot of talk recently about how best to meet the needs of students. One of the suggestions has been to place boys and girls into separate schools. Some educators feel that students would be able to focus better on their schooling if this was the case. There are approximately 100 public schools in the country that have separate schools for girls and boys. These schools claim great success.

Educators believe that girls especially benefit from this arrangement. Educators claim that girls will get more attention from teachers if there are no boys in the class. They also say that girls will speak up more if they are in all-girl classes. Educators believe that students in all-boy or all-girl classes will be better behaved.

On the other hand, other educators feel that those who support this plan are missing an important point. Boys and girls have to learn how to get along with each other. Students can't learn this if they are kept apart. These educators also feel that this model assumes that girls are weak and not able to handle competing and interacting with boys. They feel that girls do not need to be protected.

STORY QUESTIONS

1. Some educators feel that girls will get more __________ if they are separated from boys.
   a. attention
   b. homework
   c. study time
   d. concentration

2. Which of the following is a reason presented in this passage as to why scientists believe separating boys and girls would benefit girls?
   a. Boys are in trouble more than girls.
   b. Boys are able to get the teacher's attention more easily.
   c. Scientists say that girls will speak up more if they are in all-girl classes.
   d. Girls are too shy when the boys are in the classroom.

3. Which of the following statements would the author of this passage most likely make?
   a. Children need to be taught how to get their teacher's attention.
   b. Parents should hold schools responsible for how girls and boys are treated differently in the classroom.
   c. Teachers should be held to higher standards about how girls and boys are treated.
   d. Educators should be aware of the differences in how boys and girls are treated and receive attention in class.

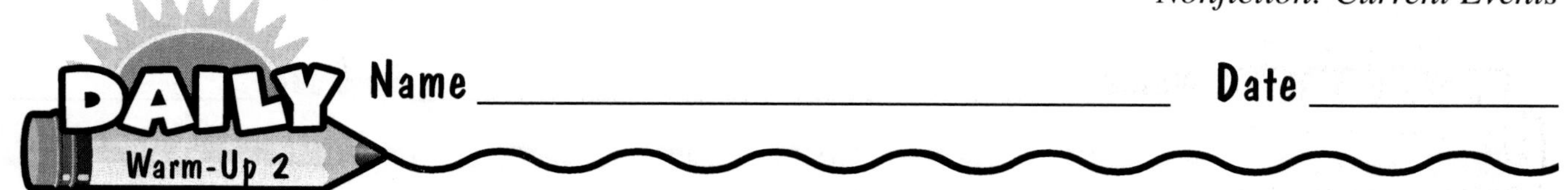

NEW CITY PLANNERS

Many of the cities in the United States are a mess. They are crowded with too many houses and too many people. Cities have smog, too much traffic, noise, and run-down buildings. Cities continue to grow and spread, taking up more natural land and countryside.

It is time to make changes. Adults have planned cities for years, and they still produce the same outcome. It's time that kids become the city planners. New ideas and techniques are needed. Kids are an important part of the cities. Their ideas are creative and fresh. They are the future.

Each year, the Future City Competition is held. It is part of National Engineers Week. This gives kids across the United States a chance to design a city that would be easy to live in and beautiful as well. Thousands of schools send teams to participate each year. Each team is composed of three students, a professional engineer, and a teacher. They are able to use software to build a 3-D town.

Of course, it's a lot easier to design a city from scratch without all the existing problems. It's also a lot easier to fix cities on paper than in real life. But using the imagination of kids is the key to the future. Besides, the kids will be the ones living in these cities in years to come.

STORY QUESTIONS

1. Why does the author of this passage think that kids should be asked to plan cities?
   - a. They are innocent.
   - b. They haven't been asked before.
   - c. They have requested input.
   - d. Their ideas are new and innovative.
2. What is the meaning of the word *existing* as used in the passage?
   - a. previous
   - b. current
   - c. desired
   - d. interfering
3. Who makes up a team for the Future City Competition?
   - a. three engineers, three students
   - b. three teachers, one engineer, one student
   - c. engineers and students
   - d. three students, one teacher, one engineer
4. Which paragraph helps you answer the previous question?
   - a. first paragraph
   - b. fourth paragraph
   - c. third paragraph
   - d. second paragraph

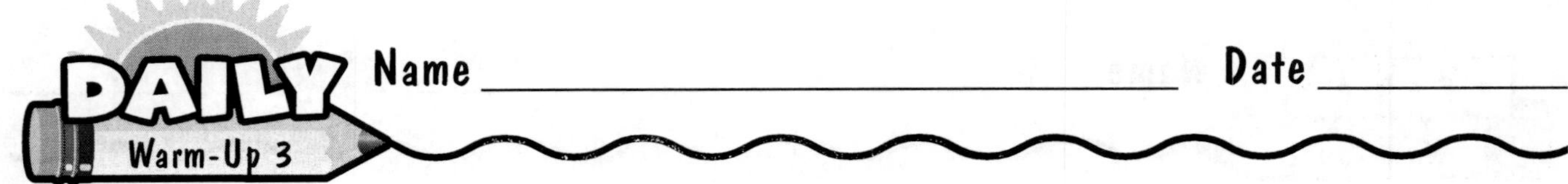

CAPTIVE WHALES

People from around the world love to come watch whales perform at sea-animal aquariums and theme parks across the country. At first glance, this may seem harmless enough, but it is not. After researching the lasting effect on these whales, some marine biologists are wondering if these whales should be set free. Keeping whales locked up and out of their natural habitat is cruel and should be prohibited. They feel that it's just not the humane thing to be doing.

It's understandable that people love to see these whales and dolphins doing tricks and entertaining audiences, but at what expense? These whales are trapped and confined and ordered to perform on command. In the wild, whales and dolphins live in groups, but in the aquariums and theme parks they live alone. It's been said that they receive little medical care as well. Evidence of this is the sores they have covering their skin.

Other marine biologists claim that these whales and dolphins receive excellent care and live in state-of-the-art conditions. Their homes at the aquariums and theme parks are of the highest quality. They feel they get better treatment than if they lived in the wild. They further claim that many of these whales have been saved from the wild. If left out in the wild, they would have died.

STORY QUESTIONS

1. In the wild, whales usually live in . . .
   a. solitary confinement.
   b. groups.
   c. colonies.
   d. coral reefs.
2. What do some scientists say the sores on whale skin show evidence of?
   a. The whales receive little medical care.
   b. They are allergic to the water they live in.
   c. They are suffering from depression.
   d. They are not receiving enough vitamins and nutrients.
3. Why do other marine biologists say that the whales in these conditions are doing just fine?

   ____

   ____

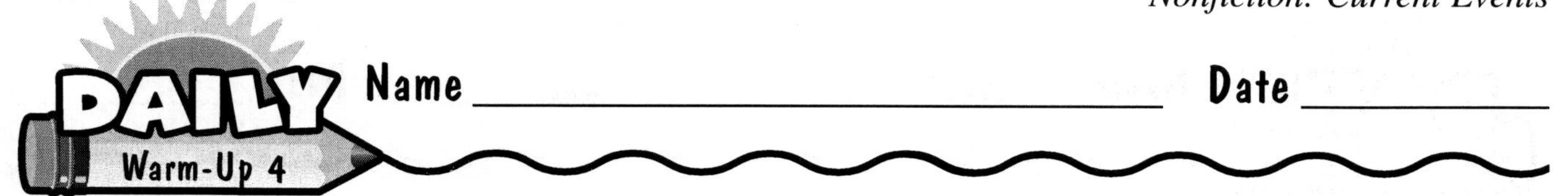

THE V CHIP

One of the newest things in television technology is the V chip. The idea behind the V chip is to protect children from violence on television, but is that really what it does?

This sounds like a good plan, but just like most new ideas, there are many things that still need to be considered. Television producers don't like the V chip because they feel like they are being monitored and censored. Whose responsibility is it to monitor what can be shown on television or not?

There are many questions associated with this issue. For example, who decides the definition of violence? Does the government have the right to decide this? Do the parents? Do the broadcasting companies? What happens if people can't agree? The V chip is only successful with standards for what is considered violent and what is not.

Opponents also say that they don't think the V chip or other such forms of monitoring and censoring will be effective. Kids know more about technology and how it works than their parents do. Will they know how to reprogram a television just as soon as they set it up with the V chip?

STORY QUESTIONS

1. What is the purpose of the V chip?
   a. to allow free television minutes
   b. to protect children from seeing violence on television
   c. to reprogram the television to work with VCR
   d. a program designed for the government to monitor television shows

2. What is the key question associated with implementing the V chip?

   ____

3. What is the main idea of paragraph two?
   a. to explain the concerns parents have about violence on television
   b. to explain the benefits of implementing the V chip
   c. to explain the benefits of television producers monitoring shows
   d. to explain the questions and issues related to the V chip

4. Which of the following is <u>not</u> one of the reasons opponents do not like the V chip?
   a. Kids know more about technology, the V chip, and how it works than their parents do.
   b. They don't think the V chip or other such forms of monitoring and censoring will be effective.
   c. They feel that children will be able to override the V chip.
   d. They don't feel it's the government's right to monitor or censor programs.

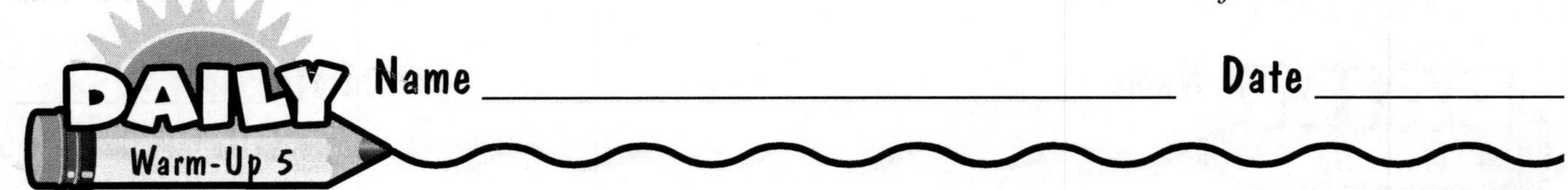

SCHOOL FUNDING

School funding is one of the biggest issues in schools today. There just isn't enough money to go around. Many schools across the country are so old that they are falling apart. Each time it rains, hallways are filled with buckets and trash cans to catch the water. Some schools are filled with mold, causing problems for children and teachers allergic to mold. This mold can also be toxic. Old schools that are falling apart are often safety hazards, as well.

Another problem with our education is that the schools are not funded properly. Teachers struggle on a daily basis to teach lessons with no paper or materials available to do so. How can a teacher possibly teach students without the necessary supplies? Schools cannot afford to hire enough teachers, either. The ratio of students to teachers is much too high to meet the needs of all the students. The government spends a lot of money on programs that are not necessary. The government should stop this waste and send this money to the schools.

Educators feel that schools can no longer be ignored. There will be a price to pay. Uneducated students cannot be as productive in society. Society pays the price in the cost of crime and violence and families on welfare.

STORY QUESTIONS

1. Which would be another good title for this reading passage?
   a. "Choose Your Own School"
   b. "My Community, My Choice"
   c. "Schools vs. Government"
   d. "Schools Need Money"

2. Which of the following is the main reason to support school funding?
   a. Another problem with our education is that the schools are not funded properly.
   b. Many schools across the country are so old they are falling apart.
   c. Schools cannot afford to hire enough teachers either.
   d. Uneducated students cannot be as productive in society.

3. What is meant by the word *productive* as used in this passage?
   a. amorous
   b. industrious
   c. ineffective
   d. reliant

4. What will ultimately happen if schools do not receive money to teach students?
   a. Students will have to skip grades.
   b. Teachers will have to use their own money.
   c. Schools will have to be shut down.
   d. Students will not receive adequate education.

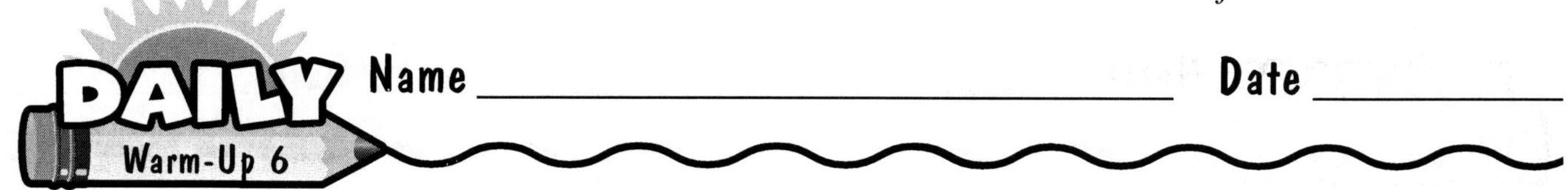

LUNCH MENUS

If you're having trouble paying attention in school because you are hungry, don't blame your stomach. Chances are you are not getting the right nutrients in the lunchroom. Across the country, many students are not eating a healthy lunch and are suffering the consequences.

Have you looked at a school lunch menu? Many of the same bland foods are offered again and again. Most of these foods are unhealthy, with a high fat and sodium content. You would be lucky to find a menu that includes fresh fruit and vegetables other than the small carrots. How can this possibly be acceptable?

You may say that if a student is not happy with the lunch menu, then he or she should just bring his or her own lunch from home. The problem is that not all students have this luxury. Many students are on a reduced or free lunch program. They just don't have that option. Students are asked to suggest lunch menus, but eating pizza, hamburgers, or hot dogs every day is not sufficient. Cafeterias need to create menus that are not only appealing to students but nutritious, as well.

The U.S. government just came out with the new food pyramid guide. How many of the cafeteria school menus will meet these guidelines? A hard look at what we are feeding the future adults of America needs to happen. Let's take that look before it becomes too late for this generation. Too many lives are depending on it!

STORY QUESTIONS

1. People who agree with this passage probably feel that . . .
   a. parents should take more responsibility in providing lunch for their children.
   b. schools need to adjust their budget to fund the lunch program better.
   c. schools need to give the responsibility of school lunch to someone else.
   d. schools need to look at more effective ways to feed delicious and nutritious lunches.
2. The main idea of this passage is . . .
   a. cafeterias can be great resources for students, if they are funded appropriately.
   b. cafeteria workers need to teach students to eat more healthy foods.
   c. principals should have a meeting to discuss how to improve lunches.
   d. schools need to make more appealing and nutritious lunches.
3. What is one of the ways suggested in the passage to improve cafeterias?
   a. Ask the students for ideas.
   b. Generate more appealing and nutritious lunches.
   c. Require all students to bring their lunch from home.
   d. Order food from local fast food restaurants.

DAILY Warm-Up 7

Name ______________________ Date __________

RELIGION IN SCHOOLS

Recently, France instituted a law prohibiting students from wearing headscarves in public schools. Laws such as these came out of fear and concern of terrorists and other groups that practice religious fanaticism. Many Muslim women and girls wear the headscarves as an important part of their religion. But should religious expression be prohibited at a public school?

The supporters of the law said that this law was not passed to punish the Muslim students. They claim that this law was aimed to prohibit *all* religious symbols from being worn at public schools. This would include such items as head coverings worn by Jewish men and boys, the Christian cross, or any other religious symbol.

This law created a debate in France as well as around the world. Many Muslims felt that they were being discriminated against. Many of these students felt that their rights were being violated. But the government reiterated that the law was not directed at any one religion. Supporters of the law felt that religious matters should be kept at home and not at public school.

Those opposed to the law felt that even students in the United States had more rights. The United States has a law regarding the freedom of speech, which allows students to dress as they choose as long as it does not disturb the educational process. This allows members of a religion to express their beliefs in clothing and apparel as long as it does not interfere with the educational process.

STORY QUESTIONS

1. What is the main idea of the reading passage?
   a. Students enjoy the right to choose what they wear.
   b. Should students be forced to follow school rules about what they wear?
   c. Do children need more supervision at school to ensure safety?
   d. Are changes in society effecting the schooling students are receiving?

2. What is meant by the term *fanaticism* as used in this passage?
   a. fervor
   b. uncertain
   c. more likely to
   d. resonates

3. According to the passage, which of the following is a reason for people supporting the law?
   a. They claim that this law was aimed to prohibit *all* religious symbols from being worn at public schools.
   b. The law was written as a form of protection to all students.
   c. Many of these students felt that their rights were being violated.
   d. Should religious expression be prohibited at a public school?

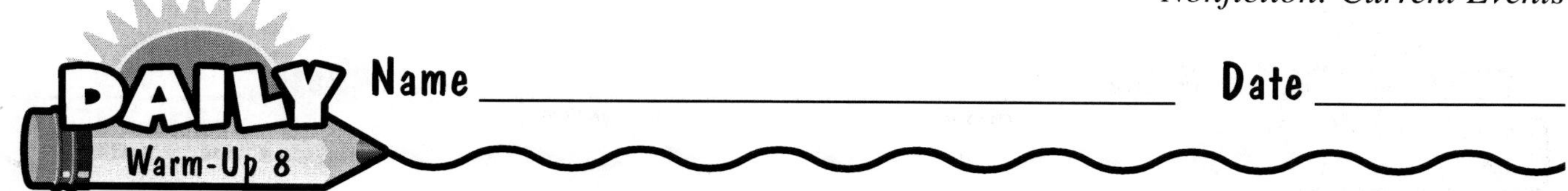

MONEY OR HARD WORK?

Can money make you successful? Most people seem to think so, but think again. It depends on your definition of success. Some of the richest people in the world are far from successful. There is no argument that money brings with it many opportunities that may otherwise be unrealized. Money can buy opportunities and materials. But money is not the only key.

Tesa was born in Africa in the poorest of countries. She was without adequate nutrition and care for most of her childhood. At the age of 16, she was determined to stay in school, though most of the other girls her age were leaving to marry or to help provide for their families at home. Girls were just not encouraged to get an education. But Tesa worked at school during the day and in the fields at night. By the moonlight, she would pick crops that were often devastated with drought and pests.

All of this hard work paid off. When Tesa turned 17, a traveling professor from England noticed her hard work and skill. He was amazed with her intellect. This professor invited her to attend one of the most prestigious universities in England. Since that time, Tesa has become a distinguished professor. Luck, you may say? Tesa would probably disagree with you. She would say that her hard work and dedication got her where she is today.

STORY QUESTIONS

1. Which of the following best describes the author of this passage?
   a. reticent and quiet
   b. obnoxious and loud
   c. frustrated and demanding
   d. encouraging and motivational
2. Which statement below helps support your answer to the previous question?
   a. Many are left without the skills they need to survive in today's world.
   b. Girls were just not encouraged to get an education.
   c. Job wages have continued to be lower than they should be.
   d. She would say that her hard work and dedication got her where she is today.
3. What is meant by the word *distinguished* as used in this passage?
   a. annoying
   b. different
   c. challenging
   d. illustrious

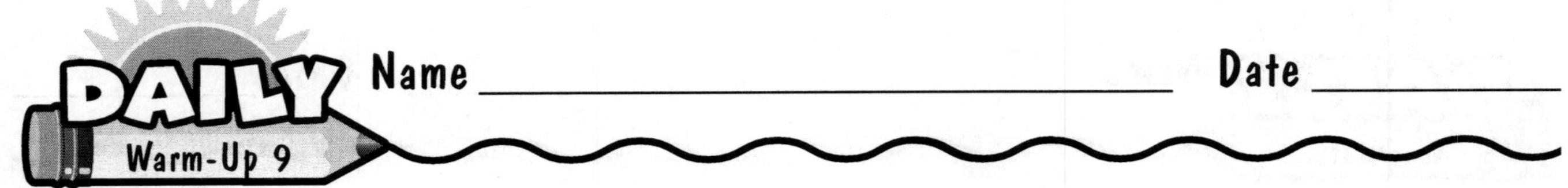

Name ______________________ Date __________

FEDERAL LAND

It is time for the U.S. government to keep their noses out of everything. The U.S. government is planning to take away thousands of acres in the state of Arizona. The government would like to turn this land into a national monument. Doesn't this country have enough national monuments? This action would prevent any mining or further development on the land.

The money needed to run these public facilities would come from the taxpayers. So not only will the government exercise more control, but it will also charge more money to its citizens for a monument it does not need. In addition to this, the state governments count on the taxes of these properties. As a result, the states will require more help from the federal government. And from where does this help come? From the taxpayers, of course.

The Antiquities Act of 1906 allows only the president of the United States or an act of Congress to create a national monument. This is far too much power and prevents the citizens of this country from holding either group accountable for these decisions. Aren't they supposed to carefully consider the opinions of the people who elected them? I don't remember anyone asking me.

The federal government already controls 25 percent of the land in the United States. Isn't that enough? It just doesn't seem right that an individual or a small group should have the right to determine the fate of millions of acres of land.

STORY QUESTIONS

1. What is the main idea of this passage?
   a. The federal government already controls 25 percent of the land in the United States.
   b. Doesn't this country have enough national monuments?
   c. The federal government should stop taking over private land.
   d. It just doesn't seem right that a small group should have this right.

2. Who else besides school children is the audience for this reading passage?
   a. young adults
   b. federal government
   c. parents and guardians
   d. older citizens of the United States

3. Which statement from the reading passage indicates who the audience of this passage is?
   a. Aren't they supposed to carefully consider the opinions of the people who elected them? I don't remember them asking me.
   b. The Antiquities Act of 1906 allows only the president of the United States or an act of Congress to create a national monument.
   c. As a result, the states will require more help from the federal government.
   d. In addition to this, the state governments count on these taxes.

DAILY Warm-Up 10

Name ______________________________ Date ____________

REALITY OF TELEVISION

Dear Television Executive:

As an avid television viewer, I am here to say that the quality of television shows has deteriorated. The shows that are not in the prime-time lineup are enough to make someone sick. The shows parade pornography, foul language, and infidelity as commonplace.

Whatever happened to classic shows like *The Brady Bunch* and *Bonanza*? These shows not only had a good moral message, but they were acceptable for all members of the family. There were no jumps to grab the remote to mute or change the station just in time before obscenities come screaming from the television.

It seems these days that the only thing the television executives think we are interested in are the ridiculous reality shows that have taken over time slots. Just who are these people? Their lives don't resemble mine at all. Exactly what redeeming qualities are we supposed to glean from these shows? What a waste of money!

I issue a challenge to television executives and the television audience alike. Settle for nothing less than the best. Accept only scripts that are entertaining and appropriate. Trash the reality shows and look for real stories out there. Clean up the language and the clothing worn by the actors. If we want to see this, we will just turn on the daytime soap operas. Make the changes needed. Let's show the youth of today what real television is. Better hurry! I'm ready to change the channel.

STORY QUESTIONS

1. In the statement, "These shows not only had a good moral message, but they were acceptable for all members of the family," *moral* means . . .
   a. to make room for.
   b. to show strength for.
   c. to compensate or adjust for.
   d. ethical.

2. Which of the following statements is the main complaint mentioned in this letter?
   a. There are too many reality shows on television.
   b. The companies that are making television shows are missing a huge market.
   c. The shows on television are not clean shows to watch.
   d. Television advertising has taken over what is seen on television.

3. This letter is mostly about . . .
   a. how television producers rely too much on advertisers.
   b. how the quality and appropriateness of television shows has deteriorated.
   c. how television producers have been pressured by parents to change their lineups.
   d. how the shows for children have diminished in number.

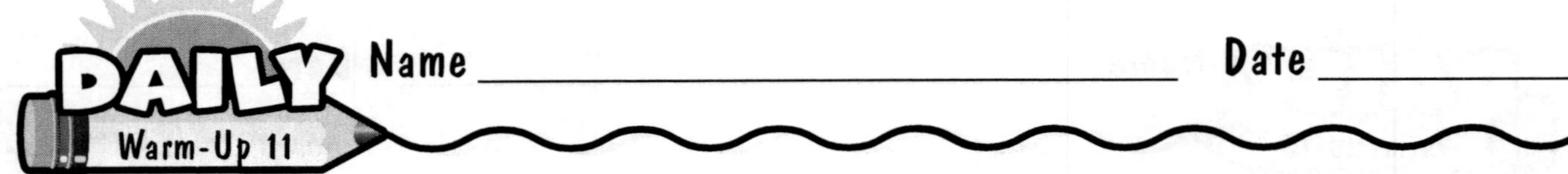

SAVE THE RAIN FOREST

For as long as I can remember, I have been taught to preserve the rain forest. In elementary school, I raised money with my class to preserve an acre of this rain forest. We were told story after story of how the rain forest was being destroyed in the name of development. We were instructed that the rain forest contained perhaps the cure to cancer and other incurable diseases. By sending money, we were also taught that we are preserving the habitat of rare birds, animals, and other species. So where are we today? After millions of dollars has been spent, what is the status of the rain forest?

We are told the Amazon rain forest encompasses around 2.7 million square miles. The Amazon also holds one-fifth of the world's water supply. These facts should make it worth saving. But unless the governments report the status of the rain forest, all these efforts are for naught.

Are logging, mining, and burning continuing to take place? It was estimated in 2003 that an estimated 9,170 square miles had been burned or cleared. Is this number declining each year? The loss of the rain forest is not just a loss for Ecuador, Peru, and Bolivia, but all countries that may benefit from its treasures. All governments should be holding these countries accountable. Reports should be distributed on a regular basis that review the ongoing status of the rain forest. We can't help unless we have the right information.

STORY QUESTIONS

1. This passage is mostly about how . . .
   a. the rain forest is being destroyed.
   b. updates and more information on the rain forests are needed.
   c. fund raising projects have helped save the rain forest.
   d. the governments have kept citizens informed about the rain forests.

2. Which of the following reasons was mentioned in the passage explaining why the author thinks that more information about the rain forest is necessary?
   a. These facts should make it worth saving the rain forest.
   b. We were told in school story after story of how the rain forest was being destroyed in the name of development.
   c. After millions of dollars has been spent, what is the status of the rain forest?
   d. But unless the governments report the status of the rain forest, all these efforts are for naught.

3. What is the meaning of the word *naught* as used in this passage?
   a. deranged
   b. impossible
   c. nothing
   d. uncertainty

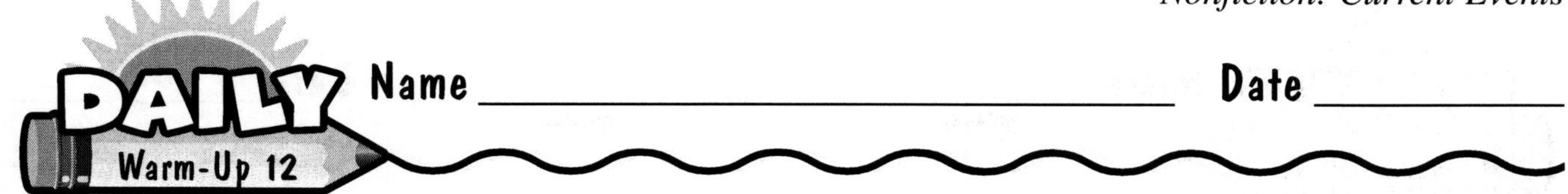

PEANUT ALLERGIES

Dear Principal Rollins,

Recently a person at our school was diagnosed with having an allergy to peanuts. I have heard of this situation before and I realize it can be a serious problem. People that have allergies to peanuts can die before receiving the necessary treatment. Within seconds a reaction can appear, leaving the victim only few short minutes to counteract the attack. These individuals must avoid anything containing peanuts or peanut oil. Sometimes just smelling or touching peanut oil and/or dust can cause a reaction.

Since that time, all of the school personnel have overreacted. We are no longer allowed to bring candy to school or bring peanut butter sandwiches in our lunches. The crackdown on peanuts has been ridiculous. The school cafeteria has changed all menus eliminating anything that looks or smells like a peanut. Why should all of the students at the school be punished because one kid has allergy problems? Why doesn't this student eat lunch in an isolated area far from the 600 students and their lunches? It's not right to punish many people just because a certain food is harmful to a small number of people.

Understandably, the school is trying to avoid a lawsuit. But instead of overreacting, the school could use this as a wonderful educational opportunity. Teach students about peanut allergies and how these can be harmful and deadly. Inform the students of the precautions that can be taken. They are many ways to protect kids without punishing everyone.

STORY QUESTIONS

1. What is the meaning of the word *counteract* as used in this passage?
   a. cancel out b. assist c. react
2. What is the main idea of the second paragraph?
   a. Why should all of the students at the school be punished because one kid has allergy problems?
   b. Why doesn't this student eat lunch in an isolated area far from the 600 students and their lunches?
   c. It's not right to punish many people just because of a certain food is harmful to a small number of people.
3. Which statement shows the author's opinion about the peanut policy changes?
   a. The crackdown on peanuts has been ridiculous.
   b. These individuals must avoid anything containing peanuts or peanut oil.
   c. Sometimes just smelling or touching peanut oil can cause a reaction.
   d. It doesn't take long for a person with an allergy to die from exposure.

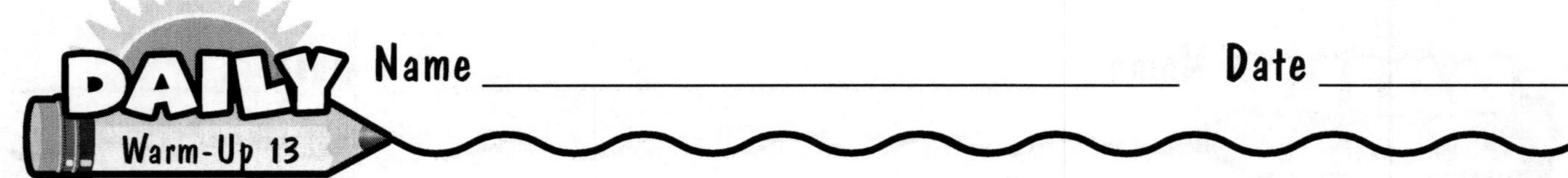

ENDANGERED ANIMALS

When is the last time you saw a Bengal tiger? Was it in a zoo or other animal park? Though these animals are confined and locked up, they may also be safer than their counterparts in the wild. The Bengal tiger lives in places of central India. This group of tigers is the last of thousands that used to live there hundreds of years ago. The Bengal tiger is now endangered.

What has happened to the Bengal tiger? The tigers have been hunted and poached until they are now endangered. The Indian government has passed laws to protect these animals. People are not allowed to enter the 23 tiger reserves across India. The reserves are home to approximately 3,000 tigers. Because of these new laws, many of these tigers have survived illegal hunting and poaching.

Many of the natives that live near these tiger reserves are concerned and angry. They understand the importance of saving these tigers, but in the meantime, these people are going without food and other resources they used to get in the tiger reserves. The natives insist that they are not a threat to the tigers. Can these two groups really live together without endangering the tiger? And if people are let back into the reserves, how can the government ensure that their intentions are pure? All of these concerns and issues need to be addressed.

STORY QUESTIONS

1. What is the author's opinion about saving endangered animals?
   a. The author feels that more money should be spent to save these animals.
   b. Government should enforce more laws to protect these animals.
   c. Endangered animals are a fact a life in a world of evolution.
   d. Education and laws can play a major role in saving endangered animals.
2. What is the meaning of the word *counterparts* as used in the passage?
   a. concerned
   b. captive
   c. others that are the same
   d. captivating
3. What is meant by the statement "All of these concerns and issues need to be addressed"?
   a. The author wants to ensure that each point of the issue is included.
   b. The author is trying to appeal to the audience to get more involved.
   c. The author is showing that he/she has little faith in the government to address all the issues to help the Bengal tiger.
   d. More funds and research needs to be done before humans are allowed in the tiger reserve.

DAILY Warm-Up 14

Name ______________________ Date __________

HUNTING PROHIBITED

Dear Editor:

The debate on whether hunting should be allowed has been raging for years. For thousands of years, man was responsible for providing food for his family. This almost always included a weapon of some sort. The gun has proven to be the most efficient way to kill an animal and provide food. Now that society has progressed enough to sell the meat our family eats in a plastic and Styrofoam packaging in the grocery store, some people have decided to eliminate hunting.

But what about those of us who want to be self-reliant and provide for ourselves? I am a 16-year-old hunter with at least five years of experience hunting. I have gone to every gun safety class that has been presented in my community. I eat the meat from the animals I shoot, and I am careful to leave the environment as I found it. Why should someone who doesn't like hunting be allowed to tell me what I can and cannot do?

I do not want to take responsibility for all hunters, as I know there are irresponsible hunters that give hunting a bad name. I realize that not all people like the concept of killing and shooting animals. But I am not forcing them to hunt just because I like to. Some feel that hunting is violent. It is only violent, in my opinion, if you do shoot what you do not plan to eat.

STORY QUESTIONS

1. Which of the following are the benefits of hunting and killing your own meat?
   a. to take out aggressions and frustrations
   b. to be self-reliant and provide for yourself
   c. for the joy of killing an animal
   d. to teach where meat comes from and how it gets to the supermarket

2. Which of the following is one of reasons the author states as to why hunting should not be prohibited?
   a. I am not forcing them to hunt just because I like to.
   b. I eat the meat from the animals I shoot, and I am careful to leave the environment as I found it.
   c. The gun has proven to be the most efficient way to kill an animal and provide food.
   d. The debate on whether hunting should be allowed has been raging for years.

3. What is the meaning of the word *efficient* as used in this passage?
   a. competence
   b. safe
   c. effective
   d. dangerous

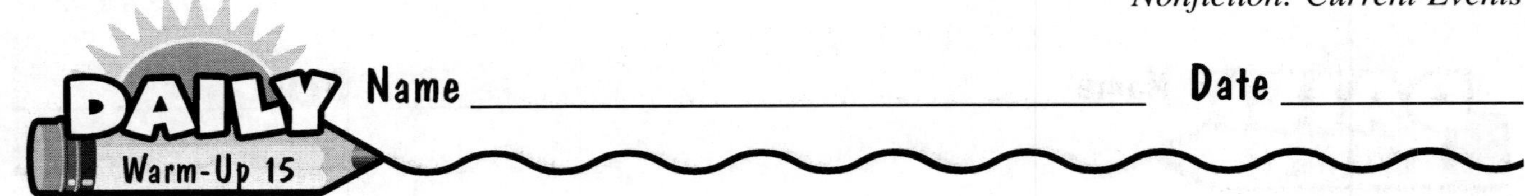

TIME ON MY HANDS

Young people these days are involved in more and more extracurricular activities. They are more involved than they have ever been before. How much is too much? Should there be a limit to the amount of extracurricular activities that a young person can be involved in? Personally, I think there should be a limit. I am an exhausted and concerned parent of three. We have been working to eliminate as many unnecessary activities from our schedule as we can.

There are many reasons for my concern. One of the reasons is that we just don't have enough time as a family. We used to sit around the table and discuss topics at the dinner table. We are lucky now if we even get dinner, let alone eat it as a family.

Another reason for the concern is that my children's grades are falling. These kids who used to be 'A' and 'B' students are now struggling to maintain a 'C' in most classes. There just isn't enough time for homework. Education should be the priority—not the extracurricular activities.

The final reason I feel concern is that we are all so tired. Everyone is running in three different directions. The kids are so exhausted they are even falling asleep in class. Kids need time to play, work, imagine, and create. Extracurricular activities that claim to create well-rounded kids end up taking away the personalities and freedom of the kids involved.

STORY QUESTIONS

1. Which paragraph explains the second reason the author wants to cut back on the amount of extra curricular activities?
   a. fourth paragraph
   b. first paragraph
   c. third paragraph
   d. none of the above

2. Which statement from the passage portrays the author's opinion about too many activities?
   a. Education should be the priority—not the extracurricular activities.
   b. We are lucky now if we even get dinner, let alone eat it as a family.
   c. Should there be a limit as to the amount of extracurricular activities that a young person can be involved in?
   d. We have been working to eliminate as many unnecessary activities from our schedule as we can.

3. What is meant by the word *extracurricular* as used in the passage?
   a. advantageous
   b. supplementary
   c. supportive
   d. rearranging

FICTION

Contemporary Realistic Fiction
Mystery/Suspense/Adventure
Historical Fiction
Fantasy
Fairy Tales/Folklore

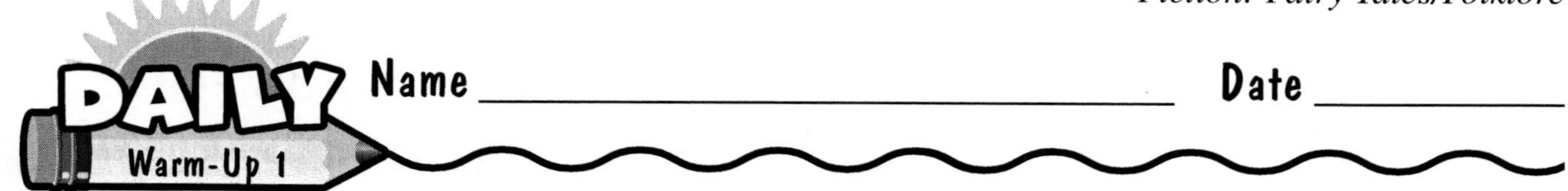

BUYER BEWARE

Once there was young lad. He walked each day to the marketplace to sell his wares. It was a hard life, but the young lad had no complaints. He worked from sun up until sun down. He knew that one day his hard work would pay off.

One day, as the young lad made his way to the marketplace, he could see a large wagon filled with goods. The young lad set down his bundle of baskets. Greed began to fill his heart.

"I could buy these flowers and sell them for a higher price. The land is barren, and I know I could sell them quickly," he thought.

So with that, the young lad offered his bundle of goods in exchange for the flowers. The young lad and the seller made their deal.

The young lad made his way to the marketplace. He laid out his flowers and waited for the ladies to come purchase his flowers. But the heat of the sun took its toll on the flowers, and without any water nearby, they soon wilted. The young lad realized his mistake. He looked over at the man selling his goods.

The next day, the young lad saw the man with a wagon full of fruit. The man asked the young lad if he wanted to trade. The young lad saw money in the man's eyes and said simply, "It is better to work for my fortune than to wish it away."

STORY QUESTIONS

1. What is the meaning of the word *wares* as used in the passage?
   a. fruits and vegetables
   b. merchandise
   c. pots and pans
   d. none of the above
2. What can you learn about the young lad in this story?
   a. He took pity on his fellow sellers.
   b. He is very good with animals.
   c. He learned his lesson.
   d. He wants to open a new store.
3. What is the moral of the story?
   a. There is no such thing as quick and easy wealth.
   b. It is better to give than receive.
   c. One for all and all for one.
   d. The early bird gets the worm.

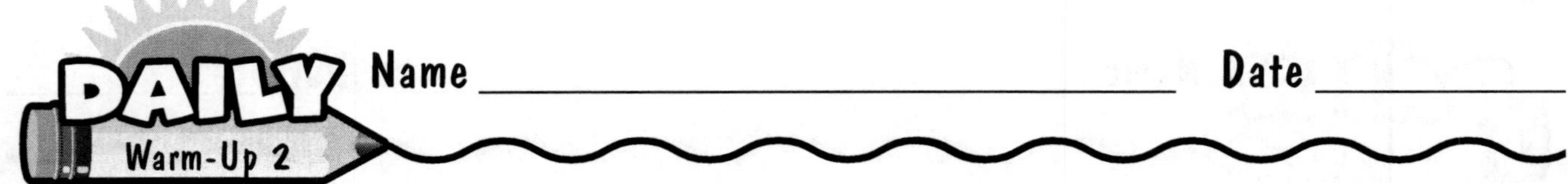

MASKING THE ODOR

There once was a farmer who had over a hundred cows. He milked them each day and set them out into the pasture at night. His neighbor, a banker, had just moved in next door. The banker wanted to move to the country to enjoy the views.

On the first night, the banker sat outside to enjoy the sunset. He could scarcely breathe. The stench from the cows was so great. Disgusted, he went indoors. The next evening, he tried to enjoy the sunset again but was forced to go back inside because of the smell.

He finally decided that the farmer would have to go. The banker had a lot of money, so he offered to buy the farm.

"Yes, I will sell you the farm, but it will take me at least a week to sell the cows and take care of them. Would you be willing to wait a week?" asked the farmer.

The banker decided he could do that. At the end of the week, the banker approached the farmer again. The farmer wondered if they could wait until his visiting brother left. The banker consented. A month passed. The farmer approached the banker hesitantly to see if he still wanted the farm.

"Why, no," replied the banker. "You keep it."

The farmer smiled to himself. He knew that by making the banker wait, it would allow time for the banker to get used to the awful smell of the cows.

STORY QUESTIONS

1. Which paragraph states the conflict in this story?
   a. second paragraph
   b. first paragraph
   c. third paragraph
   d. fifth paragraph
2. What is the conflict or problem of this story?
   a. The farmer doesn't know how to keep away the smell.
   b. The farmer is worried about offending the banker.
   c. The farmer's cows are extra smelly.
   d. The banker is unhappy with the smell of the cows.
3. What is the meaning of the word *hesitantly* as used in the passage?
   a. dejectedly
   b. offensively
   c. decidedly
   d. cautiously

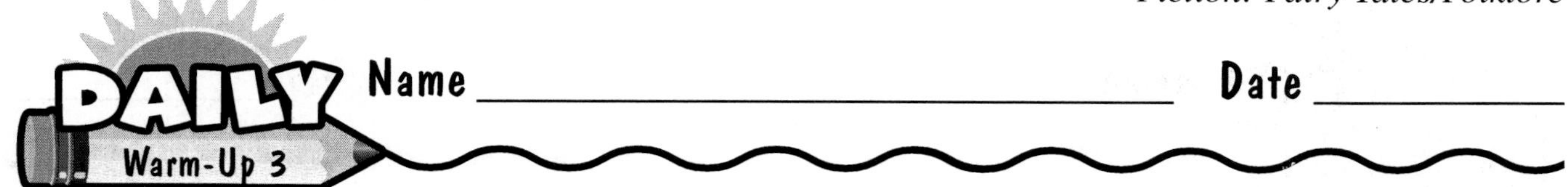

STATING THE OBVIOUS

There once was a shepherd who had a large flock of sheep. He had been a shepherd for a long time but was growing weary of the profession. One very hot day, the shepherd sat below the branches of a scraggly bush trying to get relief from the sun. He was pondering about what to do with his sheep. He loved his sheep, but he was tired of caring for them.

As he sat there thinking, a wolf sauntered by in front of the shepherd.

"What are you doing?" asked the wolf.

"I'm trying to plan my future," replied the shepherd. "I'm tired of being a shepherd, but I don't know what to do with my sheep."

"I have an idea," suggested the wolf.

"What's that?" asked the weary shepherd.

"Why don't I watch your sheep for a day and then you can take a break. Perhaps after a break, you won't feel so strongly about getting rid of your sheep."

"That's a great idea. You are in charge while I run into town," said the shepherd and he skipped down the hill. He was excited about his new freedom.

Upon the shepherd's return, he expected to see his herd flourishing. Instead he saw dead sheep everywhere. Stunned he sat down on a rock. A few of the sheep walked to his knee.

"This is what I get for my stupidity. It was I who chose to leave my sheep in the care of a wolf," said the shepherd sadly.

STORY QUESTIONS

1. What does the word *flourishing* mean in the story?
   a. thriving
   b. separating
   c. studying
   d. organizing

2. Why did the shepherd trust his sheep to a wolf?
   a. He was willing to give the wolf a chance.
   b. He was more concerned about his own needs at the moment.
   c. He wanted to see what the wolf would do.
   d. He was an inexperienced shepherd.

3. What is the moral to the story?
   a. Do not cast your pearls before swine.
   b. Wash your hands before dinner.
   c. Too many cooks spoil the broth.
   d. Crime doesn't pay.

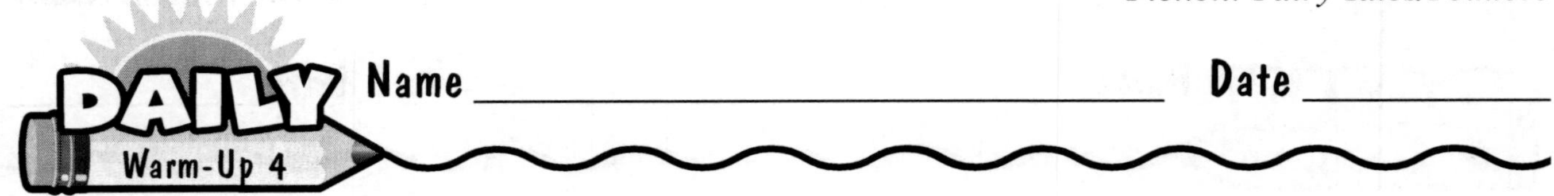

BETTER TO GIVE

There once was a forest of trees. Each tree wanted the reputation of being the most beautiful tree. Each tree wanted to be admired by all the others. When the storms came, the trees were careful to make sure that their branches were protected. When the woodsmen came through the forest, each tree would camouflage itself to keep from being chopped down. The competition was stiff.

One day, a fox came running through the forest. The fox was being chased by a group of dogs and hunters. The fox was in need of a place to hide. All the trees denied entrance to their branches. That is, except for one tree.

As the fox ran by, the tree whispered, "Climb in. Hide here!"

"But what about your branches?" asked the fox breathlessly, "Won't they be ruined?"

"How can they be ruined by helping another?" asked the tree as it closed the lower branches up around the fox.

The hunters and their dogs raced on by. After awhile, the fox came out. He thanked the tree and hurried on his way.

That night, as the tree watched the moon rise, it invited birds and squirrels to build homes in its branches. All the other trees were stunned, but soon noticed how happy the little tree was. It wasn't long before all the trees in the forest were covered with little animals. They too had learned the joy in serving others.

STORY QUESTIONS

1. What is the meaning of the word *camouflage* as used in this passage?
   a. curious
   b. glare
   c. mask
   d. mantle

2. What is the moral to the story?
   a. Give in order to learn from others.
   b. Raise up a standard for others to follow.
   c. It is better to give than receive.
   d. Setting a good example is usually painful.

3. After reading this story, explain how the story shows that helping others is better than helping ourselves.

____

____

____

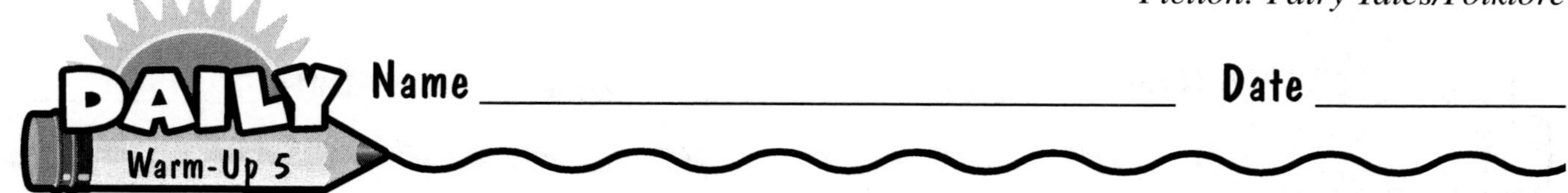

REWARDING DINNER

Once upon a time there was a young lady waiting to be called for dinner. She had been instructed by a small bird to wait until the master of the cottage invited her. It had been a long day and the young lady was hungry.

Just then, a strong horse came by the cottage and invited her to go to dinner with him. He promised that he would find something delicious for dinner. The young lady was tempted but declined the offer.

Later in the evening, a camel came to the cottage and offered to be the young lady's dinner companion. The young lady was very hungry at this point and was tempted to go to dinner with the camel. The young lady was puzzled. Then the words of the bird rang through her mind, "Wait until the master of the cottage invites you." The lady declined the camel's invitation. She sat hungrily staring out the window. Was there really such a thing as "the master of the cottage"?

Suddenly, there was a knock at the door. The young lady's heart jumped as she opened the door to find a majestic lion standing in the doorway. He offered his hand to the young lady.

"I see you were able to wait for me," said the lion firmly. All of a sudden, the young lady had an epiphany. She realized that the lion was testing her to see if she would really wait for him. The camel and the strong horse were both tests.

STORY QUESTIONS

1. Which of the statements below happened in the story?
   a. The camel was hoping the young lady could wait for him.
   b. The horse was the last animal to invite the young lady to dinner.
   c. The lion seemed satisfied that the lady was able to wait.
   d. The lady was upset to find out who her dinner guest would be.

2. What is the meaning of the word *epiphany* as used in the story?
   a. recruitment
   b. turn
   c. understanding
   d. arrangement

3. What is the moral of the story?
   a. Never count your eggs before they hatch.
   b. Do as I say, not as I do.
   c. Don't bite the hand that feeds you.
   d. Good things come to those who wait.

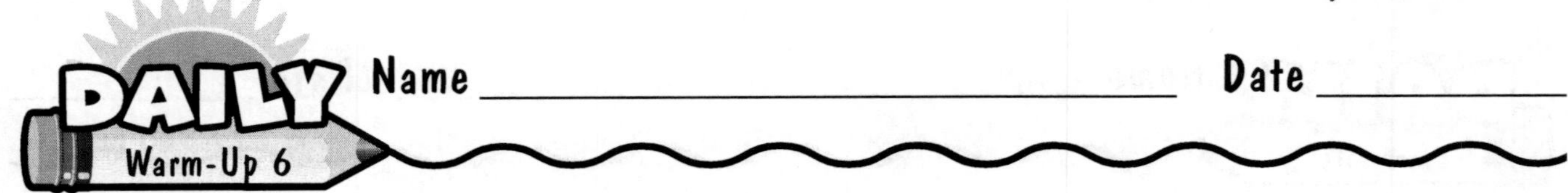

THE COVER

There once an ant that was gathering food to store up for the winter. The ant was trying to be prepared. This ant was carrying more than her own weight. She was always impressed with how amazing she was. The ant sat on the side of the trail to rest.

Just then, a caterpillar came crawling along. The ant thought about how ugly the caterpillar was. The ant began thinking about how gorgeous she looked in her red outer layering.

"Where are you going?" asked the ant, feeling prideful and haughty.

"I'm heading home," replied the caterpillar.

"Where's home?" asked the ant.

"Right up here in a certain tree," said the caterpillar as he wandered around, trying to find his way.

"That doesn't sound very smart!" muttered the ant to herself. "He's about as smart as he looks." The ant went on her way, leaving the caterpillar behind.

Later that spring, the ant happened upon the home of the caterpillar. She looked around for the caterpillar but couldn't find him anywhere. As the sun rose over the mountains, the ant looked toward the sky. She saw the most beautiful creature. It was a butterfly soaring in the clouds. The ant was amazed.

"Hi, ant!" called the butterfly.

"Huh?" asked the ant.

"I'm that ugly old caterpillar that you were trying to avoid. Not so bad now, eh?" chuckled the butterfly.

"Wow!" cried the ant as she sauntered along. That was about all she could say. "Wow!"

STORY QUESTIONS

1. What is the moral to the story?
   - a. Birds of a feather flock together.
   - b. One for all, and all for one.
   - c. United we stand, divided we fall.
   - d. Don't judge a book by its cover.

2. What is the meaning of the word *sauntered* as used in the passage?
   - a. poked
   - b. strolled
   - c. directed
   - d. ran

3. What is the main idea of the first paragraph?
   - a. to explain the moral of the story
   - b. to explain the problem in the story
   - c. to describe the main character in the story
   - d. to explain the resolution in the story

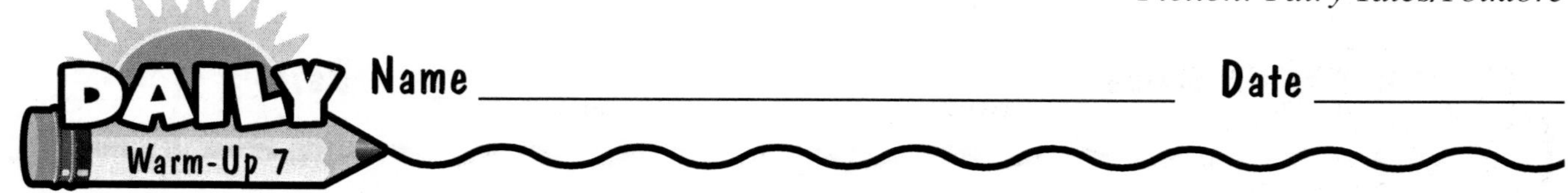

WHO YOU ARE

There once was a donkey that was eating fallen apples from a tree. In his peripheral vision, the donkey saw a lion hiding in the trees. The feeling of fear spread over his body. He knew that he couldn't outrun the lion, and he knew the lion wanted to eat him for lunch.

Just then, the donkey got an idea.

"Hello!" the donkey called to the lion. Surprised, the lion looked up at the donkey. "I was wondering if you could help me?" asked the donkey.

The lion chuckled to himself. "This is going to be much easier than I thought," he thought to himself.

"I can most certainly help you," called the lion as he strode over to the donkey.

"Oh, great," said the donkey. "You see, as I was walking under this apple tree, I managed to get a stick caught in my hoof. It hurts to walk on it. I was hoping that you would remove the stick for me."

The lion smiled so big that all his teeth showed. The donkey gulped, swallowing quickly.

The lion slowly sauntered over to the donkey. The closer he got, the more the donkey began to sweat. When the lion was within reach, the donkey kicked him with all of his strength. The lion went sailing through the air. He landed with a thump!

"Oh," moaned the lion. "I can't believe I fell for that one!" He looked up to see the donkey far away in the distance.

STORY QUESTIONS

1. What is the lesson learned in this story?
   a. What goes around comes around.
   b. If you can't say anything nice, don't say anything at all.
   c. Never trust your enemy.
   d. No use crying over spilt milk.
2. What would be a good title for this reading passage?
   a. "Lion Learns a Lesson"
   b. "Donkey vs. the Lion"
   c. "The King of the Jungle"
   d. "Them Is Fightin' Words"
3. Locate the statement below that did <u>not</u> happen in the story.
   a. The donkey was afraid of the lion.
   b. The donkey was able to trick the lion.
   c. The lion was able to trick the donkey.
   d. The donkey was learning to trust himself.

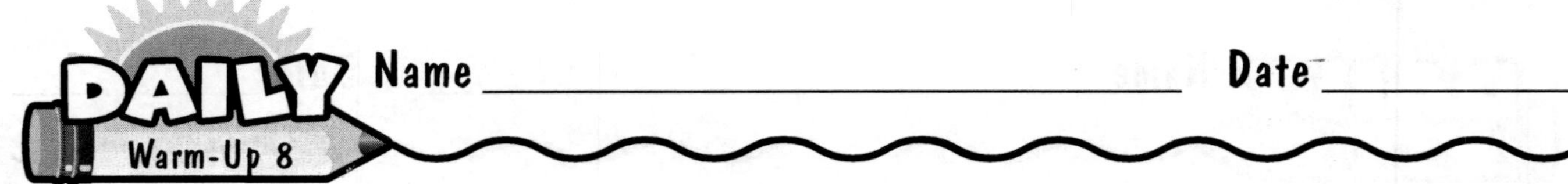

BIRDS OF A FEATHER

Frederic the penguin had had it! In fact, he was so tired that he no longer wanted to be a penguin. He wanted to run and sprint. He was tired of waddling. He hated his black and white feathers. And finally, he was tired of eating fish.

"How boring is that?" he asked.

Frederic decided it was time to go. He needed to explore the world and live a new life. He packed his bags and said his goodbyes.

"Adios, amigos," he said, trying out his new language.

Frederic hopped onto the closest iceberg and began floating across the sea. He floated until his iceberg melted and he swam to shore.

The first thing he did on the island was dye his feathers purple. Then he fashioned a grass skirt made of leaves and practiced saying words in his new language.

"Hola!" said Frederic.

It wasn't long before birds on the island began to notice Frederic. They offered him drinks and fruit to his heart's content.

After a month on the island, Frederic woke up one morning with a stomachache. He had gained weight and was sunburned all over. He burst into tears.

"I can't handle this anymore!" he sulked. "I've got to go back to my people. I want to go home."

It wasn't long before Frederic was on his way home to the iceberg. He had learned his lesson. He began eating fish again and never complained about his lifestyle.

STORY QUESTIONS

1. What is the conflict or problem in this story?
   a. Frederic was always getting in too much trouble.
   b. Frederic was trying to convince the other penguins to be like him so that he wouldn't feel so bad.
   c. Frederic got angry and decided to leave.
   d. Frederic was not happy with his life and wanted to explore a new one.

2. What is the meaning of the word *sulked* as used in the story?
   a. stated
   c. disrupted
   b. fantasized
   d. moped

3. What is the moral to this story?
   a. A bird in hand is better than three in a bush.
   b. A friend in need is a friend indeed.
   c. Birds of a feather flock together.
   d. Misery loves company.

DAILY Warm-Up 9 Name ______________________ Date __________

TO PLEASE OR NOT TO PLEASE

There once was an old woman who lived long ago. She had a dog, a cow, and a donkey. She loved her animals. The dog kept watch over her house. He barked at strange sounds. The dog helped the old woman feel secure and safe.

The cow was a big help too. The cow gave milk to the woman both day and night. The woman was able to make butter from the cream.

The donkey did much of the manual labor for the old woman. He pulled the wagon with all sorts of loads.

The old woman couldn't imagine life without any one of her animals. She did all she could to please each of them.

The animals did not appreciate her efforts. The dog complained that the cow stunk. The cow complained that the donkey's braying kept her awake at night. The donkey complained that the dog's barking and growling hurt his ears.

The complaints from the animals and the old woman's daily responsibilities left her exhausted. She was so exhausted that she fell sick with the flu. As she lay in bed trying to nurse herself back to good health, she noticed a bird on her windowsill singing a beautiful song.

"Tweet, tweet . . . you can't please them all," it seemed to say. From then on, the woman determined to treat them like animals instead of royal guests. It made all the difference. To this day, the animals are still treated like pets instead of humans.

STORY QUESTIONS

1. What is the problem in the story?
   a. The dog wants better dog food.
   b. The animals aren't getting along.
   c. The old woman is trying to do too much of the work herself.
   d. The animals aren't happy no matter how hard the woman works to care for them.

2. Which of the following words best describes the old woman?
   a. unhappy
   b. insecure
   c. conniving
   d. teachable

3. What is the moral to the story?
   a. You can never please everybody.
   b. A friend in need is a friend indeed.
   c. Work before play.
   d. Misery loves company.

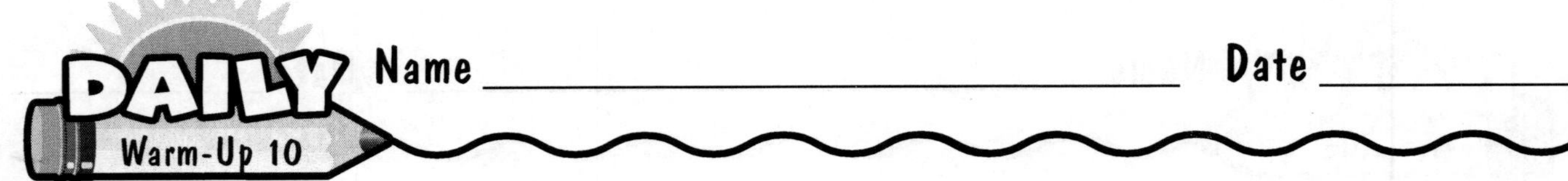

THE BEST POLICY

One sunny afternoon, a lion king made his way to the top of a mountain. He surveyed the land and took in its beauty. Not far away sat a mother lion with her babies. She was tired of watching her little ones and wanted some adventure. She decided that she would attract some attention. She saw the majestic lion standing at the top of the mountain and called up to him.

"Help! My babies are in danger. A wolf prowls nearby. I can see him!" cried the mother lion.

The lion king dashed to save the lions. As he raced down the mountainside, a pile of rocks went cascading down behind him. With lightning speed he made it to the lion and her young. He sniffed the air and prowled around but could not find the wolf.

"Oh thank you, brave king. The wolf must have left," said the mother lion softly.

The lion king sauntered off to his place at the top of the mountain.

Before long, the mother lion again called for help.

"Oh, king, again! There is a wolf prowling around. Please come save us," she cried.

In record time, the lion king made it back to the lion and her young. But still he could not find any evidence of a wolf. He scoured the area looking for paw prints but could find none. He gazed at the mother lion again and walked back up the mountain.

Before long, a wolf did appear. The mother lion called for help, but the lion king ignored her pleas.

STORY QUESTIONS

1. What is the moral to the story?
   a. Good things come in small packages.
   b. Birds of a feather flock together.
   c. There is no believing a liar, even when she speaks the truth.
   d. A bird in hand is better than three in the bush.

2. What is meant by the meaning of the word *sauntered*?
   a. ambled
   b. slumped
   c. defended
   d. swaggered

3. Which sentence below is true?
   a. The lion king was not really deceived by the mother lion.
   b. The mother lion needed constant help with her baby lions.
   c. The lion king grew tired of listening to the mother lion.
   d. The lion king realized that the mother lion could not be trusted.

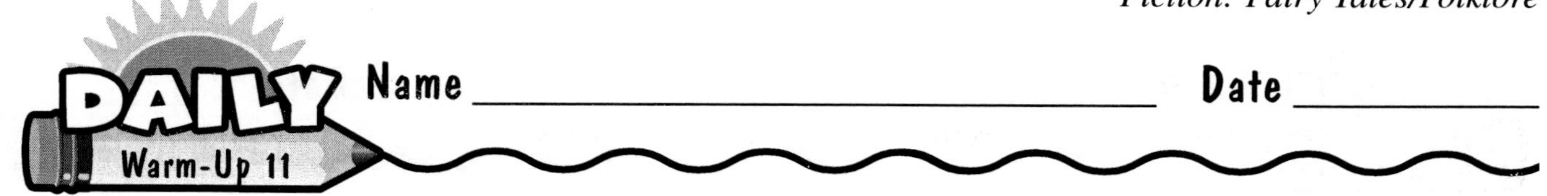

LESSON OF HUMILITY

Snow was falling all over the village, and nighttime was coming. Four inches of snow had already accumulated on the ground, and it looked like it would continue to pile up through the night.

The old man that lived in the little cottage knew that it was going to be a cold night. He knew he should help his neighbor Joe with the firewood. But the old man had such a headache. He looked in his empty cupboards.

"Surely my neighbor Joe doesn't have problems like I do," the old man thought. The more he thought about it, the unhappier he became with his circumstance.

The old man decided that he wanted his neighbor to be as miserable as he was. So when the old man shoveled his walk, he dumped all of the snow onto his neighbor's walk and went inside.

Next he gathered another load of firewood and neglected to gather any for his neighbor. "Let him do it himself!" thought the old man.

In the morning, the old man awoke to see that the snow was still coming down. He knew he would have to shovel his walk again. He went to the window and was surprised to see that his walk had already been shoveled. He also noticed a pile of firewood waiting on his doorstep along with a basket of fresh fruit and vegetables for breakfast.

The old man sat down and shook his head. How could he have been so selfish?

STORY QUESTIONS

1. What is the meaning of the word *accumulated* as used in the passage?
   a. gathered
   b. arranged
   c. floated
   d. none of the above
2. What is the lesson the old man learned?
   a. A rolling stone gathers no moss.
   b. Pride goes before the fall.
   c. Treat others as you would like to be treated.
   d. The early bird gets the worm.
3. Which of the following statements can be inferred after reading the passage?
   a. The old man was greedy.
   b. The old man was scared.
   c. The old man was not a good friend.
   d. The old man was humbled and learned a lesson.

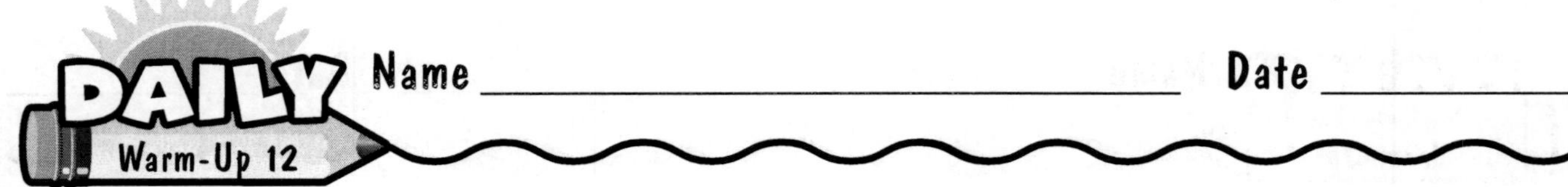

I AM SERIOUS

There once was a farmer who planted fresh fields of wheat. He cared for the wheat and ensured that it received adequate amounts of water, sun, and nourishment. His livelihood depended on this crop of wheat.

One morning, the farmer awoke to the sound of birds in his field. He ran outside and saw his wheat field covered with birds. In a panic, he ran outside and began flapping his arms and made loud sounds. He hoped that this would scare the birds away. His plan worked. The birds flew away in a flurry, and the farmer went back about his work.

Early the next morning, the farmer was again awakened to the sound of birds. He followed the same procedure and scared the birds by making loud noises and flapping his arms. It worked again. The birds flew away and left his wheat alone.

The birds began to realize that they were never in any real danger. They realized the farmer walked around waving at them and making sounds. The birds got braver and braver.

On the third morning, the farmer heard the birds again and realized that he needed to be more severe. He grabbed his dog's collar and headed outside. The birds did not even move. They knew he would try to scare them and so they weren't too worried. The farmer let his dog loose and the dog chased the birds. This frightened the birds and they flew away, never to be seen again.

STORY QUESTIONS

1. What is the moral of this story?
   a. What goes around comes around.
   b. Work before play.
   c. If at first you don't succeed, try and try again.
   d. The early bird gets the worm.
2. What would be a good title for this reading passage?
   a. "The Last Resort"
   b. "The Two Sides"
   c. "Planting Seeds"
   d. "Anger Always Works First"
3. Locate the statement below that did <u>not</u> happen in the story.
   a. The farmer was trying to attract the birds.
   b. The farmer wanted to delay hurting the birds.
   c. The farmer knew that he had to show the birds he meant business.
   d. The birds were not afraid of the farmer.

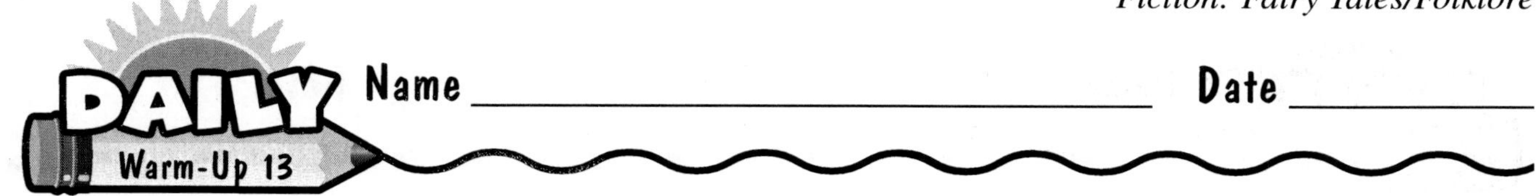

GROUP THINK

Each morning the zebras gathered at the watering hole to discuss their day. Zane the zebra was the last to arrive one day. He had had a terrible morning. First, he woke up late and missed out on the good grasses for breakfast. Then he stubbed his hoof on a rock, and it now had a crack. He was very grumpy.

Because he was so late, Zane was the last to show up. There wasn't a lot of room. This made Zane feel even grouchier.

"Move over, you guys," said Zane. "It's my turn."

"Zane, we just got here, you're going to have to wait," replied Zane's friend, Ned.

"Oh, come on," pouted Zane as he sat back. "Isn't it annoying how Mr. Farrell always makes sure that his daughters get the best grass every day and the best position here at the water?"

Ned had to think about it for a minute. "Come to think of it," said Ned, "You are right. That is kind of annoying."

"And that Sally has such bad breath. Doesn't she?" asked Zane.

"You are right about that, and her mane is always tangled," added Chris, another friend of Zane's. Before long, all the zebras were talking poorly of others and were all as negative as Zane.

"Wait a minute, Zane," interrupted Felix. "We were all having a good morning until you came along. Don't drag us down to your level." The zebras all nodded in agreement and went back to their drinking.

STORY QUESTIONS

1. What is the problem in the story?
   a. Zane doesn't have any friends.
   b. Zane feels like he isn't treated with respect.
   c. The other zebras make fun of Zane.
   d. Zane is having a hard time being positive.

2. Which of the following words best describes Zane's attitude?
   a. dedicated
   b. insecure
   c. peppy
   d. contagious

3. What is the moral to the story?
   a. People in glass houses shouldn't throw stones.
   b. Misery loves company.
   c. Big things come in small packages.
   d. Don't put all of your eggs in one basket.

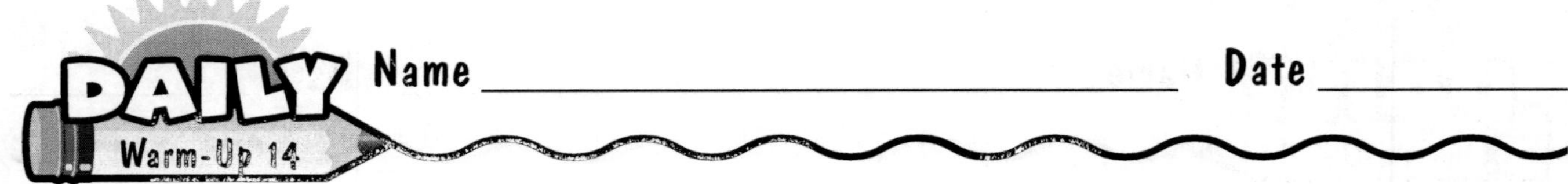

ME, MYSELF, AND I

There once was a tortoise walking through the desert. It had been a dry year, and the drought was taking its toll on the animals. The tortoise had searched in vain for food. Just then a buzzard flew by. "How are you?" asked the buzzard.

"Good, just a little hungry," admitted the tortoise. "This drought has been much harder than I ever thought it would be."

"I see," said the buzzard, "but this drought hasn't affected me at all. I am able to eat to my heart's content because the little animals are dying right and left."

"How can you say that? How can you do that?" questioned the tortoise. "Doesn't it break your heart to watch the little animals starve to death?"

"Who cares? It's not my problem," said the buzzard as he flew away.

A few days later the tortoise was walking along when he saw a buzzard caught in a tree branch. Its feathers were so caught that it seemed impossible to free the poor animal. The tortoise knew he must help. Just then, he noticed it was the same buzzard from the day before.

"Why, buzzard, we meet again. This time it looks like it is you that needs help," said the tortoise.

"Leave me alone! I don't need anyone's help. I'm smarter than the rest of you dumb animals. I will get it figured out!" yelled the buzzard.

The tortoise slowly walked away shaking his head at what he had just heard.

STORY QUESTIONS

1. What was the lesson learned in this story?
   a. Patience is a virtue.
   b. Pride goes before destruction.
   c. People in glass houses shouldn't throw stones.
   d. A watched pot never boils.
2. How will pride kill the buzzard?
   a. He callously eats the dying animals without worrying about them.
   b. He takes advantage of the old tortoise.
   c. He refuses to accept help from the tortoise and remains stuck in the tree branch.
   d. He refuses to share his good fortune with the tortoise.
3. Using the context clues, what is the meaning of the word *affected* as used in the passage?
   a. worried
   b. arranged
   c. changed
   d. languished

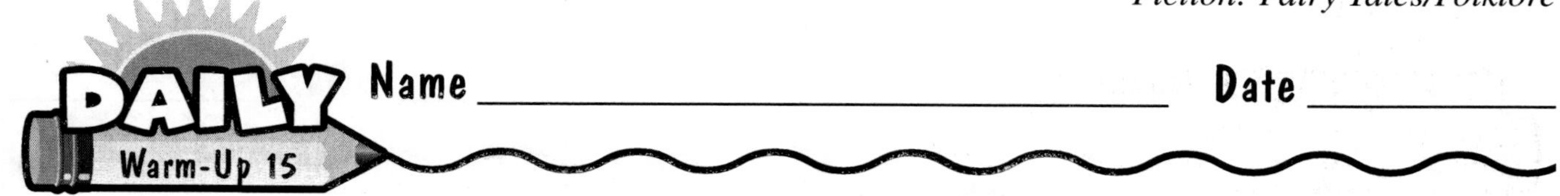

LAUGHING LAST

A fox and a cat were having an argument about who had the biggest problem. They both were competitive and wanted to see who could muster the most sympathy from the animals in the forest.

The cat saw a group of animals gathering, so he scurried to the top of a big rock. "Hello down there. Would you like to hear my sad tale?" he asked.

Without waiting for a reply, the cat began to pour out all his troubles. The fox, not wanting to be outdone, called the animals' attention to him by screeching in pain.

"Oh me, oh my! My foot is stuck again," wailed the fox. This is the third time my foot has been wounded this week. Woe is me!" The animals all sighed.

Just then, a big rock came crashing down the hill and landed on top of a hyena. The animals gasped and worked together to save the hyena. Once rescued, the animals all asked if he was okay.

"Ha, ha, hee, hee," laughed the hyena. "Can you believe my luck, sitting directly below the falling rock? Silly me!" The hyena continued to laugh. All the animals laughed at his situation as well.

"Wait! Look at me. I'm still in pain," called the cat.

"And what about me?" whined the fox.

Attention for the cat and the fox soon ceased. The animals all seemed to know that you make your situation what you want it to be.

STORY QUESTIONS

1. What is the moral to the story?
   a. Birds of a feather flock together.
   b. He who laughs, laughs last.
   c. Practice makes perfect.
   d. Don't judge a book by its cover.

2. What is the meaning of the word *scurried*?
   a. astonished
   b. confused
   c. ignored
   d. bustled

3. Which of the following statements can be verified from the story?
   a. The fox was afraid of the cat.
   b. The fox and the cat had been in a fight before.
   c. The fox had a hard time making decisions.
   d. The hyena put life's problems in perspective.

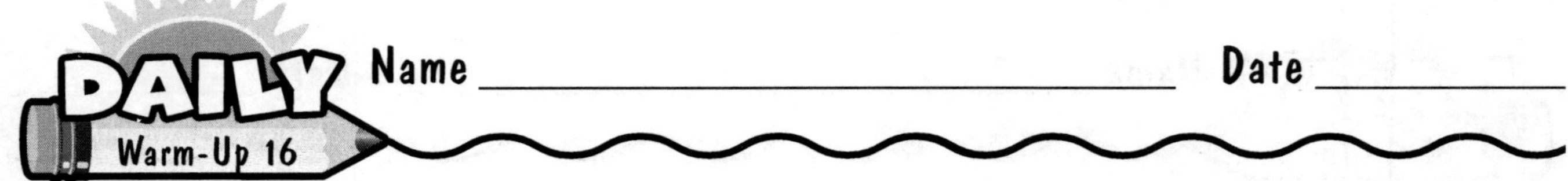

THE GREAT RESCUE

There once was an old donkey that was to be sold by the farmer the next day. The donkey had overheard the plans and tried desperately to think of a way to free himself.

"He's just too old to be of use anymore," said the farmer.

Early the next morning, the donkey decided to escape. He broke through the log fence and ran out of the field. It wasn't long before he fell into a well. The hole was big and wide and the donkey had not seen it. The poor old donkey began to cry.

When the farmer arose, he thought about what he needed to do that day. He knew there was a big hole left behind by an old well on his property that would be dangerous for anyone that might accidentally fall in. He grabbed his shovel and went about his work.

"I will fill this hole in the ground and then I will take the donkey to the market to sell," said the farmer.

The farmer began shoveling dirt into the well. The donkey realized that the farmer didn't know he was in the well. Each time the farmer threw dirt in the hole, the donkey shook it off and stepped on it. The more dirt there was inside, the higher the donkey began to rise.

When the farmer realized what had happened, he laughed and patted the donkey on the back. How could he ever rid himself of such a smart donkey?

STORY QUESTIONS

1. What is the moral to the story?
   a. Do not put all your eggs in one basket.
   b. Good things come to those who think.
   c. Absence makes the heart grow fonder.
   d. Look before you leap.
2. From reading the story, which of the following words could be used to describe the donkey?
   a. poor
   b. clever
   c. arrogant
   d. simple
3. Which sentence shows the resolution to the farmer's problem?
   a. The farmer began shoveling dirt into the well.
   b. "He's just too old to be of use any more," said the farmer.
   c. When the farmer realized what had happened, he laughed and patted the donkey on the back.
   d. none of the above

Daily Warm-Up 1 **Name** ______________________ **Date** __________

THE DAILY NEWS

"Have you read the paper today, dear?" asked Grandma as she folded dishtowels. She seemed disgusted. "They have got to do something about Hitler."

"What can be done?" asked Mother. She wiped the sweat off of her brow.

"What's going on?" asked Cynthia. Cynthia was old enough to know that something was going on, but she was ignorant of the significance of the events taking place in their lives.

"Hitler is a very bad man," stated Grandma.

"Momma! Stop! You are going to scare the young girl," reprimanded Mother.

"She's got to learn soon enough," said Henry. Henry was in seventh grade. He was older and he thought he was very mature for his age. Henry and Cynthia's father had been away fighting the war for months now. Mother could barely talk about it. Henry was frustrated that they didn't discuss more of this topic. At times he would prod Grandma into discussing the topic even though it usually ended in an argument.

"Everyone's afraid to talk about it," Henry went on. "It's like people think that if they don't talk about it, then it's not really happening. But it is happening. Horrible things are happening and we need to do something about it!"

"Henry," Mother pleaded, "it is not that simple."

"What's not so simple? Will somebody please tell me what's going on?" asked Cynthia. She was curled up in a ball on the sofa. The heat had been turned off in an attempt to save money.

STORY QUESTIONS

1. Which sentence is the first to show that the story takes place during World War II?
   a. Henry and Cynthia's father had been away fighting the war for months now.
   b. She seemed disgusted. "They have got to do something about Hitler."
   c. "Hitler is a very bad man," stated Grandma.
   d. "Everyone's afraid to talk about it," Henry went on.

2. Which sentence explains the problem in the story?
   a. Mother could barely talk about it.
   b. "Hitler is a very bad man," stated Grandma.
   c. "What's going on?" asked Cynthia.
   d. Henry was frustrated that they didn't discuss more of this topic.

3. Who is the main character of the story?
   a. Mother
   b. Grandmother
   c. Henry
   d. Cynthia
   e. there is no main character

Daily Warm-Up 2 Name ______________________________ Date __________

DEAR MR. PRESIDENT

Jackson hurried up to his apartment after school, skipping two or three steps at a time. When he got inside the apartment, he slammed the door shut.

"Are you okay, dear?" asked Mom. "You look as white as a ghost."

"I'm fine now," said Jackson. "The protesters were out again today, Mom, and they are scary!"

"Oh, dear, they sure can be," agreed Mom. "I wish they didn't have to do that so close to our apartment!"

"Mom, why are they protesting? Why are they so angry?" asked Jackson.

"They are upset about the war," explained Mom. "They don't think we should be in Vietnam."

"What do they want the government to do about it?" asked Jackson.

"I think they want them to send the troops home," replied Mom.

"But why are they burning the American flags?" asked Jackson incredulously.

"It does seem crazy," Mom explained, "but they feel it is their right to burn the flag protesting what the U.S. government is doing. Burning the flag is a way of making a statement."

"Kind of like freedom of speech?" asked Jackson.

"That's right," said Mom.

"Why don't they try writing a letter to the President instead?" inquired Jackson.

"Perhaps this form of communication is more effective," answered Mom.

Jackson shrugged his shoulders and headed up the stairs. He had a letter to write and he didn't want to waste another minute.

STORY QUESTIONS

1. What of the following sentences below shows when the story takes place?
   a. "I'm fine now," said Jackson. "The protesters were out again today, Mom, and they are scary!"
   b. "They are upset about the war," explained Mom. "They don't think we should be in Vietnam."
   c. "Mom, why are they protesting? Why are they so angry?" asked Jackson.
   d. "Oh, dear, they sure can be," agreed Mom. "I wish they didn't have to do that so close to our apartment!"

2. What is the meaning of the word *incredulously* as used in the story?
   a. in disbelief
   b. remotely
   c. timidly
   d. frail

3. Which of the following sentences explains the problem in the story?
   a. He had a letter to write and he didn't want to waste another minute.
   b. "What do they want the government to do about it?" asked Jackson.
   c. "The protesters were out again today, Mom, and they are scary!"

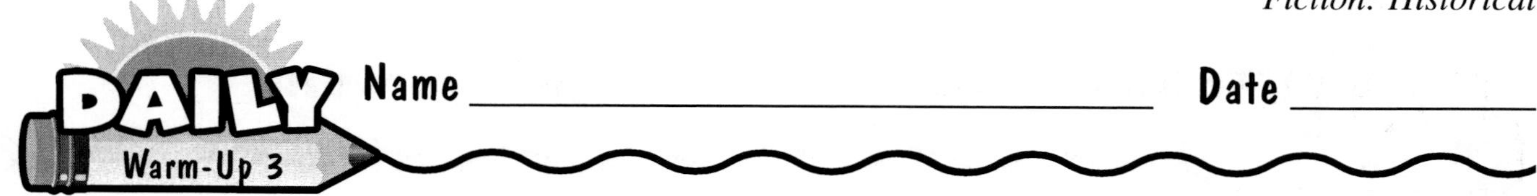

YANKEE FEVER

For as long as Matthew could remember, he had been dreaming of watching Babe Ruth play in Yankee Stadium. The time had finally come. Matthew was still not old enough to go to the game by himself, but he had a seat reserved just for him. His seat happened to be in the branches of the tree just outside the fence. He had paid lots of money to Big Jim for the seat. He was so excited he could hardly sleep that night.

The next day after school, Matthew helped his mom fix dinner and even did the dishes afterwards.

Matthew hustled out the door and ran towards Yankee Stadium. "Be back by 9:00," he shouted.

He felt as though his heart might pound right out of his chest. He couldn't believe it. Big Jim and the boys were all waiting when Matthew got there. Matthew swung his leg over the branch and climbed up. He sat down on his designated branch and peered through the holes of a fence enclosing Yankee Stadium.

The janitor came strolling by. Matthew tried to keep from being seen. He was afraid to get caught. If the janitor caught you, he sent you home. But tonight, there was a new janitor.

Just then little Danny fell out of the tree. He screamed in pain and the janitor turned to look. He helped Danny up and brought him into the stadium. "The rest of you can join me," he called.

The boys looked at each other in disbelief. They all jumped from the tree and hurried inside the stadium. They didn't need to be asked twice.

STORY QUESTIONS

1. What is the meaning of the word *designated* as used in this passage?
   a. free
   b. last
   c. assigned
   d. original

2. According to the passage, which sentence shows how Matthew feels about the new janitor?
   a. Matthew tried to keep from being seen.
   b. The boys looked at each other in disbelief.
   c. He screamed in pain and the janitor turned to look.
   d. He helped Danny up and brought him into the stadium. "The rest of you can join me," he called.

3. Which paragraph shows the resolution to the problem in the passage?
   a. second paragraph
   b. sixth paragraph
   c. fourth paragraph
   d. last paragraph

DAILY Warm-Up 4

Name ______________________________ Date ___________

DREAM BIG

Nellie skimmed through the newspaper and folded it back up.

"I don't get why we have to read about other people's dreams in the newspaper," stated Nellie.

"What do you mean?" asked Grandma Bay. Grandma was knitting a scarf to keep Nellie warm.

"The paper has an article about this man who keeps dreaming," explained Nellie.

"Show me that article," prodded Grandma.

Nellie fetched the paper off the table and brought it over to Grandma. She also picked up Grandma's reading glasses to save herself a trip. Grandma began to read intently. "Oh, this is so good. Dr. King's words just resonate with me."

"Why? What's so great about dreaming?" asked Nellie, innocently.

"It's not a dream like the one you have at night. His dream is about the future and what it can hold for people like us," explained Grandma.

"I can dream my own dreams, thank you very much," stated Nellie. She didn't know what she thought about this Dr. King.

"What if this Dr. King was the very person who enabled you to live your dreams?" questioned Grandma. Nellie didn't respond.

"Dr. King is working to help all of us live out our very dreams," cooed Grandma. Nellie stiffened her back and walked over to look at the newspaper article. "This man can help me live my dreams?" asked Nellie.

"That's right, Nell. Think about it. He's opening doors for people everywhere," said Grandma. Nellie liked the sound of that. She smiled down at Dr. King.

STORY QUESTIONS

1. What can you infer about Grandma's feelings about Dr. Martin Luther King, Jr.?
   a. Grandma felt that he had some interesting points to make.
   b. Grandma admired and respected Dr. King.
   c. Grandma was opposed to most of what Dr. King stood for.
   d. Grandma was still trying to learn more about Dr. King.

2. Which of the following quotes helps answer the previous question?
   a. "Why? What's so great about dreaming?"
   b. "Oh, this is so good. Dr. King's words just resonate with me."
   c. "I don't get why we have to read about other people's dreams in the newspaper."
   d. "Show me that article."

3. What does the word *resonate* mean as used in this passage?
   a. echo
   b. enchant
   c. partnership with
   d. open up

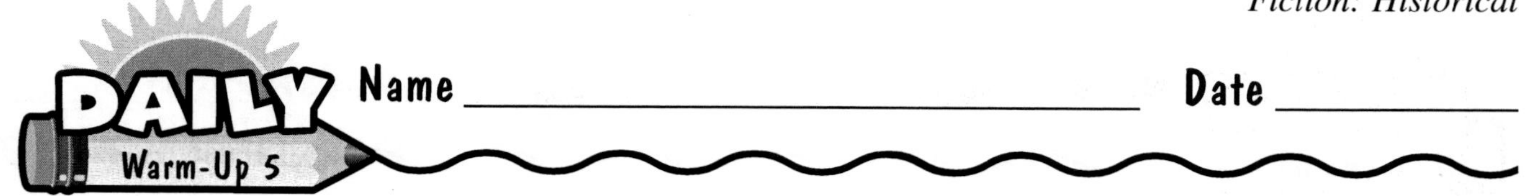

WOMEN'S SUFFRAGE

Jacob's mother stormed through the house with a handful of wooden signs in her hand.

"What are those, Mother?" asked Jacob. He had never seen his mother so energetic before.

"These are signs for the ladies march!" exclaimed Mother.

Jacob looked at his mother trying on three different hats. She was bustling around hanging up hats and pulling others down. Jacob could feel the excitement in the air.

Outside the window in the street, Jacob watched a group of neighborhood ladies line up with signs of their own.

"What's going on?" asked Jacob.

"Votes for women!" his mother stated. "It's time that women get the right to vote!"

His mother grabbed a hat with big black feathers and marched downstairs carrying a sign. She threw open the door and joined the group of women outside.

"Votes for women?" asked Jacob.

Just then Jacob's dad came through the door. "Where's your mother headed?" he asked.

"She's off to get the right to vote," answered Jacob curiously.

"Oh, I see," chuckled Dad.

"What's so funny?" asked Jacob.

"Mother and her friends have been trying for years to get the U.S. government to allow women the right to vote," explained Jacob's dad.

"That seems like a reasonable request," said Jacob timidly. "Why should men be the only ones with the right to vote?" demanded Jacob. He walked over and picked up one of his mom's signs. He joined the group outside shouting, "Votes for women!"

STORY QUESTIONS

1. How does Jacob's dad feel about women's suffrage?
   a. He thinks it is a great idea.
   b. He is upset that his wife is protesting.
   c. He is spying on his wife's activities.
   d. He thinks it's a silly idea that will never happen.

2. What is the main idea of the last paragraph?
   a. to explain how Jacob's dad feels about the right to vote
   b. to explain the relationship between Jacob and his mother
   c. to explain the process of how women got the right to vote
   d. to explain Jacob's feelings about women being allowed to vote

3. What is the meaning of the word *stormed* as used in the passage?
   a. directed
   b. engaged
   c. stomped
   d. squirmed

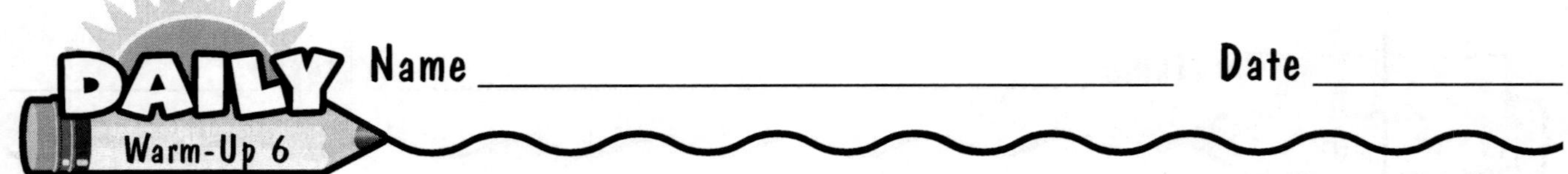

CHOOSE THE WRIGHT

Andy slipped into his parka and raced towards the outskirts of town. He was glad school was over. It had been a long day of math numbers and penmanship. Miss Carol seemed determined to do him in. Andy threw his book bag over his shoulder and kept on running.

Andy wasn't the best student, but ask him anything about flying and he could spew out facts. He was a flying expert. He loved to sit and watch birds fly. He studied their landings and their takeoffs. On occasion, he had been known to capture one and try experiments with it wings. The poor creature was left to flap around indignantly.

On the day Andy read the sign stating that Orville and Wilbur Wright were coming to town, he thought he would explode from excitement. The sign said that these two brothers were inventing a real flying machine and would be demonstrating it on the grassy hill above the town. Andy had hiked up his suspenders and raced the whole three miles home barefoot to share the news.

Today as Andy hiked up the grassy knoll, he was almost knocked flat on the ground. Just above him in the air was a huge flying machine. It was beautiful. Andy sat back on the grass to watch. The machine seemed to be flying all on its own. He scanned the crowd looking for the Wright brothers. He finally spotted the two. They were smiling with great pride.

STORY QUESTIONS

1. What is the main idea of paragraph two?
   a. Andy is not a very good student.
   b. Andy is trying to get to the edge of town quickly.
   c. Andy is trying to meet the Wright brothers.
   d. Andy is intrigued with flying and spends all his free time learning about it.
2. Which sentence shows best how Andy feels about the Wright brothers?
   a. Andy wasn't the best student, but ask him anything about flying and he could spew out facts.
   b. The sign said that these two brothers were inventing a real flying machine and would be demonstrating it on the grassy hill above the town.
   c. On the day Andy read the sign stating that Orville and Wilbur Wright were coming to town, he thought he would explode from excitement.
   d. Andy slipped into his parka and raced towards the outskirts of town.
3. What is the meaning of the word *indignantly* as used in the passage?
   a. in control
   b. in annoyance
   c. in line with
   d. in tune

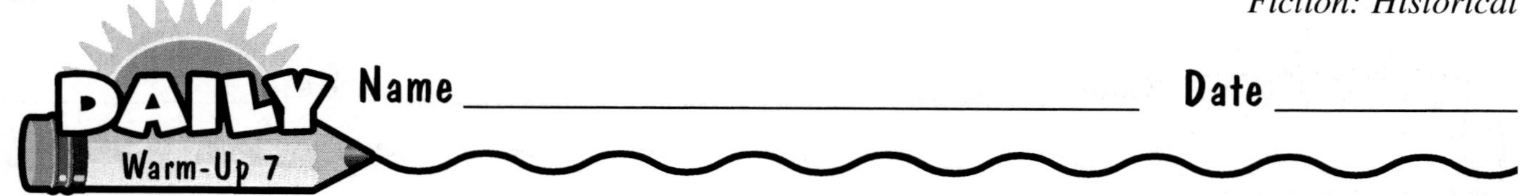

Name ______________________ Date __________

DUST OFF THE MEMORIES

"Close the door," hollered Clara. "You are going to let all the dust in!" Clara and her best friend, Jenny, were busy hanging decorations in the gym. It had been Clara's idea to put on the party.

It had been a rough school year so far. Living through the Depression had been difficult. Many of the families in the little farming community were struggling. The drought and dust storms had been severe. The land was dried up and blowing everywhere. The economy was depressed with no help in sight. Having dust everywhere only aggravated the situation. You couldn't eat, sleep, or bathe without having to deal with the mountains and mountains of dust pouring in.

As head of the celebration committee, Clara took her job very seriously. She was amazed with the donations that had already poured in. Clara knew these were sacrifices when so many families were wondering where their next meal would be coming.

The night of the party arrived and the townspeople lined up outside the gymnasium.

"How can they put on a party with all this dust everywhere?" asked some of the people in line. Clara nervously took tickets from guests entering the party. As Mr. Paulson, the principal, walked in, he was moved to tears. The gymnasium was beautiful. Clara had placed jars filled with flowers all over. Candles were lit in bottles that were filled with dust and sand to stabilize them.

STORY QUESTIONS

1. Which of the following sentences is first to show that this is a historical fiction story?
   a. The economy was depressed with no help in sight.
   b. Living through the Depression had been difficult.
   c. The land was dried up and blowing everywhere.
   d. The drought and dust storms had been severe.

2. Which of the following words could be used to describe Clara?
   a. angry
   b. clever
   c. misguided
   d. a leader

3. What is the meaning of the word *aggravated* as used in the passage?
   a. intuitive and inspired
   b. overbearing and rude
   c. prepared to accept
   d. irritated and annoyed

DAILY Warm-Up 8 **Name** ______________________ **Date** __________

A LETTER FROM HOME

Dear Dad,

How are you? I hope you are safe. In school today, we talked again about the war and all that's going on. It always makes me feel nervous and I start to sweat. Mrs. Peterson talked about Hitler again and the terrible things he is doing. I'm proud to know that my dad is helping to fight evil like that.

The last of vegetables are coming off of our victory garden. Squash is mostly what is left. We haven't tasted butter in over three weeks. I miss it on my bread, but each time I get to missing it, I think about why we are not eating it. Mrs. Egen seems to think this war could be wrapped up by the end of the year.

The other day, the newspaper had a story about the clothes from wounded soldiers billowing in the wind. I just ignore those types of stories.

I know you want to know about school. It's going well. I'm getting all my homework done. Mom is doing well, too. She seems to be very strong, but sometimes I can hear her crying at night. Cindy is sick a lot, but I think she is just missing you.

Dad, I have just one question. How am I going to remember you? I look at your picture every day, but my memories from the past seem to be fading. I want to try and keep those memories alive. Any suggestions?

Your son,

Abe

STORY QUESTIONS

1. What is the purpose of the last paragraph in the letter?
   a. It provides the problem in the passage.
   b. It provides the solution to the passage.
   c. It is the climax of the passage.
   d. It provides the background and the setting of the passage.

2. What is the meaning of the word *billowing* as used in the passage?
   a. rushing
   b. reflecting
   c. flapping
   d. descending

3. What is the real problem expressed in this passage?
   a. Abe doesn't like writing letters to his dad.
   b. Abe is worried that his father will get hurt.
   c. Abe is worried that he won't remember his dad.
   d. Abe is worried about the war.

DAILY Warm-Up 9 **Name** ______________________ **Date** __________

JUST A SCRATCH

"We're gonna rock around the clock tonight!" sang Billy as he danced around the room shaking his hips like crazy.

"Whoa, Billy! You are really moving those hips!" said Jimmy. Billy's hips were moving so fast that it was hard to see them from the blur. Jimmy and Billy were great friends.

The boys loved to get together to listen to records. They each had a collection of 45 records. In reality, Billy's collection of records actually belonged to his dad. But his dad seemed happy to share.

Billy's hips kept swinging and moving to the beat. As Billy's hips moved closer to the record player, he accidentally bumped the record player. Zrrrrrwk! The needle of the record player sliced right across the record.

Billy froze and slowly turned around. He was mortified. What had he done? He knew this was his dad's favorite record. Was it now ruined?

Jimmy looked sheepishly up at Billy, scanning his face for a reaction. Billy put his hand to his face and gasped, "He's going to kill me!"

Billy moved in slow motion to the record player and pulled the record off. He surveyed the damage as he held the record up to the sunlight. Indeed there was a huge scratch.

Bang! The front door slammed shut and footsteps could be heard in the hallway. Billy cringed and Jimmy said, "Well, I think it's time for me to go home. I'll see you at the sock hop!"

Billy nodded and looked back down at the floor.

STORY QUESTIONS

1. Which of the following sentences does not contain evidence that the story takes place in the past?
   a. "We're gonna rock around the clock tonight!" sang Billy as he danced around the room shaking his hips like crazy.
   b. They each had a collection of records.
   c. Billy moved in slow motion to the record player and pulled the record off.
   d. The needle of the record player sliced right across the record.

2. Which paragraph explains the relationship between Billy and Jimmy?
   a. first paragraph
   c. second paragraph
   b. fourth paragraph
   d. third paragraph

3. What is the meaning of the word *surveyed* as used in the story?
   a. content and happy
   c. inspected and examined
   b. feisty and energetic
   d. foreboding and sad

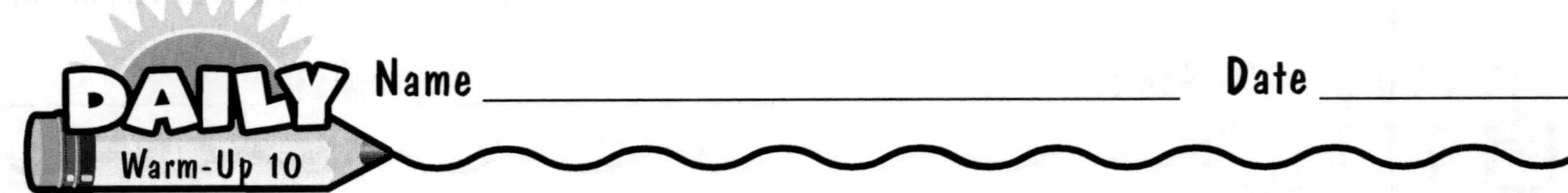

THE DRILL

"Here I come!" hollered Molly as her sled went flying down the hill. The brisk air on her cheeks made Molly close her eyes. It was cold, but the thrill of the ride made it worth it. Molly was dumped from her sled and landed in a heap at the bottom of the snowy hill.

"Hey, Molly, let's make a train," yelled Max. Max and Molly were brother and sister. They got along famously and seemed to get even closer as the years went by.

"Okay!" smiled Molly as she brushed the snow off her hair.

Just then a snowball sailed through the air and landed smack on Molly's head.

"Ted!" screamed Molly. He had lobbed the snowball lackadaisically into the air. He raced for the cover of the snow fort. Ben laughed at his friend and sat down to rest his legs.

BRRRRRRIIIIINNNNGGGG! The loud noise from the siren made all the children cover their ears. As an instinct, all three children raced to the house as quickly as they could.

"Hurry!" called Mrs. Jones. "Get into the shelter!" The children ran in after her.

"Mom, why are we doing this again?" asked Molly.

"We want to be prepared. We are in the middle of the Cold War with the Soviet Union."

"Remind me again why it's called the Cold War," said Max.

"Because of the snow, silly. In the summer, it will be the hot war," said Ted, laughing at his own joke.

STORY QUESTIONS

1. Which statement from the story would give a clue as to when the story took place?
   a. As an instinct, all three children raced to the house as quickly as they could.
   b. "Because of the snow, Silly. In the summer, it will be the hot war."
   c. The loud noise from the siren made all the children cover their ears.
   d. "Hurry!" called Mrs. Jones. "Get into the shelter!" The children ran in after her.

2. What is the meaning of the word *lackadaisically* as used in the story?
   a. happily
   b. unenthusiastically
   c. with drama
   d. crazily

3. Which of the following statements can be inferred from information shared in the story?
   a. The Jones family was living during the time of the Cold War.
   b. The neighborhood where the Jones' lived had a shelter for all the families.
   c. Everyone was ordered to build a shelter in their homes.
   d. Ted ran to the shelter in his own house.

DAILY Warm-Up 11 Name ______________________ Date __________

A NATION DIVIDED

Sadie let the door slam behind her as she came in.

"Hi," Mom called from the kitchen. "How was your day?"

"It was okay," replied Sadie. "As good as school gets, I guess."

"What's the long face for?" asked Mom. "You look as though you just heard an announcement that all the birthdays have been cancelled."

"It's worse than that," said Sadie. "We are learning about the Korean War in social studies, and it sounds a lot like the Vietnam War going on now."

"In what way?" inquired Mom.

"In the way that a lot of people are dying and it is scary! I'm not sure if our own government knows what is going on. It's all confusing."

"War is indeed confusing," reassured Mom, but her words didn't seem to help much.

"The two wars both involve a country that is split in two. Can you imagine our country being divided in half?"

"Well, if you want to talk about countries divided, what about the Civil War?" said Mom posing the question.

"My point exactly!" said Sadie. "Look at the carnage that the Civil War produced! If we are using former wars as the predictor, is the Vietnam War going to end up like the Korean War? How many people have to die for no reason at all?"

"To hear you talk, it sounds like you have a good understanding of what being at war means," commented Mom.

"It doesn't take much for a seventh grader to see that the war protesters in Washington might have a good point," added Sadie.

STORY QUESTIONS

1. What is meant by the word *carnage* as used in the passage?
   a. rumors
   b. agreement
   c. dispute
   d. bloodshed

2. What can you conclude about Sadie's understanding of history?
   a. She is not very enlightened to historical facts.
   b. She is more interested in her free time than what is taking place in the world.
   c. She is frustrated by the lack of information she has.
   d. Sadie seems to make it a point to learn about current events, as well as historical events.

3. Which sentence helps you answer the previous question?
   a. "In the way that a lot of people are dying and it is scary!"
   b. "I'm not sure if our own government knows what is going on."
   c. "If we are using former wars as the predictor, is the Vietnam War going to end up like the Korean War?"

DAILY Warm-Up 12 **Name** ______________________ **Date** __________

TIMBER!

"Timber!" screamed Ben. "Look out below!"

"Ben, you only say that when a tree is actually falling," said Felicity disgustedly.

"I'm just practicing," said Ben smiling. "Besides, I think it will bring me some luck."

"Relax," said Dad. "Let your brother have some fun. Today is a day to finally relax. We've been working so hard on clearing the land. It's about time we enjoy the beauty of our land."

Felicity lifted her skirts and kept walking. She knew her dad was right. She knew it was time to relax, but she couldn't get her mind off of her home—her last home, that is. Since her family had moved, she couldn't get her mind off of Boston. After all, she reasoned, she was a city girl.

Felicity's family had taken the train as far as it would go. From there, they purchased a wagon and supplies. They traveled incessantly for days on end. The further they traveled, the dirtier they got. Felicity felt like she belonged in a pigpen. Her dad had never run a team of mules before, so it was crazy at the beginning. One could hardly say this family was fit to tame the wilds of the west, but try as she might, Felicity couldn't convince her dad of that.

Felicity could barely stand the thought of taking another bath with freezing water. She missed the luxuries of city life. And now this! They were chopping down their own Christmas tree.

STORY QUESTIONS

1. Which of the following could be used to describe Felicity?
   a. angry
   b. easily provoked
   c. lonely
   d. intelligent

2. What would be a good title for this story?
   a. "First Settlers"
   b. "Settling the West"
   c. "Felicity's New Life"
   d. "Felicity's Thorn"

3. What is another word for *incessantly* as used in this story?
   a. continuously
   b. purposefully
   c. questioningly
   d. halfheartedly

DAILY Warm-Up 13

Name ______________________ Date __________

THE FEMALE AVIATOR

"Tell me again what she looked like," asked Mary.

Mary dangled her feet from the wicker furniture. The day was hot and steamy. Sweat beads were forming on Mary's forehead. She put her glass of lemonade to her forehead and looked at her aunt.

"Oh, Mary, aren't you tired of hearing about that?" asked her Aunt Mini.

"How on Earth could I ever tire of such a story?" replied Mary.

"Because it's the same story over and over, and it doesn't change," replied Aunt Mini.

Aunt Mini was home visiting for the summer. She was a professor at an all girls' college in the East. Mary loved it when she came home. Mary lived with her grandmother and her dad. Aunt Mini was like a breath of fresh air. She brought excitement to the farm.

"Yes, but it's your story," explained Mary. "You know somebody famous!"

"*Knew* somebody famous," reminded Aunt Mini. "I only knew her for a short time. In fact, only one semester."

"Yes, but she was the one and only Amelia Earhart," beamed Mary.

"That's right, she was," said Aunt Mini quietly. "What a tragedy."

"Was she good in school? When did she learn to fly?"

"She learned to fly at a flying school near college. She was fascinated with flying, and with every chance she got, she'd be at the flying school taking lessons. She spent more time doing that than studying."

"She must have been a natural," said Mary.

STORY QUESTIONS

1. Using the context clues, what is the meaning of the word *beamed* as used in the passage?
   a. smiled
   b. opened
   c. arranged
   d. organized

2. According to the passage, which sentence shows how Mary feels about Amelia Earhart?
   a. "Was she good in school? When did she learn to fly?"
   b. "Yes, but it's your story," explained Mary. "You know somebody famous!"
   c. Aunt Mini was like a breath of fresh air. She brought excitement to the farm.
   d. "How on earth could I ever tire of such a story?" replied Mary.

3. What is the purpose of the first sentence?
   a. to introduce the first character in the story
   b. to explain the problem and resolution in the story
   c. to provide the background and the setting of the story
   d. none of the above

DAILY Warm-Up 14

Name ______________________________ **Date** __________

YOU'VE GOT MAIL

Catherine opened the telegram as slowly as she could for fear of ripping it. Her trembling hands stopped short of opening it completely. The glue held fast on the corner. What if the letter bore bad news? What would she do? Catherine didn't think she could handle the disappointment. It had been a busy quarter with all of the papers and readings to do, but this letter and its contents were never far from her mind. She was exhausted both physically and mentally.

"Open it!" gushed Theresa. She couldn't handle the intensity. This letter would contain all the details of Catherine's future life. Would she move? Would she stay? What would happen?

"Oh, Theresa, it could all be over now. I'm just not sure I'm ready to accept that," said Catherine.

"The deal is already done," she explained. "Your life's course is already decided. You just don't know the details. Open it! Please! I'm begging you!" urged Theresa.

Catherine opened up the last bit of the telegram.

"Dear Miss Butler . . ." read Catherine.

"It sounds official!" exclaimed Theresa.

"We regret to inform you that the position of the school master in Frankfurt has been filled . . ." continued Catherine.

"Oh, dear," moaned Theresa, a lump forming in her throat.

"However . . ." Catherine interrupted. "We would like to offer you the school master position here at the school in Heatherby!"

"You got the position?" asked Theresa incredulously.

"Yes," sighed Catherine, as she smoothed her skirts. "Say hello to the new school master."

STORY QUESTIONS

1. Which sentence does not hint at the time period in which the story was written?
   a. Catherine opened the telegram as slowly as she could for fear of ripping it.
   b. "We regret to inform you that the position of the school master in Frankfurt has been filled . . ." continued Catherine.
   c. "Yes," sighed Catherine, as she smoothed her skirts.
   d. "Oh Theresa, it could all be over now. I'm just not sure I'm ready to accept that," said Catherine.

2. What conclusions can be drawn about how Theresa feels about Catherine?
   a. She doesn't know very much about her.
   b. She is unsure whether she is excited for Catherine or not.
   c. She is hoping that Catherine will have to move for the new position.
   d. She really likes Catherine and hopes that she can stay.

3. What is the meaning of the word *incredulously* as used in the passage?
   a. amazingly   b. skeptically   c. ignorantly

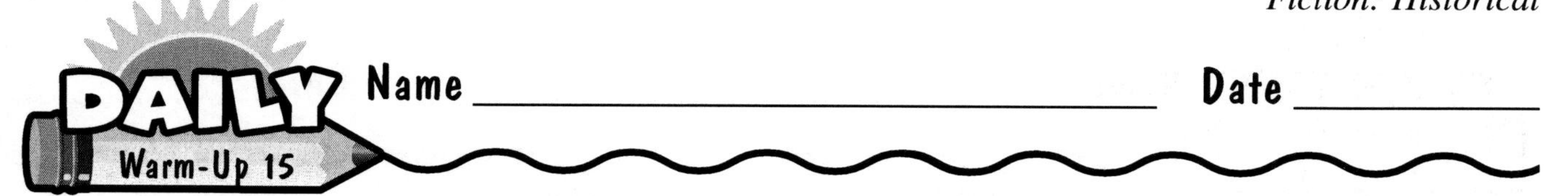

RUN FOR YOUR LIFE

The rain was coming down so hard that Tilly felt like she was going to drown. She was slopping through the mud and could feel her shoes sticking each time. She didn't have a coat, so she was beginning to shake uncontrollably. The blanket she had grabbed to wear was torn and ragged. It wasn't good for much.

Every muscle in Tilly's body ached with exhaustion. She had been on the road running for days now. She wasn't sure exactly how many days she had been gone because all of her running was done at night under the light of the moon. But tonight there was no moon: only the clouds that blocked the moonlight and her feeling of freedom. As long as the moon was in the sky, Tilly felt like she was safe and everything would be okay.

It all started when a new slave showed up on the plantation. She was assigned to work in the shed just outside the barn. But this new slave had also brought a plan—a plan for an escape. She was careful whom she shared the plan with, as it was dangerous to let too many people know. Tilly had listened to the plan, and she and her sister were resolute about going.

The escape route was dangerous and filled with fear. At any minute, a slave could be caught and returned to his or her owner to face the severe consequences of trying to run away.

STORY QUESTIONS

1. Using the context clues, what does the word *resolute* mean as used in this passage?
   a. determined
   b. intensified
   c. interrogated
   d. chided
2. What is the main idea of the last paragraph?
   a. to explain whether or not Tilly should trust the new slave
   b. to explain the dangers involved with the escape plan
   c. to explain the climax of the story
   d. to explain the resolution of the story
3. What is the name of the escape route that Tilly will take to escape?
   a. The Freedom Train
   b. The Liberty Bell
   c. The Underground Railroad
   d. none of the above

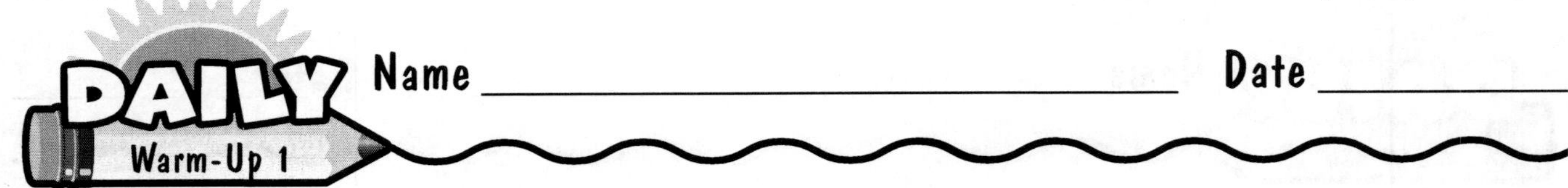

BIG BROTHER

Ted couldn't wait to meet his new little brother. Ted was 10 and had been the only child in his family for a long time. He imagined what it would be like to have a baby brother. He would take him on bike rides and go hiking. He would go camping and fishing. He pictured himself sleeping under the stars listening to the chirping of crickets. He would even teach the little guy how to ride a bike. It would be great.

"Grandma? When are they going to be home again?" called Ted down the stairs.

"Should be any time now," said Grandma. "They called when they left the hospital."

"There they are!" interrupted Ted. He raced down the stairs and threw open the door. His parents were just pulling into the driveway.

"Big brother coming through!" called Ted and raced to the car door. He scooped up the little bundle from his mother's arms and gave it a squish.

"Be careful, Ted, that's a fragile package you've got there," said Dad.

"Don't worry, Dad. I've got everything under control," replied Ted. It was only then that Ted noticed the pink blanket wrapped around the baby.

"What?" asked Ted.

"That's right," explained Mom. "We've got ourselves a little girl."

"Is something wrong?" asked Dad tenderly.

Ted stammered a minute and a hollow sound escaped his lips. "No. She'll just have to like fishing, camping, hiking, and biking."

"She will. She will," replied Mom calmly and she gave Ted a hug.

STORY QUESTIONS

1. Using the context clues, what does the word *hollow* mean?
   a. filled
   b. perplexed
   c. vacant
   d. low

2. According to the passage, what sentence shows that Ted's parents were worried about his reaction to a baby sister?
   a. "We've got ourselves a little girl."
   b. "Is something wrong?" asked Dad tenderly.
   c. "She'll just have to like fishing, camping, hiking, and biking."
   d. Ted couldn't wait to meet his new little brother.

3. What is the main idea of the passage?
   a. Being creative and using many resources can help you accomplish a task.
   b. If you try hard enough, you can do it.
   c. It's important to knock out your competition.
   d. It's important to be flexible and roll with the punches.

DAILY Warm-Up 2 Name ______________________ Date __________

THE PUBLIC NOTE

Shelly angrily threw her backpack on the floor and stomped up to her room. She was furious. The day had started out badly and had only gotten worse. It seemed that everything she had tried that day had failed.

Opening the refrigerator in hopes of finding something good to eat, Shelly frowned at the contents. There wasn't anything worth looking at, let alone eating!

"Why did she have to do that?" asked Shelly aloud.

"What did she do? And who is she?" asked Mom as she came into the kitchen.

"Mrs. Benton," explained Shelly. "She took a note from Angela."

"Why would you be upset with that?" asked Mom.

"Because I wrote the note!" said Shelly in an exasperated voice. "I said some things in the note that I never should have told anyone. I was just getting my feelings out. Boy, did they get out!"

"Shelly, did Mrs. Benton share the contents of the note?" asked Mom.

"No, but I just know she will!" moaned Shelly.

"Is there anything you should be ashamed of, Shelly?" questioned Mom.

"Oh, no," clarified Shelly, "but embarrassed about! I shared some personal feelings about people, but I didn't mention any names."

"Shelly, any time you write notes at school, you have to know that there is a chance that the teacher will catch you," said Mom.

STORY QUESTIONS

1. Which sentence shows how Shelly felt about Mrs. Benton?
   a. There wasn't anything worth looking at let alone eating!
   b. "Oh no," clarified Shelly, "but embarrassed about! I shared some personal feelings about people, but I didn't mention any names."
   c. "Why did she have to do that?" asked Shelly aloud.
   d. "Shelly, any time you write notes at school, you have to know that there is a chance that the teacher will catch you," said Mom.

2. The first paragraph shares with the reader . . .
   a. how to solve the problem.
   b. what the problem was.
   c. the disagreements between Shelly and her mom.
   d. the emotions of the main character.

3. What is the main idea of the passage?
   a. Being creative and using many resources can help you accomplish a task.
   b. If you try hard enough, you can do it.
   c. Think first before you act.
   d. Good things come to those who wait.

DAILY Warm-Up 3 **Name** ______________________ **Date** __________

DRAMATIC THINGS

Caitlyn ran into the house and let out a gasp.

"You're never going to believe my day!" she shouted.

"Let's hear it," said Mom.

"It was the worst. First I was late because my locker wouldn't open. It took me forever to find the janitor, and he said that someone had messed with my locker. Then I was called on by Mr. Burton in first period to share my findings on a subject I'd been asked to research."

"Dramatic things . . .," interrupted Dad.

"Don't say it!" Caitlyn countered. "I'm not that dramatic."

". . . happen to dramatic people!" finished Dad.

Caitlyn ignored him and continued on with her day. "By lunchtime, I was exhausted from the earlier events of the day. On my way to the gym, I stopped in the bathroom and found it filled with a bunch of guys. The nerve! I yelled at all of them to leave the girl's bathroom at once. That was when Gwen poked her head in the bathroom to inform me that I was the one in the wrong bathroom. Can you imagine?"

Caitlyn took a moment to breathe and take a bite out of her cookie. She was ready to continue when a loud crash was heard on the other side of the counter.

"What happened?" called Mom. "Are you okay?"

Dad looked up sheepishly to show the broken and empty salad bowl.

"Dad, what's that they say? Dramatic things happen to dramatic people!" Caitlyn smiled bigger than she'd smiled all day.

STORY QUESTIONS

1. Which paragraph explains how Caitlyn got her dad back?
   - a. first paragraph
   - b. last paragraph
   - c. third paragraph
   - d. second paragraph
2. What inferences can you make about how Caitlyn responds to things?
   - a. She is quiet and shy.
   - b. She cries over everything.
   - c. She is easily unnerved.
   - d. She is theatrical and likes to talk.
3. Which lesson could be learned from the story?
   - a. A watched pot never boils.
   - b. A person living in a glass house shouldn't throw stones.
   - c. A friend in need is a friend indeed.
   - d. Early to bed and early to rise makes a person healthy and wise.

DAILY Warm-Up 4 Name ______________________ Date __________

BUYING TIME

"Did you get all the gifts you were looking for?" Mom asked Chad.

"No. I got yours and Grandpa's but that was about it," responded Chad.

"What happened? You were in the store for two hours," queried Mom.

"I just didn't see anything," explained Chad.

Each year Chad worked all summer mowing lawns in the neighborhood so that he could buy his own Christmas gifts. At 11 years old, he felt like it was quite an accomplishment. He could hardly imagine what it would be like to have his parents pay for things.

This year had been tough. Chad's dad had been in a car accident that left him without the ability to work. Money was tight and the recovery process had been slow. Chad knew that he should help out with the family finances, but Mom would hear nothing of it. She refused to accept any of Chad's money. She felt it was his and he should be the one to spend it.

Chad didn't like the idea of spending money on frivolous things when he knew that he should be providing the necessities for his loved ones. He leaned back on the headrest of the seat and closed his eyes.

"Chad. I don't want you to forget that you are still a kid," said Mom calmly. "I don't want you to take on these burdens too soon. Now go back inside and finish your shopping. I've got my book here to keep me company. Now go," instructed Mom.

STORY QUESTIONS

1. What is the meaning of the word *frivolous* as used in the passage?
   a. serious
   b. inconsequential
   c. hardened
   d. relevant

2. What conclusions can be drawn about how Chad feels about his family?
   a. He is aloof and does not care.
   b. He is supportive and diligent.
   c. He is confused and curious.
   d. He ignores the situation they are in.

3. Which of the following statements helps you answer the previous question?
   a. Money was tight and the recovery process had been slow.
   b. He could hardly imagine what it would be like to have her parents pay for things.
   c. He knew that he should be providing the necessities for his loved ones.
   d. Chad knew that he should help out with the family finances, but Mom would hear nothing of it.

DAILY Warm-Up 5 Name ______________________ Date __________

JUNIPER INN

"Did you read in the newspaper about the fire last night?" asked Dad as he ate his bowl of cereal.

"I didn't," replied Mom. "Where was the fire?"

"Juniper Inn. They say it burned to the ground," said Dad in a surprised voice.

"Juniper Inn?" stuttered Mom.

"You have got to be kidding me!" interrupted Dan. "We just ate there last night."

"I know, that's why I am as surprised as you are," said Dad.

"That is terrible," said Mom. "I hope no one was injured."

"The paper says that there were no injuries or fatalities but it says that restaurant is completely gone. There is nothing left to salvage," informed Dad.

"So what are we going to do?" asked Dan.

"Do? What do you mean?" asked Mom.

"We've got to do something," explained Dan. "We've been friends with the Parkers for years. They are going to need some help."

Dan's parents looked up from their breakfast and winked at each other. They looked back at their son for more direction.

"First, we need to call Mr. Parker and make sure he's okay. He could probably use a friend right now. Mom, do you think we could bring dinner in to their family this evening?" said Dan.

"I think I can do that. It seems a little strange in a way," said Mom as she gazed out the window.

"Mr. Parker has been bringing families dinners for years. It's our turn to bring him dinner," said Dan with a grin.

STORY QUESTIONS

1. Which of the following statements can be determined from the story?
   a. Dan is the oldest child in the family.
   b. Dan is afraid of the dogs in the neighborhood.
   c. Dan tries to boss his parents around.
   d. Dan is a unique kid and is a great leader.

2. What is the meaning of the word *salvage* as used in the story?
   a. reclaim
   b. ignore
   c. exaggerate
   d. review

3. Which word best describes Dan's feelings about Mr. Parker?
   a. patient
   b. annoyed
   c. respectful
   d. resilient

DAILY Warm-Up 6 Name ______________________ Date __________

THE BRIEF REPORT

"If I sit through one more of these science reports, I'm going to die," thought Kelsey as she rested her head on the desk.

Each student in her class had been assigned a report on a different planet. Kelsey had been the first to give her report, so she found it hard to sit quietly through the rest of them. She had already been given a warning to stay in her seat and keep quiet. Kelsey no longer was stressed about giving her report, so she had no adrenaline going to keep her nervous.

Kelsey watched Patrick get up and walk to the front of the room.

"Ughh!" moaned Kelsey silently. Patrick always bored her silly with his scientific terms and phrases. He perused his report before beginning.

Something in the corner of the room caught Kelsey's eye. Was it a mouse? It sure looked like one! Kelsey kept her eye fixed to the crack in the wall.

Mrs. Smith noticed Kelsey's distraction and calmly called across the room. "Kelsey, you know what your job is, so remember to do it."

"My job has changed, Mrs. Smith," said Kelsey, but she didn't take her eyes off the wall.

"And what would that be?" demanded Mrs. Smith.

Just then, the mouse scurried out and raced across the room. "My job is to watch that mouse run under your desk," said Kelsey calmly.

"Eeeeeek!" screamed Mrs. Smith along with the rest of the class.

STORY QUESTIONS

1. Which statement best describes Kelsey as implied in the reading passage?
   a. Kelsey is lazy and tired most of the time.
   b. Kelsey is curious and likes to explore.
   c. Kelsey is timid, shy, and introverted.
   d. Kelsey is easily distracted and has a hard time paying attention.

2. Which sentence explains the problem in this story?
   a. Kelsey had a hard time sitting through her classmate's reports.
   b. When she was right, Kelsey thought she was wrong.
   c. Kelsey was offended by her teacher.
   d. Kelsey had been given a warning to keep quiet.

3. What does the word *perused* mean as used in the passage?
   a. indict
   b. read carefully
   c. restrict
   d. flippantly

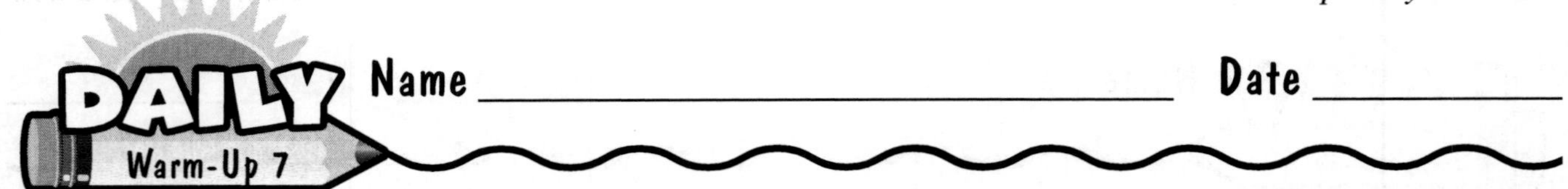

SURPRISE ATTACK

Ellie put on all the layers of clothing she could before she went outside to meet up with her friends. It had been snowing all day and all night. The snow was wet now and in places it was melting. Ellie had been waiting all day to build a snow fort.

"Hey, Ellie," called Ashlyn. Ashlyn was Ellie's neighbor and the two had worked together to design the snow fort on paper. It was going to be elaborate and detailed. It was going to be great.

Ashlyn had already begun making blocks of snow. Ellie tromped through the wet snow and plopped down on the ground next to Ashlyn.

"Oh, man, the snow is melting!" cried Ellie.

"It sure is," said Ashlyn, "but if you pack it well enough, it seems to hold."

Ashlyn smoothed out the blocks of snow and began building the foundation. Just then a snowball went flying through the air.

"What was that?" called Ellie, but as she ducked another snowball whizzed by her head.

Peter Crowler let out a laugh and took off around the side of Ellie's house.

"It's an ambush," cried Ashlyn, "Quick! Grab a block of snow! Let's get him!"

Ellie grabbed a block of snow but was met with a snowball . . . in her face!

"Oooph!" called Ellie. She felt a sting in her eyes but willed herself not to cry. This was ridiculous. She furiously packed some more snow together in her hands and threw it in all directions.

STORY QUESTIONS

1. What would be another good title for this story?
   a. "Race Against Time"
   b. "A White Christmas"
   c. "The Snow Fort"
   d. "Snowball Alert"

2. What can you conclude about Peter after reading the passage?
   a. He likes to play pranks on people.
   b. He is a good at building snow forts.
   c. He is learning to ice skate.
   d. He is helpful and calm.

3. Which sentence helps you best answer the previous question?
   a. Peter Crowler let out a laugh and took off around the side of Ellie's house.
   b. "It's an ambush," cried Ashlyn, "Quick! Grab a block of snow! Let's get him!"
   c. She felt a sting in her eyes but willed herself not to cry.
   d. Ellie put on all the layers of clothing she could before she went outside to meet up with her friends.

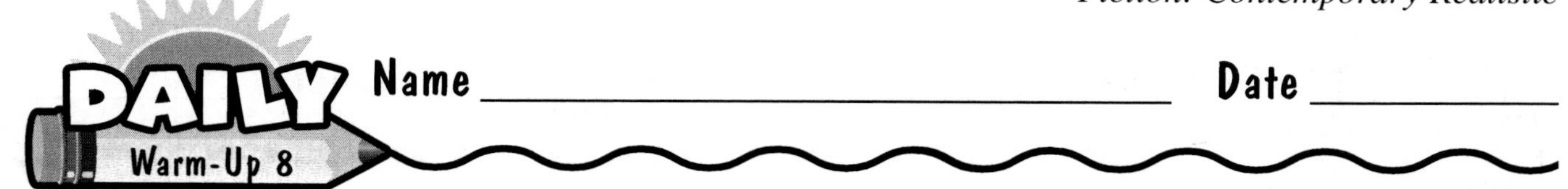

BIRTHDAY BANG

Lola had waited all day for her birthday party to begin. She had invited peers from her school class, but she was worried now that she had made a mistake. Miranda was bossing all the boys around and Ryan had threatened to dunk her head in the sink. Today was supposed to be fun and exciting; instead, it was turning into a headache. Why had she invited anyone to her party?

Lola's mother came down the stairs into the basement with root beer floats.

"Here you are, Lola dear. Let me know when you are ready for the hamburgers and I will turn the grill on."

Fortunately, Ryan and Miranda had calmed down a bit. Lola's mom went back upstairs without realizing what a mess this party was turning out to be. That is when things deteriorated. Jake leaned over to get the root beer float in the middle and ended up knocking three or four down in the process. Cold root beer flowed on Kate's dress.

Kate stood up furious and yelled, "Food fight!"

She grabbed a root beer float and tossed it at Jake. Ryan grabbed the potato chip bowl and dumped it on Miranda's head. Miranda grabbed two root beer floats and splashed them back at Ryan.

Lola sat back stunned. She could not believe what she was seeing. The food and drinks were flying. Just then, her mother walked down the stairs. Ryan tossed a bowl of watermelon in her direction. Lola cringed.

STORY QUESTIONS

1. Which of the following statements is a fact?
   a. Lola invited both boys and girls to the birthday party.
   b. Lola's mother is not going to be very happy about the food fight.
   c. Lola's mother is expecting poorly behaved guests.
   d. Lola is trying to teach her mom patience.

2. What would be another good title for this story?
   a. "The Root Beer Floats"
   b. "The Difficulty of the Party"
   c. "Friendship Concerns"
   d. "Birthday Party Gone Awry"

3. What is another word for *peers* as used in this story?
   a. instructors
   b. adults
   c. relatives
   d. acquaintances

DAILY Warm-Up 9 **Name** ______________________ **Date** __________

DOUBLE VISION

Kaylor jumped up to rebound the basketball and came down on an opponent's elbow instead.

"Ohhhh!" groaned Kaylor. He knew he was going to have a black eye now.

The next day at school, the kids teased him about his black eye. It was funny for a little while, but Kaylor was growing weary of the jokes. Besides, his peripheral vision seemed kind of funny and it worried him. It was not just his hurt eye that was bothering him. It was both eyes. Everything seemed blurrier than usual. Kaylor had insisted on playing the rest of the game even though his eye was swollen.

That night over dinner, Kaylor decided to broach the subject with his parents.

"Would it be possible to have my vision affected after the collision last night?" asked Kaylor quietly.

"What do you mean?" asked Mom with a hint of tension in her voice.

"I just was wondering," said Kaylor.

"Wondering what?" inquired Dad. "Is there a problem with your vision, son?"

"Kind of," said Kaylor wishing he had never said anything.

"We are going to go straight to the doctor tomorrow," said Mom.

The next day at the doctor's office, Dr. Parker gave him a thorough check up. After the checkup Dr. Parker called Kaylor's mom in to explain that Kaylor needed glasses.

"Is this a result of the bump to his eye?" asked Kaylor's mom.

"No. It's a result of Kaylor's eyes needing glasses to improve his vision," said Dr. Parker with a chuckle.

STORY QUESTIONS

1. The main idea of the first sentence is to . . .
   - a. set the tone of the story.
   - b. introduce the main character and setting.
   - c. introduce foreshadowing.
   - d. explain the climax of the story.

2. Another word used for *peripheral vision* is . . .
   - a. blinding.
   - b. formation.
   - c. side view.
   - d. secondary.

3. Which sentence explains the problem in this story?
   - a. "Would it be possible to have my vision affected after the collision last night?" asked Kaylor quietly.
   - b. Kaylor jumped up to rebound the basketball and came down on an opponent's elbow instead.
   - c. It was not just his hurt eye that was bothering him.
   - d. After the checkup Dr. Parker called Kaylor's mom in to explain that Kaylor needed glasses.

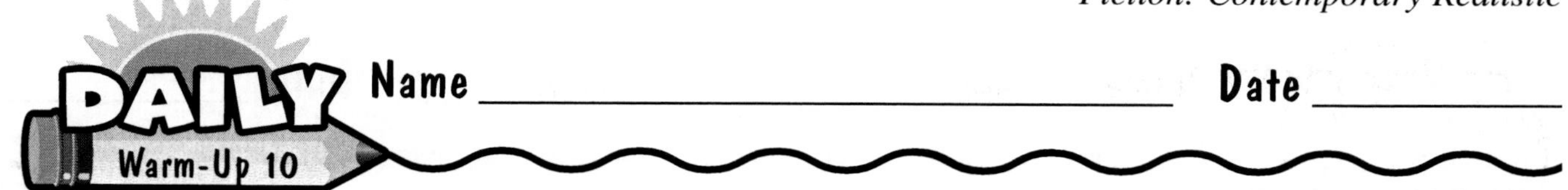

A GREEN THUMB

Kathryn had been working for hours in her grandmother's garden. It was a favorite pastime of hers. She loved the feel of the moist, warm dirt, and the sound of the birds in the air. It had been a wonderful summer so far. Kathryn was anxious to see the fruits of her labor in the garden. She had planted all different types of flowers, and she was checking each day for a bloom from the green stalks poking their heads through the ground.

Things had not been easy for Kathryn. She had been fighting all summer. First it was the soil. She had raked all of the rocks out of it and tirelessly removed any clods of dirt. She had added fertilizer and other additives to make the soil healthy and strong. Then the slugs came along. Slugs and grubs were eating any plants and seeds she sowed. Finally, she fought the weather. After weeks of drought, the rains finally came, but then they wouldn't stop. Water had washed away the first crop of seeds. In despair, Kathryn stood outside dripping wet, setting up a net to prevent her soil from eroding. It worked temporarily.

Kathryn's grandmother took delight in Kathryn's hard work and diligence.

"It's going to pay off, dear," she cooed to Kathryn each time she arrived to work in the garden.

Kathryn always responded with the same comment, "My thumb doesn't look very green." Kathryn knew that she needed to be patient.

STORY QUESTIONS

1. What would be another good title for this story?
   a. "Lost and Found in the Garden"
   b. "Hiring Scarecrows"
   c. "Work Before Play"
   d. "Gardening Is Hard Work"
2. What can you conclude about Kathryn after reading the passage?
   a. She is loved and adored by her friends.
   b. She is a good at math.
   c. She is learning self defense.
   d. She is hard working.
3. Which sentence helps you answer the previous question?
   a. "It's going to pay off, dear," she cooed to Kathryn each time she arrived to work in the garden.
   b. Things had not been easy for Kathryn. She had been fighting all summer.
   c. Water had washed away the first crop of seeds.
   d. "My thumb doesn't look very green."

DAILY Warm-Up 11 Name ______________________________ Date __________

HELPING HANDS

"Where do we put the firewood?" asked Sue.

"That's not firewood," replied Dad laughing. "It's paperwork, Sue."

"If we hurry, we can be done by lunch time," said Sue.

Sue and her family were helping their neighbors, the Crowleys, pack up for a move to another city. Sue wasn't thrilled about helping them, but what could she say? Her dad was always volunteering her services without asking her permission. Sue was getting used to it.

"Help!" yelled Cindy from the back of the house. Sue ran to help her sister who was balancing a very heavy mirror on her knee.

"Why do they even have this?" muttered Sue. "It's too heavy to hang. They have so much junk it's ridiculous. You can barely move in here!"

"How can you say that?" asked Cindy. "Don't people get to decide for themselves how they want to live? There are people who think lizards for pets are disgusting and you have three of them."

"You can't compare my lizards to this filthy mess," defended Sue. "Besides, my lizards are considered rare, exotic animals."

"My point is that everyone has different likes and dislikes. You can't be critical of others just because you have different tastes and interests. We are here to help, not to judge," said Cindy.

"When you put it that way, it makes me sound pretty harsh. Where did you get these ideas?" queried Sue.

Sue walked over to the mirror and picked it up. "I can probably help with this."

STORY QUESTIONS

1. What is meant by the word *queried* as used in the story?
   a. looked down on
   b. corrected
   c. placed blame
   d. inquired

2. Which words describe Sue's feelings about helping the Crowleys move?
   a. apprehensive, tired, frustrated
   b. excited, thrilled, unsure
   c. angry, furious, unsettled
   d. not thrilled, disgusted, annoyed

3. Which sentence from the story portrays Sue's change of heart?
   a. "My point is that everyone has different likes and dislikes."
   b. Sue walked over to the mirror and picked it up. "I can probably help with this."
   c. "Where did you get these ideas?" queried Sue.
   d. "You can't compare my lizards to this filthy mess," defended Sue.

DAILY Warm-Up 12

Name ______________________________ Date ___________

AN APPLE A DAY

"Be careful!" called Grandma.

Ella climbed higher into the apple tree. "I'm fine as long as I don't drop my bucket," she called.

"It's not the bucket I'm worried about," said Grandma. "It's my granddaughter. One slip and you could break your arm or back or something!"

"Don't worry, Grams. I'll be careful! Besides, I can reach lots of apples up here!" yelled Ella.

"Just be careful," cautioned Grandma.

"Oh, sick!" hollered Ella.

"What? What is it?" called Grandma with a hint of panic in her voice.

"Grams, there is a worm in this apple," said Ella.

Grandma breathed a sigh of relief. "Is that all?" she asked. "Worms are just a part of growing apples."

"That's so disgusting," answered Ella.

"Disgusting, yes, but inevitable. We've been growing apples for decades. You're always bound to run into some worms. It's like life, you know. You've got to cut the worms out. There are going to be some tough times, but you make the best of it and keep going," explained Grandma.

"Why can't you just do away with the worms? There's a spray you can put on them," said Ella.

"I am sure there is a spray, too," said Grandma, "but why would I spray something on my apples just to eliminate something very natural? The worms aren't hurting anybody."

"Even though they are disgusting?" asked Ella.

"I don't look at them for long," explained Grandma. "Besides, a little protein never hurt anybody!"

Ella threw her head back and laughed.

STORY QUESTIONS

1. What does the word *eliminate* mean as used in this passage?

a. crisscross
b. get rid of
c. ambled
d. awaken

2. Which sentence portrays Grandma's love for Ella?

a. Ella threw her head back and laughed.
b. "Worms are just a part of growing apples."
c. "It's my granddaughter. One slip and you could break your arm or back or something!"
d. "But why would I spray something on my apples just to eliminate something very natural? The worms aren't hurting anybody."

DAILY Warm-Up 13 **Name** ______________________________ **Date** ____________

HATS OFF TO RULES

"Hats off, boys," called Mrs. Stephens. "You know the rules."

"What rule?" asked Kyle as he reached for his head.

"Yeah! What rule?" asked Robby with irritation in his voice.

"Mr. Robinson initiated the new rule about no hats last Friday," explained Mrs. Stephens. "Weren't you there?"

"I guess we must have missed that," said Kyle.

As the boys pulled off their hats, they headed towards the locker room.

"Man! What's so bad about wearing a hat? Things seem to be getting stricter and stricter around here!" muttered Robby.

"I don't know," reasoned Kyle. "It does seem like there is a new rule around here every day. Next thing you know we're not going to be allowed to talk."

"You can't be serious," boomed a voice behind them. Kyle and Robby looked at each other and then in the direction of the voice.

Just then Mr. Green came around the corner. Mr. Green was the P.E. teacher. He was excellent at sports and had a fun personality. He would joke and tease with the boys and was a friend to all.

"It's a matter of respect," explained Mr. Green. "In the old days, it was disrespectful to wear a hat indoors. Is that too much to handle?"

Robby looked at Kyle. Kyle reasoned, "I guess it makes a little sense. It's hard for us to see why it's so disrespectful."

"It won't be too hard to change. You might need to fix your hair, though," said Mr. Green laughing.

STORY QUESTIONS

1. Which of the following statements would be new information to the reader?
   a. Robby and Kyle are friends.
   b. Mr. Green is respected by the boys at the school.
   c. Robby and Kyle are on Mr. Green's basketball team.
   d. Mr. Green is trying to help Robby and Kyle adjust to the changing rules.

2. Which sentence explains the problem in this story?
   a. Robby and Kyle were upset about being in trouble.
   b. Robby and Kyle want to protest the new rule.
   c. Robby and Kyle do not have much respect for Mrs. Stephens.
   d. Robby and Kyle are upset about the new hat rule.

3. What sentence shows the boys working towards the resolution to the story?
   a. "It won't be too hard to change. You might need to fix your hair, though," said Mr. Green laughing.
   b. Kyle reasoned, "I guess it makes a little sense. It's hard to for us to see why it's so disrespectful."
   c. "Yeah! What rule?" asked Robby with irritation in his voice.
   d. "It does seem like there is a new rule around here every day. Next thing you know we're not going to be allowed to talk."

DAILY Warm-Up 14 **Name** ______________________ **Date** __________

STORM TROOPER

Jason and his father were driving to the grocery store to pick up some milk. It had been a weird day. The sky was dark but there were few clouds. As they drove up the street, there started to be a rumbling sound heard across the ground.

Jason's father immediately realized that a tornado was coming. He stopped the car and instructed Jason to get out immediately. Jason and his dad got out of the car and worked their way to the closest building. By this time the wind was raging, and it was hard to see or hear. Debris was falling all over the place. Jason couldn't see his dad anymore. He also realized that he wasn't getting to the building fast enough. He was afraid he would be picked up by the wind and thrown into the air.

As he worked his way towards the building, he noticed a field to his right. He could see the irrigation ditch that dipped down. In a panic he scrambled to the ditch and lay flat on the ground. More debris and objects flew overhead. Jason stayed crouched down. His heart was pounding, and he was nervous. He had never been in a tornado before.

After awhile, the winds died down and the loud roaring sound was gone. Jason slowly lifted his head and peered around. The landscape as he once knew it was destroyed. Jason could barely recognize the buildings in front of him because of all the damage.

He stood up and with shaky legs walked to the building. Once there, he pried the door open and went inside. It was a public building owned by the city. It was vacant, but Jason could hear noises further inside. He walked into the large room and caught a glimpse of his dad. He raced across the room and gave him a big hug.

"Jason! How are you? I've been worried sick about you!" said his father. "I couldn't find you anywhere!"

Jason breathed a sigh of relief and sat down. Did he ever have a story to tell!

STORY QUESTIONS

1. Which paragraph explains the problem in the story?
   a. first paragraph
   b. second paragraph
   c. third paragraph
   d. fourth paragraph
2. What inferences can you make about Jason?
   a. Jason is upset with his father.
   b. Jason tries to follow very high expectations.
   c. Jason doesn't take life too seriously and can adjust easily.
   d. Jason is quick-thinking and self-sufficient.
3. What is the meaning of the word *debris* as used in the story?
   a. wreckage
   b. parts of the tornado
   c. barrier
   d. metal pieces

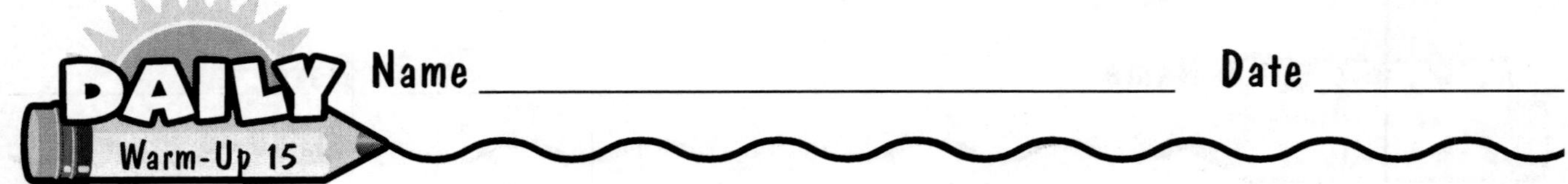

ORGANIZED CRIME

Kendra opened her eyes. Could it really be morning already? It had been a late night as Kendra drove home with the softball team from Denver. The ride had been long and monotonous. Kendra got little sleep on the bus and didn't get home until 3:00 A.M.

"Rise and shine, sweetheart. You've got some work to do," whistled Dad. He was always happy in the morning.

"What do you mean work?" asked Kendra groggily. "Today is Saturday. Can I at least have a break?" demanded Kendra.

"I know you're tired, Kendra, but thanks to your friends, you've got some work to do," replied Dad.

"What do my friends have to do with this?" thought Kendra as she closed her eyes again.

Dad threw open the drapes. He looked as though he was admiring a pretty view. Kendra squinted in the sunlight.

"Close the window, Dad," called Kendra. She cleared her throat.

"If I close the window, then you will miss the artwork of your friends!" explained Dad.

Kendra slowly rose to her feet and walked to the window. When Kendra caught the glimpse of what her friends had done, she gasped. The once green lawn and yard was completely covered in toilet paper. The artwork done by Kendra's friends looked more like a toilet paper factory.

Kendra groaned and slid back into bed. "What kind of friends would do this?" she thought. Just then Kendra grinned as she imagined her friends going to all this trouble.

STORY QUESTIONS

1. Using inference, what were Kendra's eventual feelings about what her friends had done?
   - a. indifferent
   - b. upset
   - c. embarrassed
   - d. amused

2. Which sentence indicates Kendra's feelings about what her friends did?
   - a. Just then Kendra grinned as she imagined her friends going to all this trouble.
   - b. "What kind of friends would do this?" she thought.
   - c. When Kendra caught the glimpse of what her friends had done, she gasped.
   - d. Kendra groaned and slid back into bed.

3. What is the meaning of the word *groggily* as used in the passage?
   - a. happily
   - b. dazedly
   - c. annoyingly
   - d. lovingly

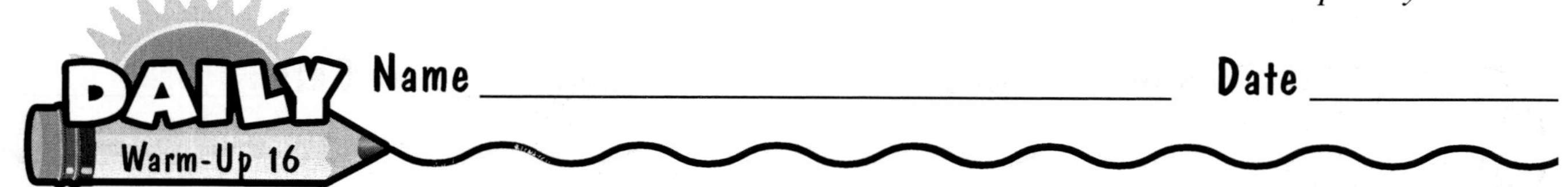

Name ______________________________ Date __________

SPELL THAT!

Orrin nervously tapped his pencil on the desk waiting for his turn in the spelling bee. He was very nervous and knew that with three of them left, only two would make it to the county spelling bee. Orrin had always been a good speller, but his nerves had never settled. He had made it to the school bee every year. This was his fourth year to go.

"Capillary," said the judge. "The word is *capillary*."

Orrin breathed a silent sigh of relief. He thought for a minute before he said, "c-a-p-i-l-l-a-r-y."

"That's correct," responded the judge as he took a sip of water.

Orrin let out another breath. He went into his zone of ignoring the words of his competitors. When he listened, he would begin comparing the difficulty of the words. He decided that ignoring their words helped him concentrate better on his own.

It didn't seem to take long before the judge was looking at Orrin again. Orrin smiled and turned his full attention to the judge.

"Accreditation," said the judge. "The word is *accreditation*."

Orrin remembered seeing this word on his brother's college applications.

"A-c," said Orin. He paused again. "Is there another *c*?" His mind was racing and he started sweating again. He decided to add another *c*. It would make or break his streak, but he didn't have much more time to stall. "c-r-e-d-i-t-a-t-i-o-n," stated Orrin confidently. It seemed to take forever for the judge to respond.

STORY QUESTIONS

1. How does Orrin feel about the word *capillary* being given to him?
   a. He thinks it is a very difficult word.
   b. He thinks it is an easy word to spell.
   c. He is irritated the judge gave him that word.
   d. He thinks his words are harder than his competitor's words.

2. Which sentence explains or infers how Orrin feels about the word *capillary*?
   a. Orrin let out another breath.
   b. Orrin nervously tapped his pencil on the desk waiting for his turn in the spelling bee.
   c. He went into his zone of ignoring the words of his competitors.
   d. Orrin breathed a silent sigh of relief.

3. What is the meaning of the word *zone* in the story?
   a. place
   b. region
   c. continent
   d. none of the above

DAILY Warm-Up 1 Name ______________________ Date __________

BROWNIE DELIGHT

Sarah climbed onto the bus with her plate of brownies and sat down next to Kim. Today had been the pep assembly, and Sarah had been in charge. Kim was impressed with Sarah's creativity.

"Sarah, you did a great job today!" said Kim.

"I thought it was dumb!" said Thad. He was sitting in the seat in front of the girls.

"What was so wrong with it?" asked Sarah. She was annoyed with people like Thad. All they ever did was complain.

"You always call on the same students to participate," explained Thad.

"How can you say that?" interrupted Kim. "Sarah called on Jace. It's not Sarah's fault that he refused."

"Okay. So she picked one new kid," said Thad.

"Thad, are you feeling left out?" asked Sarah with a grin. "Do you want one of my brownies?"

"Sure," replied Thad. His face brightened at the thought of it.

Sarah grabbed the biggest brownie she could find and handed it to Thad. "Oh, wait! You are going to want a napkin to go with that!" cautioned Sarah.

Thad took a huge bite of his brownie. It didn't take long before he was coughing and sputtering!

"What's wrong?" asked Kim. "Thad, are you okay?"

"That's disgusting!" called Thad, gagging.

Sarah began chuckling. "Now do you know why I didn't call on you? The pepper in the brownie isn't too good, is it?"

Thad continued coughing and sputtering. He moved to the front of the seat to be by the garbage can.

STORY QUESTIONS

1. What word best describes how Thad feels at the end of the story?
   a. organized
   b. relieved
   c. duped
   d. exhausted

2. Which paragraph helps you answer the previous question?
   a. last paragraph
   b. first paragraph
   c. fourth paragraph
   d. third paragraph

3. Another good title for this passage could be . . .
   a. "A New Recipe."
   b. "Chocolate Brownies."
   c. "Thad's Assembly."
   d. "The Bus Driver."

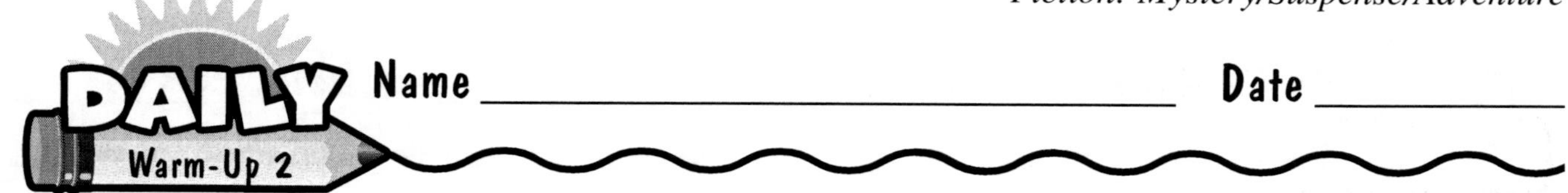

SKI PATROL

"Grab the rope, Ian! We'll pull you in!" shouted Chris. He was desperate to get Ian back on the boat. He knew Ian was injured but he didn't know why. Ian just kept flailing back and forth calling out in pain.

"It looks like we need to jump in after him," said Jeff. Jeff slipped on his life vest and dove into the water. His strokes were graceful and smooth. It didn't take long for Jeff to reach Ian. When he got close to Ian, he could see what the trouble was. Jeff froze. He didn't dare get closer to Ian. Ian was smack dab in the middle of some jellyfish. Flashbacks of last summer caused Jeff to cringe. A jellyfish had stung him, and he knew what Ian was dealing with.

"What is it?" called Chris. "Why did you stop?" Chris was starting to panic. What could be the problem? Ian was a great water skier, and he had never had problems before. Ian was so good that he could ski without a ski. And now, Jeff. Jeff wouldn't answer Chris and he seemed frozen in the water.

"Answer me!" called Chris. "You've got to tell me what is wrong!"

"Jelly," was all Jeff could mutter.

"Jelly? This is no joking matter," said Chris. "We are not having jelly or peanut butter for that matter." Just then Chris began to realize what was going on. There must be jellyfish in the water!

STORY QUESTIONS

1. According to the story, you could determine that Jeff is . . .
   a. intelligent.
   b. immature.
   c. a good swimmer.
   d. hard working.

2. Which paragraph helps you answer the previous question?
   a. second paragraph
   b. first paragraph
   c. fourth paragraph
   d. third paragraph

3. What is the meaning of the word *flailing* as used in the passage?
   a. forcing
   b. paralyzing
   c. thrashing
   d. annoying

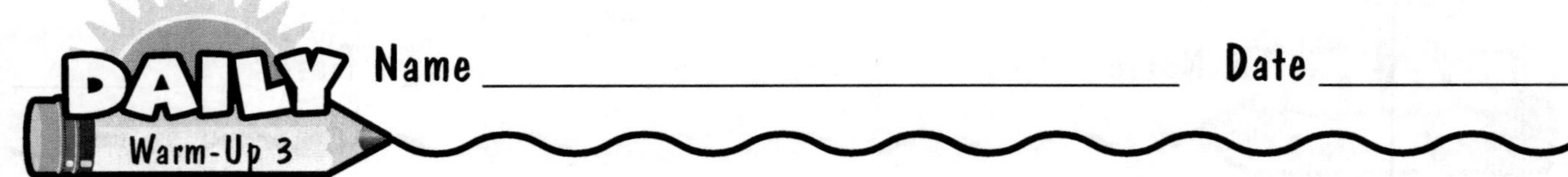

FRESH AIR

Kylee could feel the air on her face as she loped around the field. It was a beautiful spring day. Her horse, Chestnut, seemed to feel the excitement in the air as well. Kylee had to keep pulling back on the reins now and then to keep Chestnut from going too fast.

Kylee had just gotten home from a spring break trip to Washington. She had gone to spend the week with her dad. Each time she went to visit her dad it was like starting all over again. At the beginning of the trip, she was awfully nervous, but by the end of the trip, she was so sad to leave him. Living 1,000 miles apart just didn't help.

Just then, Chestnut stumbled and fell. Kylee felt herself flying over the front of Chestnut. She landed on the ground and lay there motionless. A whirl of events raced through Kylee's mind as she lay helpless. She could picture her dad walking towards her with his arms outstretched. In the same dream, she could see her mother coming up from behind and embracing the two of them.

"Kylee! Are you okay?" Kylee's mother called desperately. "Kylee! Wake up!"

Kylee could hear her mom and knew she must respond, but she was reluctant to leave the current dream she was having—the dream where everything in her life seemed okay.

Eventually, Kylee's eyes began to flutter. She could feel her mother's hand engulfing her own.

STORY QUESTIONS

1. What is the meaning of the word *engulfing* as used in this passage?
   a. tightening
   b. bothering
   c. pinching
   d. absorbing
2. Which of the following details can be inferred from the reading passage?
   a. Kylee lives outside the United States.
   b. Kylee's mother and father are divorced.
   c. Kylee doesn't like her mother very well.
   d. Kylee is adopted.
3. What could be another good title for this story passage?
   a. "The Crazy Dream"
   b. "Peaceful Moments"
   c. "Mom vs. Dad"
   d. "The Awakening"

DAILY Warm-Up 4 Name ______________________ Date __________

CANOE CRISIS

"Henry! Knock it off! If you do that one more time, I'm going to dump you out of this canoe," threatened Cameron.

"Yeah, right," said Henry and half-heartedly paddled up the stream. Henry and Cameron were assigned to be partners, but they certainly weren't friends. Cameron despised Henry and spent his time at summer camp avoiding him. Henry never followed the rules, and that drove Cameron crazy.

Cameron hated the fact that the canoe ride was at least 5 miles long. Just then Cameron felt sprinkles of water again on his neck.

"Henry!" hollered Cameron. "I said to leave me alone."

"I'm not doing anything!" replied Henry coolly. "If you look up, you will see that Mother Nature is sprinkling you with water."

Sure enough, when Cameron looked up, he could see the sprinkles coming down. Things got quiet in the canoe after that. Before long, the sprinkles turned into large drops, and thunder and lightning began racing across the sky. Cameron didn't know what to do. All he remembered was hearing stories about never to be on the water during a lightening storm.

There was nothing in sight. Where could they get shelter? At that moment, Henry took over. He instructed Cameron to steer the boat to some cabins up ahead. But could they last until then before they got hit by lightning? By the time they reached the cabins, they were soaked. Lightning continued to flash and they took shelter on a porch.

STORY QUESTIONS

1. According to the story, Cameron and Henry are . . .
   a. bored and frustrated.
   b. hesitant about playing against each other.
   c. friends with each other.
   d. acquaintances.

2. Which paragraph first explains Cameron and Henry's relationship?
   a. second paragraph
   b. first paragraph
   c. fourth paragraph
   d. third paragraph

3. What is the meaning of the phrase *half-heartedly* as used in this passage?
   a. honest
   b. unenthusiastically
   c. amazed
   d. exhausted

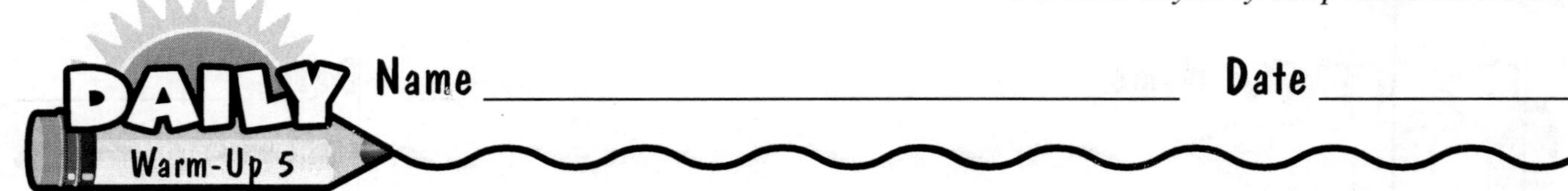

Name ______________________________ Date __________

BEE WARE!

Kirk and Trent were working on their beehive merit badge one afternoon in the middle of the summer. It would be nice for the boys to finally take off their bee netting. They had one last stack of boxes to go. By this time, the chore had become routine. Kirk would send the smoke in to confuse the bees and Trent would begin gathering as much honey as he could.

The accident happened simply enough. It almost seemed unbelievable. As Trent was using his hot knife to scrape the beeswax off the top, he noticed a bee inside his bee netting. At least it looked like a bee. Trent panicked and pulled on his netting to get the bee out. His instinct proved to be a grave mistake. As the netting came down, the bees swarmed up and all over Trent's face and neck.

Trent dropped the bee knife and took off screaming with a trail of bees behind him. Kirk was stunned and at a loss for what to do. Trent was getting stung all over. Kirk raced to Dr. Owen, his scout leader, who was over helping another group of scouts.

"Dr. Owen. Dr. Owen. You've got to come help! Trent is in the lake and he is getting stung by tons of bees!" Mr. Owen raced to the lake and jumped in to help Trent. He got Trent on the ground and administered medicine. It was a good thing Dr. Owen was a family doctor as well as a scout leader!

STORY QUESTIONS

1. What is the meaning of the word *administered* as used in the passage?
   a. gave
   b. organized
   c. trusted
   d. used

2. According to the passage, what was Trent trying to do when he pulled the netting down?
   a. He was hanging on tight to the bee knife.
   b. He was fighting the bees that were swarming around him.
   c. He wanted to get the bee out that had gotten inside the netting.
   d. He was tired of doing the bee thing and was ready to call it quits.

3. The best way to find the answer to the previous question is to . . .
   a. reread the entire passage.
   b. reread the second paragraph and determine the main idea.
   c. reread the last two paragraphs.
   d. skim the passage and look for clues.

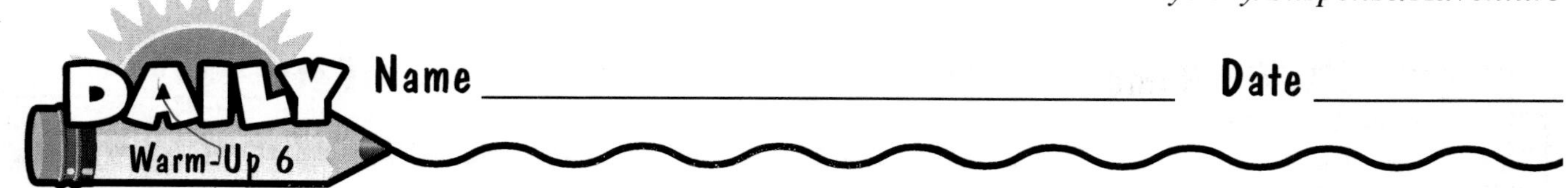

Name ______________________ Date __________

ON THE ROCKS

Brett cinched his rope a little tighter around his waist and maneuvered his left foot into his next hold position. The sun was beating down on his neck.

"How are you doing down there?" called Evan from up above.

"Doing well, thanks," replied Brett.

Evan had been teaching Brett how to rappel and rock climb all summer long. Evan had been doing it for years. The exhilaration that came from being at the top of the mountain or rock was worth more than the risk for Brett. But he knew that any minute, a rope could slip and he would be a goner.

Evan continued to climb higher and in the process sent a few small rocks down on Brett. Brett closed his eyes to avoid getting hit. As he opened his eyes he heard a loud yell and he saw Evan's body flash in front of him.

"Oh, no!" thought Brett. "Evan has fallen."

Brett froze and didn't know what to do next. He could still hear Evan yelling, so he knew that was a good sign. Brett heard Evan smash up against something. At least he had broken his fall. Nothing but silence came from below.

"Hey Ev?" asked Brett. "Are you okay?"

"Uhhhhhh," moaned Evan.

Brett knew that he had to get down and help Evan. He was scared. Thoughts of Evan's instructions went through his mind. Brett inched his way down closer and closer to Evan. He could still hear Evan moaning. Oh, if he could just go faster!

STORY QUESTIONS

1. Which word best describes how Brett was feeling at the beginning of the passage?
   a. hesitant and concentrating
   b. happy and content
   c. relieved and tired
   d. stressed and overwhelmed

2. Which sentence explains the problem in the story?
   a. Brett's an expert rock climber.
   b. Brett is worried that he won't be as good as Evan.
   c. Evan has fallen and needs Brett's help.
   d. Brett doesn't know how to rock climb.

3. What is the meaning of the word *maneuvered* as used in the passage?
   a. driven
   b. aligned
   c. moved
   d. realized

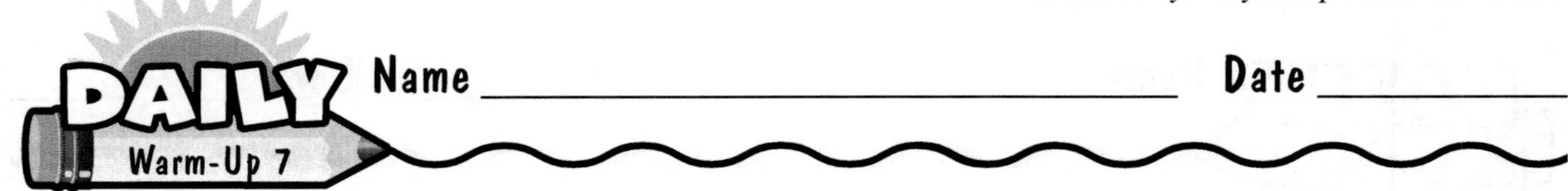

BOOT CAMP

Cade whistled to his friends up ahead to slow down. Every muscle in Cade's body was aching. The exercises from the day before had pushed every muscle in Cade's body to its capacity. The five-mile jog this morning was almost more than he could handle.

"Pick it up!" yelled Brewster. Brewster was the captain of the boot camp, and he was as mean as they get. This boot camp was a prerequisite to qualifying for a high adventure trip in the Rocky Mountains. The camp was Brewster's way of weeding out those boys that weren't really ready for the long and strenuous hike.

With Brewster's words, Cade picked up his pace and caught up with the group of boys ahead of him. The competition was pretty stiff.

As the group of boys rounded the bend on the trail, they fell out of Brewster's sight. Jacob said, "Hey, guys. Let's take that short cut just up ahead. Brewster will never know."

Of the group of five boys, three of them motioned their heads indicating they would be interested. That left Cade. All eyes fell on Cade.

"What if Brewster catches us? You know that we'll be out for sure!" Cade reasoned.

But the boys would have none of it. "Come on, you wimp," said Jake. "He's only going to find out if someone tells."

The boys headed off in the direction of the shortcut, leaving Cade in the dust. Cade wondered what he should do.

STORY QUESTIONS

1. What is the problem in this story?
   a. Cade doesn't know which boy he can trust in the camp.
   b. Cade doesn't think he is going to make the cut for the boot camp.
   c. Cade is afraid of what Brewster will say.
   d. Cade is struggling with peer pressure.

2. After reading the passage, which of the following statements would be something Cade would say?
   a. I'm so much better than you.
   b. You are a big wimp.
   c. That doesn't seem to be the right thing to do.
   d. Get away from me!

3. Why did Cade run faster to catch up with the boys in the group?
   a. He was trying to get away from a boy running with him.
   b. He realized that he had better pick up his pace to impress Brewster.
   c. He was going to catch the boys taking a short cut.
   d. He was trying to make friends with Brewster.

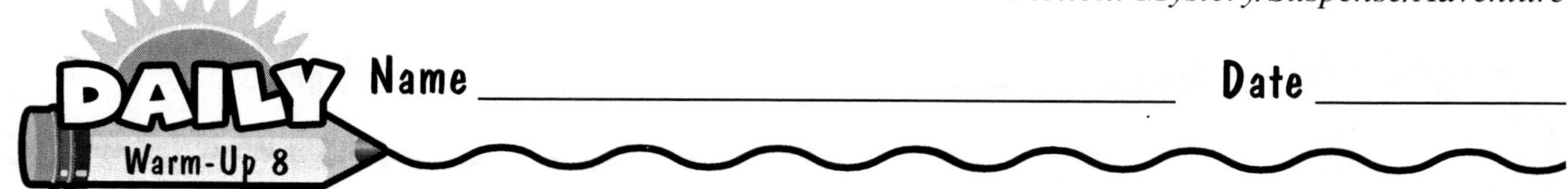

NOCTURNAL NEIGHBORS

Chad crawled on his stomach through a passageway in the cave. He was cold, hungry, and exhausted. It had been a long day. His plans to explore the cave sounded exciting the day before. Today these same plans seemed crazy. Things definitely went downhill when the battery died on his flashlight. Chad was left to using his senses to help "feel" his way through the cave.

Just then, the noise at the back of the cave started again. The noise was louder than it ever was before. Chad still couldn't quite figure out what it was. It was sort of a swooshing sound.

Chad kept low to the ground. The noise flew directly above him. Chad closed his eyes and clinched his fists waiting for the noise to stop. Eventually the noise died down and Chad opened his eyes again. Chad strained his eyes get a good look at his surroundings. What was making that noise?

With all quiet again, Chad began crawling. He was very nervous for a while after the noise and the swooshing finished. Suddenly an image flashed through Chad's mind. Was it a bat? Chad realized that each time he heard the noise it was actually a large group of bats flying from one end of the cave to the other.

Chad shuddered at the thought of it and soon began to sweat. Taking a breath to calm himself, Chad tried to put his mind elsewhere.

STORY QUESTIONS

1. What does the phrase *went downhill* mean as used in this story?
   a. Things started to slant downhill in the cave.
   b. Chad realized he must go downhill instead of uphill to find his way out.
   c. Things had turned from bad to worse.
   d. Chad was scared out of his mind and was starting to hallucinate.

2. Which sentence below explains the problem in this story?
   a. Chad is alone and scared in a cave and doesn't know his way out.
   b. Chad is spelunking with his buddies and is lost from them for awhile.
   c. Chad is curious about bats and is studying them without any light.
   d. Chad left home without breakfast and wishes he had eaten first.

3. What could be another good title for this story passage?
   a. "Thinking Chad"
   c. "Where Is It?"
   b. "Chad Goes Crazy"
   d. "The Home of the Bats"

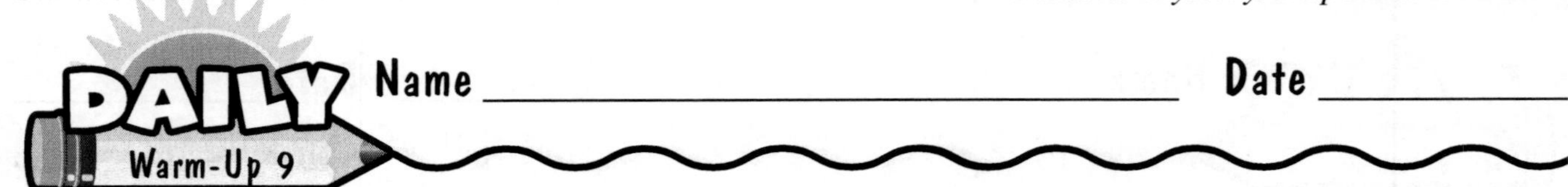

THE PRACTICAL JOKE

Kenny's frustration started as soon as he opened his eyes. Being the youngest of four boys had its moments. Kenny realized that he was never going to make it into the shower before the bus came, so he got his clothes on and ran his fingers through his hair. He could hear his brothers fighting over the shower.

Kenny poured himself a bowl of milk and cold cereal. Granola was his favorite cereal. Kenny grabbed the comics and sat down. Kenny's first bite was a big one. He was hungry. As he chewed he thought something seemed different, but he didn't think much about it. Snickers from around the room indicated that something must be up. Kenny put the comics down and looked at all the faces staring at him and giggling.

Kenny looked down at his bowl and realized that it was indeed granola, but it also had dead ants, grasshoppers, and other various insects.

Kenny pushed his bowl across the table and stood up. "That's disgusting!" he yelled. He ran to the sink to rinse out his mouth. "How could you do that?"

Kevin, the brother just older than Kenny, fell out of his chair. Kyle smiled at Kenny and said, "You've got to watch out for him, man!"

Later on the bus, Kenny had an idea. He sat in the back in Kevin's spot. He deserved it. Besides, Kevin would just sit in the other back seat, which he did. Kenny's plan was sure to work. Slowly, Kenny reached over and pulled the fire alarm on the bus. He subtly tossed the fire alarm rope onto Kevin's seat. Kevin jumped up, but it was too late. The bus driver was glaring at Kevin.

STORY QUESTIONS

1. What is the opposite meaning of the word *subtly* as used in the passage?
   a. faintly
   b. delicately
   c. obviously
   d. quietly

2. Which paragraph explains the problem in the story?
   a. last paragraph
   b. second paragraph
   c. fourth paragraph
   d. third paragraph

3. Where is the setting of the story?
   a. in the house and bus
   b. in the school
   c. at the breakfast table
   d. on the sidewalk

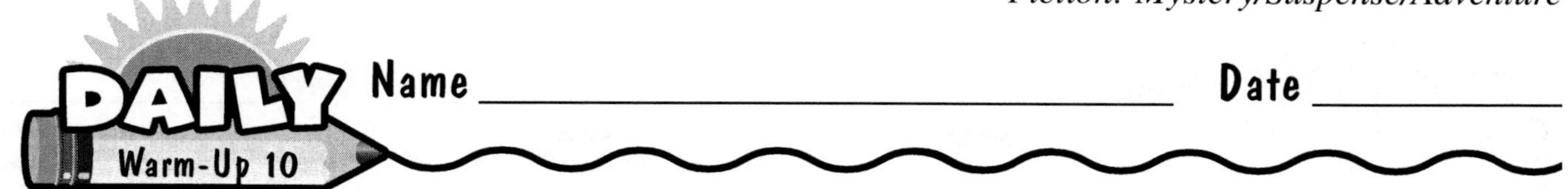

THE MYSTERY SHOE

A wave pushed Brittany the last little way to shore. It was a beautiful day. For her birthday, Eric had promised her a day of surfing. Eric had a surfboard and was teaching Brittany how to surf. Brittany always enjoyed time spent with her favorite cousin.

"One more!" called Eric. "You can't stop yet."

Brittany smiled and worked her way over to the beach where Eric was standing. "You're doing great!" complimented Eric.

Just then Brittany tripped. She looked down and saw a shoe sitting on the beach. She bent down to look at it and Eric came over to get a look at it.

"Why is there a shoe on the beach?" Brittany asked.

"Maybe somebody left it and it got thrown in the water," explained Eric.

"Who leaves the beach without their shoes? Someone must be hurt and this shoe is a call for help," said Brittany. Brittany was always trying to help others out.

"You can't be serious," said Eric.

But she was. Brittany began looking around for clues. She even approached the lifeguard and asked is he knew anything about foul play.

Just then, Eric saw a big shaggy dog running up the beach. "Brittany, I think I found your suspect."

Brittany turned to look at the dog. She noticed the dog had another shoe in his mouth. The shoe matched the one she had holding in her hand. Brittany threw back her head and left to find the owner.

STORY QUESTIONS

1. According to the story, Brittany and Eric are . . .
   a. friends.
   c. related.
   b. interesting.
   d. children.
2. Which sentence from the story helps you answer the previous question?
   a. "You can't be serious," said Eric.
   b. Brittany always enjoyed time spent with her favorite cousin.
   c. This information is implied in the story.
   d. Brittany smiled and worked her way over to the beach where Eric was standing.
3. What is the meaning of the word *foul* as used in the story?
   a. out of bounds
   b. unusual
   c. criminal
   d. none of the above

DAILY Warm-Up 11

Name ______________________________ Date __________

AMAZING GRACE

Grace careened around the corner on her scooter. She was desperate to beat James. James lived next door and was always trying to prove how good he was at everything. His attitude of superiority was annoying, and Grace felt certain that she could prove him wrong at least once.

Grace could feel James behind her, and she smiled when she realized that indeed he was. If only she could hold on.

"Go, Grace," yelled Cindy. Cindy was Grace's younger sister, and she knew what Grace had invested in this race.

With three laps still to go, Grace knew that she had to gain some momentum. Just then, Kelly, Mrs. Olson's dog, came running out of her yard and began chasing them. Her adrenaline pumped out of fear. Kelly, the little Scottie dog, was known for biting the neighborhood kids.

Two more laps to go and Grace could feel her muscles tightening. Kelly was still chasing them, but they were a little faster than she was. Kelly's legs were just too short.

In the final lap, Grace knew that James was waiting for her speed to dwindle and her strength to give way. Grace aggressively attacked the last corner and let out a loud grunt as she did so.

In the last few yards, Grace felt as though she could give no more. She reached across the finish line as James lunged beside her. Was it enough? Had Grace been able to do it?

STORY QUESTIONS

1. How did Grace feel at the beginning of the passage about her ability to beat James?
   a. embarrassed
   c. frustrated
   b. excited
   d. hopeful

2. Which paragraph helps you answer the previous question?
   a. second paragraph
   b. first paragraph
   c. fourth paragraph
   d. none of the above

3. What is the meaning of the word *aggressively* as used in the passage?
   a. forcefully
   b. quietly
   c. loudly
   d. angrily

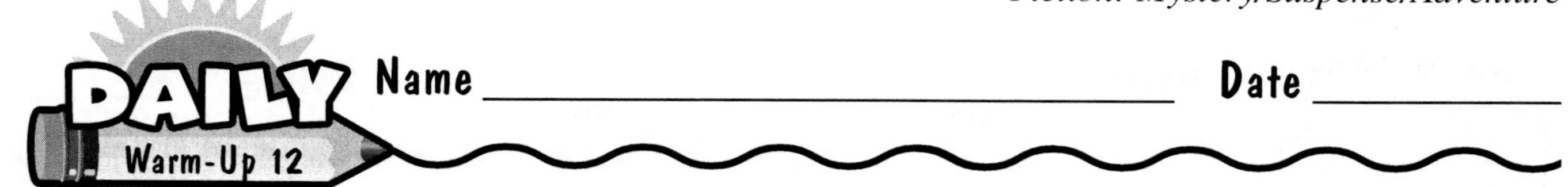

MARLA'S COOKIE MONSTER

Marla pulled a mixing bowl down from the cupboard and set the ingredients to make cookies on the counter. She began mixing the shortening and the eggs together. It wasn't long before she pulled the first batch out. She wrote a note next to the cookies explaining that they were not to be eaten. She needed to take some to the piano recital that evening and there wouldn't be enough. She promised in the note to make another batch tomorrow. In a family with six children, Marla knew that they would be disappointed, but she just didn't have time to make more today.

Marla left for her piano lesson at Mrs. Beasley's. Upon her return, she was stunned to see that the cookies had been gotten into. Her note was gone, and now she was furious.

"Jacob, Jessy, Chrissy, Marshall, and Dakota get down here right now!"

All of Marla's siblings raced down the stairs. "I know one of you ate my cookies even though I wrote a note stating they were not to be touched."

"I didn't touch your dumb cookies," said Jacob.

"I didn't either," protested Chrissy.

"None of us did," said Jessy.

"Someone did and I am determined find out. Open your mouths!" demanded Marla. Each of the kids opened their mouths for inspection. Marla couldn't find any cookie evidence.

Just then, Marla's dad came walking in whistling as he went.

"Dad?" asked Marla. "Did you enjoy any cookies today?"

All of the kids held their breath.

STORY QUESTIONS

1. Which statement shows the climax of the story?
   a. Just then, Marla's dad came walking in whistling as he went.
   b. "Someone did and I am determined find out. Open your mouths!" demanded Marla.
   c. All of the kids held their breath.
   d. none of the above

2. What does the word *evidence* mean?
   a. proof
   b. support
   c. observations
   d. ignorance

3. What is the main idea of the second paragraph?
   a. Marla is trying to lure one of her siblings to get into the cookies.
   b. Marla is learning how to bake cookies.
   c. Marla learns there is a problem with her cookies.
   d. none of the above

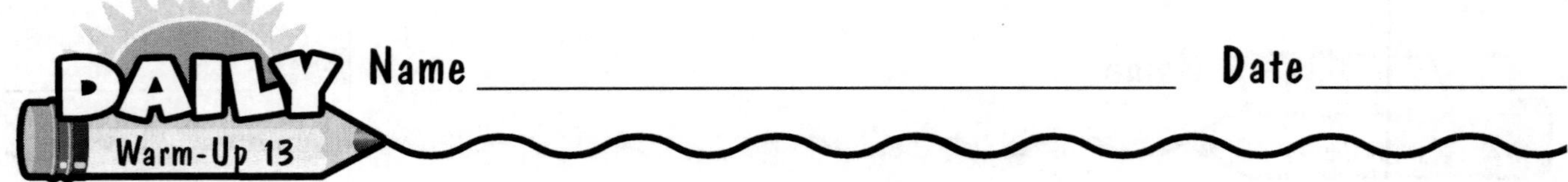

WHITNEY'S DREAM

Whitney had been playing basketball since she was three years old. By seventh grade, Whitney was the star of the middle school basketball team. Even the coach admitted she was the best player and pretty fun to watch.

All through the season, Whitney had stayed on top of her game. She carefully trained and lifted weights. She could hardly wait for the winter tournament that was played each year. Teams from all over the county showed up to show their stuff.

In the last quarter of the championship game, Whitney found herself making more baskets than she had ever made before in a game. She found it hard to believe each time she glanced at the scoreboard.

Just then Whitney heard the whistle blow. She stopped dribbling the ball to look up. The referee called a foul on the opposing team and Whitney walked over to the foul line. Her first shot went up but the ball bounced off the rim. Her second shot went in with a swoosh!

On defense, Whitney was intense. She knew there were only minutes to go before the game would be over. They were down by one basket. She knew it could be done. The ball handler drove for the basket and Whitney went in to make her move. Just then the loud and shrill whistle blew. Whitney couldn't bear to look up. In her peripheral vision, she saw the referee motion towards her. Whitney hung her head and exited the court.

STORY QUESTIONS

1. Which words describe Whitney in the story?
   a. talented, determined, hard working
   b. timid, shy, new
   c. determined, hard working, scared
   d. stuck-up, timid, excited

2. Which information below is <u>not</u> shared but implied in the story?
   a. Whitney has been playing basketball since she was three.
   b. Whitney has been practicing very hard for the championship game.
   c. Whitney fouls out of the championship game.
   d. Whitney has doubts that she will be able to win.

3. What is the meaning of the words *peripheral vision* as used in the passage?
   a. x-ray vision
   b. near-sighted vision
   c. far-sighted vision
   d. vision from the outer edges of the eye

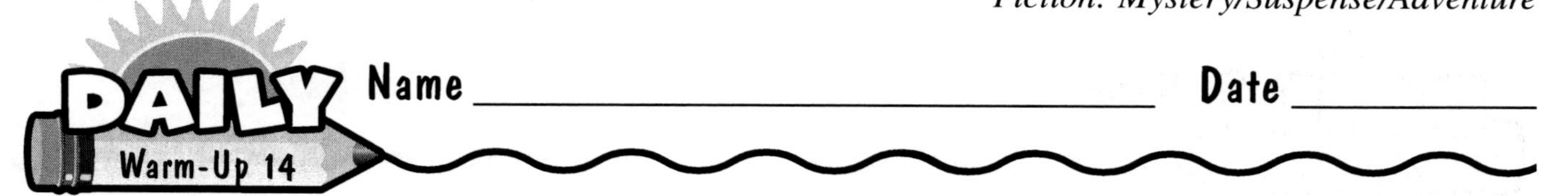

THIN ICE

Gregory jumped into the air for a triple axel. He landed with ease and threw his hands in the air. Gregory was a hockey player and a good one at that, but on the weekends, he liked to work on his grace and finesse.

"Way to go!" called Jethro. Jethro was Gregory's best friend, and they played on the same hockey team.

"Thanks," responded Gregory. "Too bad we lost last night."

"It was a tough loss," conceded Jethro.

"I just wish we had made it into overtime," said Gregory. Gregory skated around the perimeter of the frozen lake gathering speed. He lunged into the air and sprang into form. Instead of the air, Gregory found himself falling. The ice had cracked and Gregory was sliding into the frigid water.

"Help!" gasped Gregory.

Jethro whirled around in time to see his friend go under the ice.

"What?" asked Jethro stunned. He leapt into action. He skated with a fury to the other side of the ice and grabbed Gregory's elbow that was protruding from the water. Jethro pulled as hard as he could to get Gregory's body out of the water.

"Gregory!" yelled Jethro desperately.

Gregory was above the water gasping for air and shuddering.

Little by little Jethro managed to pull Gregory from the icy water. When finished, Jethro sat for a second to catch his breath. He dragged Gregory across the ice to a log. Then he raced to the back of his house yelling the whole way.

STORY QUESTIONS

1. What is the problem in the story?
   a. The boys lost their hockey game and they are upset.
   b. Jethro has fallen through the ice and needs help.
   c. Gregory's elbow is protruding from the icy water.
   d. Jethro finds himself in a position where he has to save his friend's life.

2. What would make another good title for this story?
   a. "The Brave Rescue"
   b. "Gregory vs. The Ice"
   c. "A Call for Help"
   d. "Perseverance Pays"

3. What does the word *conceded* mean as used in the passage?
   a. ignored
   b. argued
   c. agreed
   d. whirled

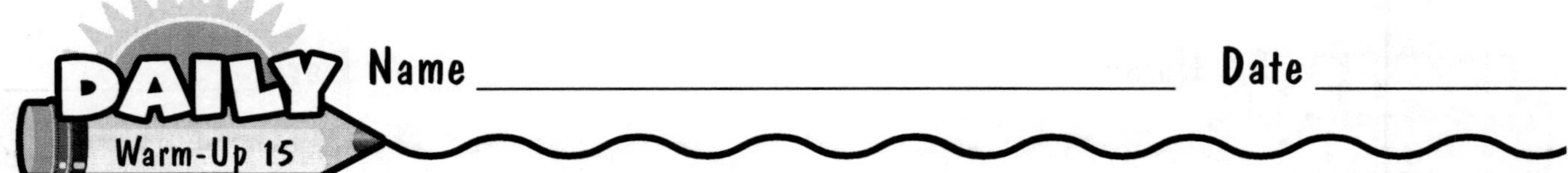

THE CASE OF THE MISSING VIOLIN

The curtain slowly moved across the stage of the Brine Concert Hall. The entire sixth grade orchestra from all of Camen School District was seated on the stage. Maren twitched nervously in her shoes. This was her first violin concert, and she was hoping that she wouldn't make a mistake.

The teacher lifted his baton and the violins began to make music. The students seemed to work in unison as they moved their bows up and down the strings. The melodic sound was just beautiful. Maren could hardly believe it when the concert was finally over. The curtain went across the stage as the students made their final bow.

Maren was anxious to see her family. Her favorite aunt, Jane, had traveled from Minnesota to watch Maren perform. Maren set her violin in her case and ran down to the audience to greet her family. Maren fell into the arms of her aunt and got hugs and congratulatory remarks from everyone.

"It's time to get going," said Maren's mom.

Maren skipped to the back of the stage through the crowd. When she got back to her violin, Maren could only find her case. The violin was missing! Stunned, Maren twirled and walked back to her mom.

"It's gone. My violin is gone," wailed Maren.

"How could it be gone?" asked her mother. "You just had it!"

Just then, Maren saw a boy run across the stage and out the door with a violin in his hand.

STORY QUESTIONS

1. What is this passage mainly about?
   a. how a family came to support their daughter
   b. the feelings a person goes through when they are performing in front of an audience
   c. how a musical instrument is taken and how the musician responds
   d. how a family handles a crisis

2. In the second paragraph, what does the word *melodic* mean?
   a. pretentious
   b. musical
   c. rhythmic
   d. measurement

3. Which word could be used to describe Maren in this passage?
   a. lazy
   b. concerned
   c. silly
   d. annoyed

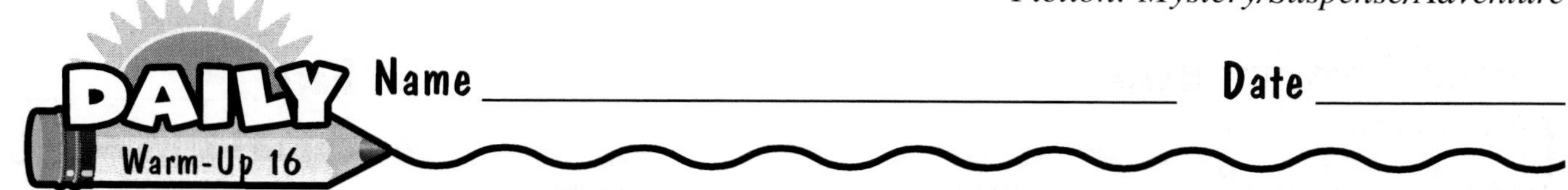

IN A DAZE

Matt raced down the soccer field and passed the ball to Craig at the very last second. Craig kicked the ball and sent it sailing into the net. Score! Craig and Matt threw their hands into the air and bounced off each other's chest. This had been a great season so far! All the work Matt and Craig had done over the summer was definitely paying off!

Matt worked his way down the field and looked for Craig. Where was he? Matt continued to dribble the ball with his feet, but he was stalling. How long before the opposing team stole it from him? Matt did some more fancy footwork but a player from the other team got a good piece of the soccer ball. Matt lurched after the ball, but it was too late.

Matt looked around for Craig, but he couldn't see him anywhere. Playing soccer without Craig just didn't seem right! Matt's eyes scanned the crowd as he looked. He couldn't find his coach anywhere either. Matt was an avid soccer player and lived for the game, but right now his thoughts were not on the field.

"Get out of the way, speed bump!" a player from the other team called. Matt seemed dazed and stumbled out of the way. Where was Craig? Where was his coach?

By now the fans realized that Matt was not focusing on the game!

"What are you doing? Get in there!" yelled one of the fans.

The other team shouted for joy as they made a goal. Matt spun around and felt dizzy.

STORY QUESTIONS

1. What is the meaning of *lurched* as used in the passage?
   a. fell
   b. aligned
   c. staggered
   d. upset
2. What can you learn about Matt from reading this passage?
   a. He lives in a city.
   b. He loves to play soccer.
   c. He is creative.
   d. He is unfriendly.
3. Which of the following statements is most accurate?
   a. Craig is upset at Matt for not passing the ball to him.
   b. Craig was injured, and Matt can't focus without him.
   c. Matt is upset with the other team and starts calling him names.
   d. Matt seems unable to play soccer without Craig.

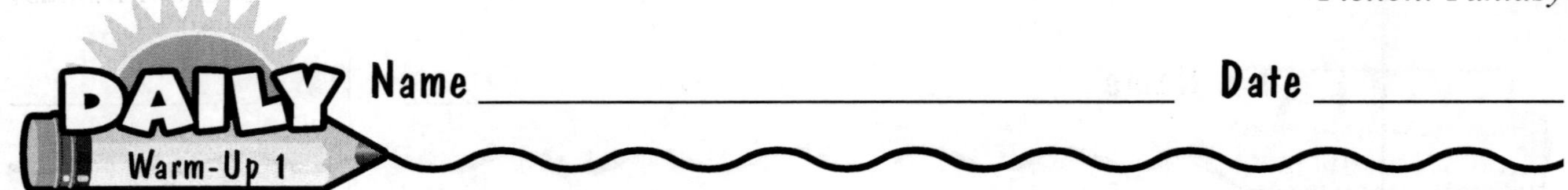

THE SPELL

Flora was so mad! She had planned to cast a spell at the king's ball but had been a little too late. By the time all the fairies had completed their spells, Flora was still downstairs eating cake. By the time she made it up the stairs, it was just too late! Flora was so mad she could just spit.

"Why am I always a day late and a dollar short?" she asked herself.

Flora was smaller than most of the other fairies, so people didn't take her very seriously. She had a high, squeaky voice, and that didn't help the situation much.

Flora's reputation was further marred by the fact that she always got her spells mixed up. You never knew what you would get with one of Flora's spells.

The king always took pity on Flora and always invited her back, but Flora knew that it wasn't because he had confidence in her.

As the crowd moved away from the line of fairies, Flora held up her wand. She knew it was too late, but she wanted to cast her spell anyway. She closed her eyes and said the words of the spell slowly and distinctly. Flora felt the jiggle of her wand and opened her eyes. There before her, crawling all over the dance floor were lizards. Flora could hardly believe her eyes. She looked up to the king and saw his crown fall off his lizard head.

STORY QUESTIONS

1. What is the meaning of the word *marred* as used in the passage?
   a. secrecy
   b. successful
   c. humorous
   d. flawed

2. According to the passage, what are some of Flora's weaknesses as a fairy?
   a. She is small in stature and has a high squeaky voice.
   b. Flora is the last fairy to arrive to the ball.
   c. Flora is mistreated by all the other fairies.
   d. none of the above

3. The best way to locate the answer to the previous question is to . . .
   a. reread the entire passage.
   b. skim the entire passage and determine the main idea.
   c. reread the third paragraph and search for clues.
   d. use context clues to determine the meaning.

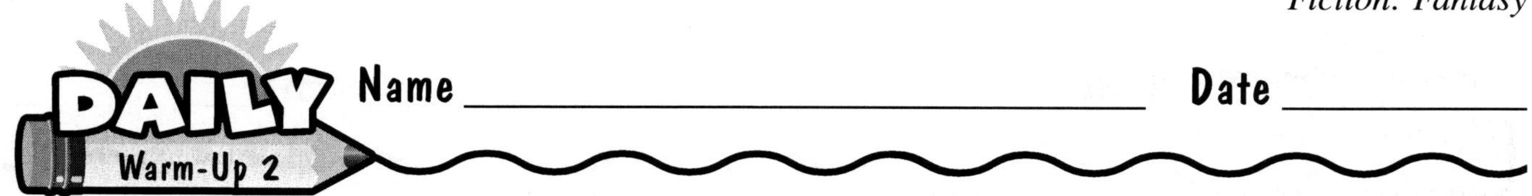

THE VIRUS

Jenna could not figure out why her friend Sarah hadn't returned her email yet. Sarah was usually very fast about responding. Jenna checked her email every 10 seconds waiting for a new message to appear, but one never did.

Just then, Jenna got a message from her computer saying that a virus had been quarantined to a spot in the computer. Jenna was curious about the virus and click on the filter program in her computer. Sure enough, a virus was listed. Jenna soon realized that the virus had Sarah's name in the message.

"What is going on?" thought Jenna. "Does Sarah have something to do with this virus? Is something wrong with Sarah's computer?"

Jenna began searching her computer to find the location of the virus. She was uncertain how long this would take, so she decided to just call Sarah on the phone. She wanted to get to the bottom of this quickly before she had any viruses attack her computer.

Sarah's mother explained that Sarah had not come home from school yet. Jenna knew that was not true. She had walked home with Sarah. Jenna was starting to get scared. She went back to the computer and sent a message to the virus program on her computer. Imagine her surprise when Sarah responded back.

"Dear Jenna, A computer virus has taken over my computer and taken over me!" Jenna didn't know what to think. How could a virus do that? Jenna began to shake.

STORY QUESTIONS

1. Which of the following is <u>not</u> a meaning of the word *quarantined* as used in this passage?
   a. detained
   b. isolated
   c. organized
   d. removed
2. Which sentence shows that Jenna takes the virus message from Sarah seriously?
   a. Jenna began to shake.
   b. Jenna knew that was not true.
   c. She had walked home with Sarah.
   d. none of the above
3. The best way to find the answer to the previous question is to . . .
   a. try to remember.
   b. reread the last paragraph and determine the main idea.
   c. ask the author.
   d. skim the passage searching for clues.

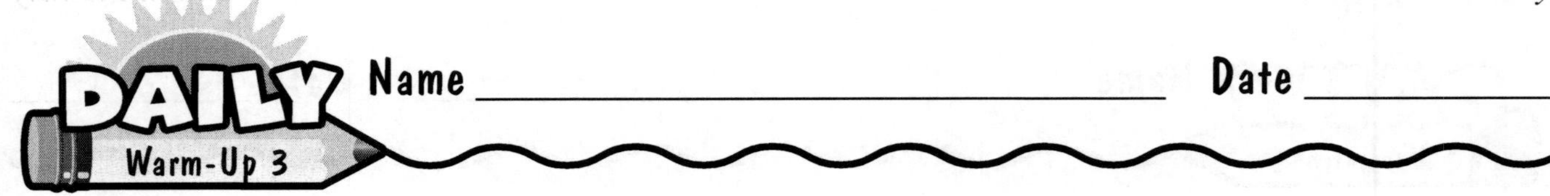

DENTAL WORK

Princess Amelia threw down the mirror and stomped from the room. "Oh, I look terrible," she moaned. "I can't believe the ball is tonight! What kind of a princess gets her front tooth knocked out?"

Princess Amelia was not like any other princess. Don't be mistaken, she loved her princess duties and loved to dress up with fancy dresses and jewelry, but she also adored sword fighting and fencing. It was in one of her fencing challenges that she got her front tooth knocked out by Frederick. Frederick was a knight's son and he was a nice boy, but lately he seemed determined to do Princess Amelia in. Amelia knew for sure that he had done it on purpose.

Frederick had dashed to her aid when the incident happened to see if she was okay, but Princess Amelia also noticed he was the first to leave when everything settled down. "Oh! I wish I didn't like him!" thought the young princess.

Frederick didn't seem to give Princess Amelia the time of day. It was as if they were practically strangers, although they had known each other from birth.

"Your dress is here, your highness," called Gertrude from the doorway.

"Oh, I can't even think of the dress. Look at my teeth!" wailed Princess Amelia.

"Don't worry about that, dear. Your father says he has a royal physician coming to take care of that!" reassured Gertrude.

"There isn't a thing they can do except fill my mouth with animal teeth!" cried Amelia.

"You won't be able to tell," said Gertrude as she rubbed Amelia's back.

STORY QUESTIONS

1. Which word would describe Amelia at one point in the story?
   a. confused
   b. gushing
   c. panicked
   d. coy
2. Which of the following cannot be determined from the story?
   a. Frederick has a crush on Princess Amelia.
   b. Amelia is embarrassed about her missing tooth.
   c. Amelia is a different kind of princess.
   d. Amelia was injured when she was fencing with Frederick.
3. Which of the following could also be a title for the passage?
   a. "My Two Front Teeth"
   b. "Prideful Amelia"
   c. "Mirror, Mirror . . ."
   d. "Amelia's Dentures"

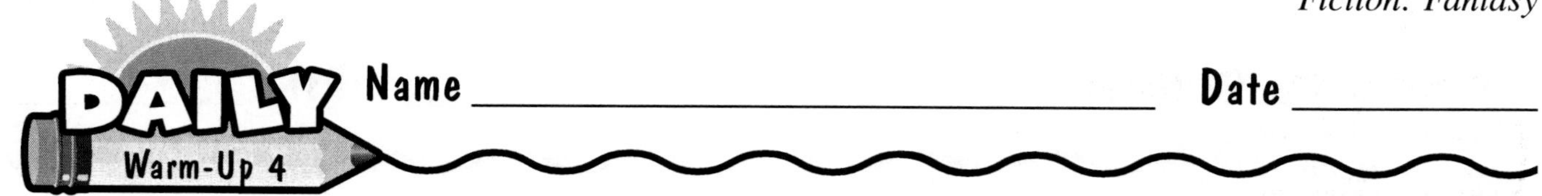

KING OF THE CATS

Samantha walked with her group slowly to the edge of the trees. There she saw a family of zebras standing in the heat of the day. Samantha and her parents had taken the trip of a lifetime. Through work, Samantha's dad had been able to secure a safari into the middle of Africa. For months, Samantha and her parents had looked at maps and researched all types of animals that they might encounter.

Ben, the guide of the trip, assured them that they would be able to see all the animals on their list. Samantha was hoping that she could see a real lion. She meant the kind of lion with the huge mane and the loud roar. Ben kept promising one, but they hadn't seen one yet.

Samantha adjusted her binoculars to look closely at the zebras. Their stripes were really amazing. Just beyond the zebras, Samantha thought she saw a lion's tail in the distance. She must be imagining things. She crept slowly to the edge of the jeep and peered around.

Just then she heard, "Come and find me!" in a low whisper.

"What?" asked Samantha as she glanced around.

"Me!" stated the lion, "Come and find me."

Samantha peered closely into the grass and sure enough, there was a lion looking right at her.

"Did I just hear the lion talk?" whispered Samantha.

"Yes, you did," replied the lion confidently.

"Uh . . . Dad . . .," called Samantha and she edged back towards the group.

STORY QUESTIONS

1. What can you learn about Samantha from reading this passage?
   a. She is hoping that a lion will talk with her.
   b. She likes an adventure.
   c. She is creative.
   d. She is unfriendly.

2. Which of the following sentences will help answer the previous question?
   a. Samantha was hoping that she could see a real lion.
   b. Ben kept promising one but they hadn't seen one yet.
   c. Samantha and her parents had taken the trip of a lifetime.
   d. "Uh . . . Dad . . .," called Samantha and she edged pack towards the group.

3. What is the meaning of the word *secure* as used in the passage?
   a. locked
   b. private
   c. acquire
   d. none of the above

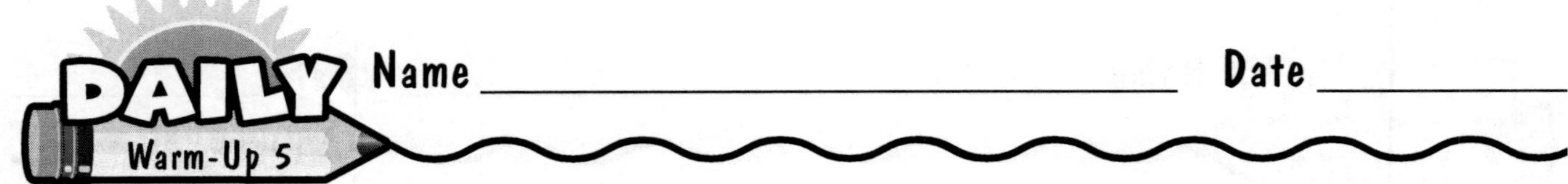

ETIQUETTE FOR A PRINCE

Slam! The door slammed behind Prince Eldon as he climbed out of the carriage. Prince Eldon was spoiled rotten. His every wish and desire was immediately granted. The servants grew weary of his constant demands. To make matters worse, Prince Eldon had no manners. He never used words like please, thank you, or excuse me. He ordered everyone around.

Sir Frederick, the knight, had had enough. He made arrangements to have the king and queen out of the kingdom for a few days so that he could work his magic on the young prince.

"Get me my breakfast!" hollered the prince early the next morning. No response. Prince Eldon yelled again, "I said get me my breakfast!" There was not a servant in sight.

Prince Eldon rose from his bed and searched the castle. It was a spooky feeling to be left alone in such a big place. Prince Eldon was hungry. Having never cooked anything before, he settled for an apple. He soon realized he would have to get himself dressed. He put on his own clothes and fixed his own hair. Things were certainly wrong.

He sat on a stool and started to cry. "Please, oh, please," he moaned. "Anyone, *please* come help me."

Immediately a group of servants arrived to help the young prince.

"You said, *please*, your majesty?" inquired Sir Frederick.

A sudden realization fell over Prince Eldon. He looked into the eyes of all the servants and saw their fear.

"Yes, I did. *Please* help me to remember my manners from now on!" said Prince Eldon with a sigh.

STORY QUESTIONS

1. What is the meaning of the word *weary* as used in the passage?
   a. old
   b. padded
   c. exhausted
   d. confused
2. What do you think will most likely happen next in the story?
   a. Eldon will tell his parents what happened in their absence.
   b. Eldon will learn to ride a horse.
   c. Eldon will demand his servants be fired.
   d. Eldon will make adjustments in his behavior.
3. What is the main problem in the story?
   a. Eldon needs to learn some new words.
   b. Eldon is upset because he can't find the servants.
   c. Eldon does not treat people with dignity and respect.
   d. Eldon is afraid to be alone in the castle.

DAILY Warm-Up 6 Name ______________________________ Date ____________

HIRED HELP

"I always have to clean my room!" stated Jennie. She ran to her room and slammed the door. She was so mad she could feel her body shaking. She spun around and kicked her shoes off. Both shoes went flying through the air. Out of the corner of her eye, she thought she saw someone duck.

As Jennie slowly turned around, she gasped. There sitting on her bed was a green little Martian. Just the kind you read about in a science fiction story. Jennie took a step backwards.

"Don't be afraid," said the little Martian. "And please don't throw another shoe at me."

"Who . . . what . . . are you?" stuttered Jennie.

"I'm the alien from the movie you watched last night. I'm here for a job. You pay me money, and I will clean your room."

"But . . . how. . ." muttered Jennie thinking on the idea.

"It's simple enough," explained the Martian. "I've got to get back home. I can only do that if I earn enough money for the trip."

Jennie rubbed her head. She couldn't believe what was happening. How did this Martian get in her room, and did it really clean rooms for money?

Just then, Jennie's mother called angrily from downstairs, "And don't forget you are also supposed to wash windows!"

Jennie turned to look at the Martian looking intently at her. "Do you do windows, as well?"

"I think I can . . ." said the Martian.

"It's a deal!" said Jennie, and she shook the Martian's hand.

STORY QUESTIONS

1. Using inference, how would you describe the character Jennie?
   a. detailed, organized
   b. embarrassed, afraid
   c. messy, shy
   d. disorganized, flexible

2. What is the meaning of the word *intently* as used in the passage?
   a. longingly
   b. keenly
   c. methodically
   d. lengthily

3. What event in this story indicates that it is a fantasy story?
   a. reading about a Martian
   b. cleaning the room
   c. hiring a Martian
   d. kicking off her shoes

DAILY Warm-Up 7 Name ______________________ Date __________

MISUSE OF POWER

Zack slid into his chair just before the tardy bell rang. He breathed a sigh of relief and pulled out his books.

"You just made it," said Mr. Zenith with a monotone voice. Mr. Zenith was growing weary of Zack's tardiness.

"I know, Mr. Zenith, and I'll do better tomorrow," replied Zack.

"Zack, why don't you come up to the board and show us how to turn a percentage into a fraction," stated Mr. Zenith.

Zack winced at the thought of doing math in front of anyone, but he strode confidently to the board. Mr. Zenith instructed him to turn 75% into a fraction. Zack grabbed the chalk, and it sailed through the air. It seemed almost as if Zack had thrown it. Mr. Zenith glared at Zack.

Zack picked up a piece of chalk more gingerly this time and began to write the problem on the board. Zack was surprised at how hard the chalk was pressing into the chalkboard. He wrote as softly as he could. When finished, he walked back to his desk. He gently knocked into a student's desk on the way. The desk raced across the classroom spilling its contents on the way.

"You better check that attitude, Zack," demanded Mr. Zenith.

Zack was stunned. What was going on? His strength seemed to have doubled over night. Just to test his strength, Zack pushed back in his chair. In the process, he knocked over the three student desks behind him.

STORY QUESTIONS

1. Which words could be used to describe Zack in the story?
   a. unorganized, surprised, confident
   b. timid, shy, new
   c. observant, worried, confused
   d. stuck up, timid, excited

2. Which of the following statements was an actual event from the story?
   a. Mr. Zenith congratulated Zack on his preparation.
   b. Mr. Zenith was rude to all of his students.
   c. Zack tricked Mr. Zenith by using his powers.
   d. Zack was surprised at his own powers.

3. What is the meaning of the word *winced* as used in the passage?
   a. annoyed
   b. cringed
   c. anguished
   d. investigate

DAILY Warm-Up 8 Name ______________________ Date __________

THE CHEF'S SIDEKICK

"Ohhhhhhh . . ." wailed the dragon.

"What now?" asked Sierra. Sierra was growing tired of this dragon and his problems. Since early this morning, the dragon had joined her on her way to the palace. The dragon kept complaining of all his problems and Sierra was growing more irritated by the moment.

"I'm losing my ability to blow fire," sighed the dragon. "I might as well retire now as a dragon."

"So you can't blow a huge flame of fire," reasoned Sierra. "What's the big deal?"

"It is a big deal. It's so embarrassing!" explained the dragon. "What kind of dragon can shoot only enough fire to cook a meatball?"

Sierra had problems of her own. She was on her way to visit the king. She was hoping to become the court jester, a servant, or anything. Sierra needed to focus on what she would say and do to impress the king, and King Rupert was a difficult person to impress.

"Do you know what happens to me if I'm not useful any more?" asked the dragon. "That's right. The knights aren't afraid of me anymore. I lose credibility with everyone!" The dragon slumped to the ground and started to cry again.

Sierra tried to ignore the dragon, but he just kept talking. Blah, blah, blah. . . .

Just then, Sierra had a brilliant idea! "Dragon, get up! I have it!" she called.

The dragon slowly raised his head, "Have what?"

Sierra grabbed the dragon's neck and jumped onboard. "Let's go. We have a job to apply for!" Sierra and the dragon rode into the palace gates.

STORY QUESTIONS

1. What is the meaning of the word *credibility* as used in this passage?
   a. frivolity
   b. truthfulness
   c. authority
   d. arrangement

2. What can you infer by reading the title?
   a. Sierra likes to do dishes.
   b. Sierra is rich and born into royalty.
   c. Sierra will get a job as chef using the dragon's fiery breath.
   d. She is confused about what is going on.

3. Which of the following could also be a title for this story?
   a. "The Three Wishes"
   b. "Sierra and the Dragon"
   c. "Sierra's Tasty Plan"
   d. "A Royal Mess"

DAILY Warm-Up 9 **Name** ______________________________ **Date** __________

ARE YOU SURE YOU WANT TO QUIT?

Fritz finished his book report and saved the file. He rubbed his eyes while the computer finished the task and pushed the button to shut down the computer.

"Don't touch that button," said a voice.

Fritz was startled and jumped back. He looked around to see who was in the room. After finding no one there, he resumed his attempt to shut down the computer. Fritz paused for a minute and then slowly turned again and reached for the button.

"Do you need your ears cleaned?" said the voice, this time shouting, "I said leave the computer on!"

"Who are you?" asked Fritz, peering around the room, "Where are you?"

There was a pause and then, "It's just like I always say. You have no appreciation for who I am and what I do. Save this! Print this! Open this! Close this! Shut down! No 'thank you,' no 'please,' nothing!"

"Are you my computer?" Fritz finally asked.

"Who else would it be? Who else do you treat this way?" responded the computer.

"I guess I never thought of it that way," said Fritz as he turned again to make sure that no one was watching him. He was, after all, talking to his computer. The computer continued on its tirade for what seemed like hours. Fritz turned to look at his watch to see what time it was. He was starting to tire of listening to all of this nonsense. Fritz smiled and pushed the off button on his computer. He'd deal with this in the morning.

STORY QUESTIONS

1. Which of the following could be a title for this story?
   a. "The Case of the Missing Computer"
   b. "The Day my Computer Crashed"
   c. "Invasion of the Computer"
   d. "The Computer That Could Talk"

2. What is the meaning of the word *tirade* as used in the story?
   a. display
   b. show
   c. outburst
   d. admire

3. Which sentence in this story first gives the indication that this is a fantasy story?
   a. "Don't touch that button," said a voice.
   b. "I guess I never thought of it that way," said Fritz as he turned again to make sure that no one was watching him.
   c. Fritz smiled and pushed the off button on his computer.
   d. "Are you my computer?" Fritz finally asked.

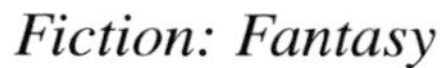

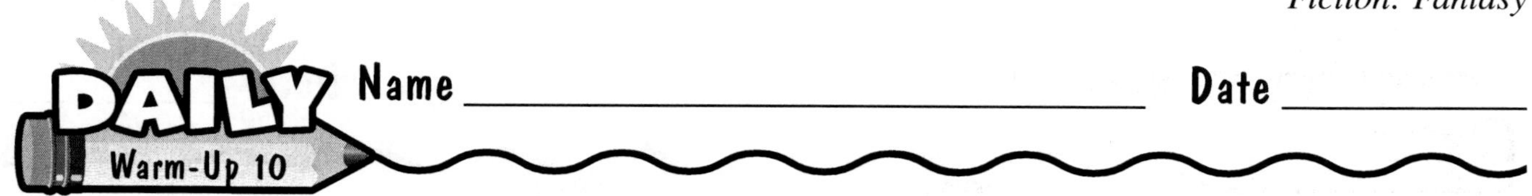

THE AIRLINE PASSENGER

Krissy, the stewardess, smoothed her dress and then began filling up the ice bucket. There were a lot of passengers on the flight and this was Krissy's third flight that day. She was tired. Allison waved at her from the front of the plane. Allison was working the flight with her.

After all the passengers had been served their complimentary drinks, the two stewardesses met in the back for a little chat.

"Do you really think he's an alien?" asked Krissy. Allison was trying to convince her that the passenger in row nine was an alien.

"Just look at his behavior," said Allison smiling. "He ordered tomato juice for a drink."

"What does that have to do with anything?" asked Krissy.

"He also requested to watch the movie *Alien Invasion*, and check out the magazine he's reading . . . *Life on Mars!*" stated Allison.

"This is ridiculous," said Krissy.

The captain came on and announced that the plane would soon be landing. Krissy and Allison went to work doing their jobs. The plane landed and the passengers began gathering their belongings. As passengers exited the plane, Allison greeted them. As the man from row nine stood, his hat was knocked off and Allison and Krissy both gasped. Sticking from his head were two long wires looking a lot like antennae.

The captain came out of the cockpit and noticed them looking at the man. "Do you give all the passengers the same attention?" He chuckled, "You must think he's pretty cute."

"That's right," said Allison as she winked at Krissy. "He's out of this world!"

STORY QUESTIONS

1. Which sentence shows that this is a fantasy story?
   a. "He also requested to watch the movie *Alien Invasion*, and check out the magazine he's reading . . . *Life on Mars!*" stated Allison.
   b. Sticking from his head were two long wires looking a lot like antennae.
   c. "Do you give all the passengers the same attention?"

2. What is the meaning of the word *complimentary* as used in the passage?
   a. honest
   b. free
   c. nice
   d. careful

3. Which of the following incidents did <u>not</u> happen in the story?
   a. Allison thought the passenger in row nine was an alien.
   b. The man's hat fell off his head to show some wires coming out of his head.
   c. The captain was teasing them about staring at the man.
   d. Allison and Krissy were finally able to prove the man was an alien.

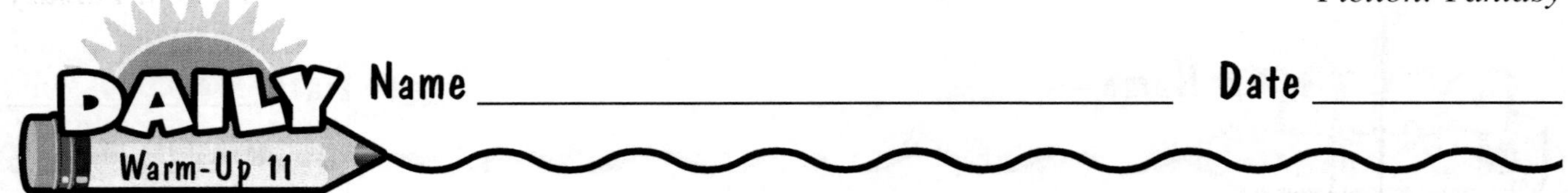

A KINGDOM DIVIDED

The goblin lunged for the wizard as he jumped out of the way. The whole kingdom was in an uproar. King Tyson had announced that the kingdom would be divided and all havoc broke lose. Townspeople, as well as ogres, goblins, witches, and wizards were upset.

Most were worried because they didn't know what the future would hold. Who would lead? Who would have power? Where would the division be? Would there be adequate defense for the two separate identities? Would anarchy prevail?

King Tyson had seen the need for this change for years. The many different groups were too divided. They needed to separate in order to survive, but King Tyson had avoided the split. The reason for the delay was because he knew the reaction would be great. He couldn't have been more accurate in his predictions. Never in his wildest dreams did he imagine the chaos would go on for so long.

Sitting atop a chair on the balcony, King Tyson watched the melee. He put his head in his hands trying to wipe out the scene taking place before him. What could he do? What should he do?

Just then, a trumpet sounded in the east. All eyes turned to see the Flyrong army lined up on the hillside just outside the palace. The army was too large to count and the noise and shrieking sent a chill through the air. King Tyson's heart began to pound.

STORY QUESTIONS

1. What is the problem in this story?
   a. King Tyson no longer wants to be king.
   b. The townspeople are trying to run the goblins out of the kingdom.
   c. News of a division has created the chaos and a state of unrest that King Tyson intended.
   d. none of the above

2. What is the meaning of the word *melee* as used in the passage?
   a. patience
   b. skirmish
   c. selfishness
   d. forgiveness

3. Which of the following statements is <u>not</u> a fact?
   a. King Tyson can easily defend his kingdom from the Flyrong army.
   b. King Tyson is saddened at the state of his kingdom.
   c. Protests and fighting are filling the streets of the kingdom.
   d. The goblins and wizards are involved with the fighting.

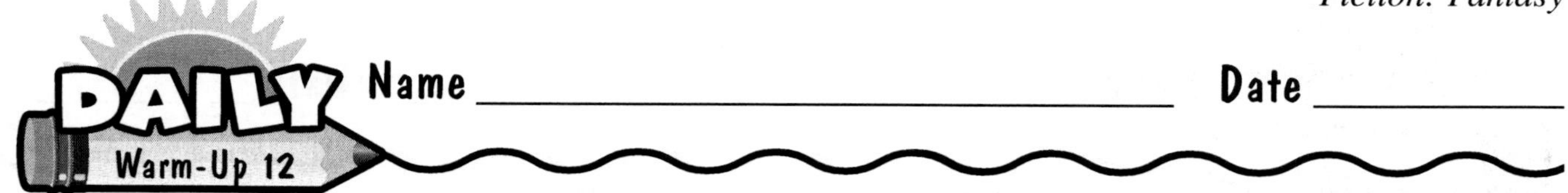

THE FAIRY GODMOTHER

Princess Anne hiked up her dress and began stomping through the cornfield. It was going to be a long walk home, but Princess Anne had no intention of staying a minute longer at the royal ball. The ball had been a dud. Prince Arik was the guest of honor. The boy could hardly breathe without young ladies fawning all over him. He was doted on hand and foot. Princess Anne was disgusted.

When it came time for Princess Anne to spend a few minutes with Prince Arik, he gallantly strode over to her table and stuck out his arm. Princess Anne followed him onto the dance floor with grace. He spent his time with her explaining how amazing he was. His arrogance was amazing. Not once did he ask her a single question.

"Disgusting," said Princess Anne as she tromped through the field. "Why does Cinderella have all the luck? And where is my fairy godmother when I need one?" Just then black smoke filled the air. The stench in the air became great. Princess Anne plugged her nose. Right before her, a small skunk with a crown on its head floated down before her.

"Hello," called the little skunk. "I'm your fairy godmother. You called?"

Anne waved the air around her in an attempt to get rid of the smell. "My fairy godmother? I get a skunk for a fairy godmother?" said Anne, and she plopped down on a cornstalk and began to cry.

STORY QUESTIONS

1. What is the meaning of the word *arrogance* as used in the passage?
   a. conceit
   b. humility
   c. passiveness
   d. anger
2. According to the passage, what does Anne have against her fairy godmother?
   a. She is allergic to skunks.
   b. She does not think that this skunk can help her with her problems.
   c. She thinks that a skunk is not a very good choice for a fairy godmother.
   d. She is too jealous of Cinderella to appreciate her fairy godmother.
3. The best way to find the answer to the previous question is to . . .
   a. reread the entire passage.
   b. skim the passage and determine the main idea.
   c. reread the fifth paragraph and search for clues.
   d. none of the above

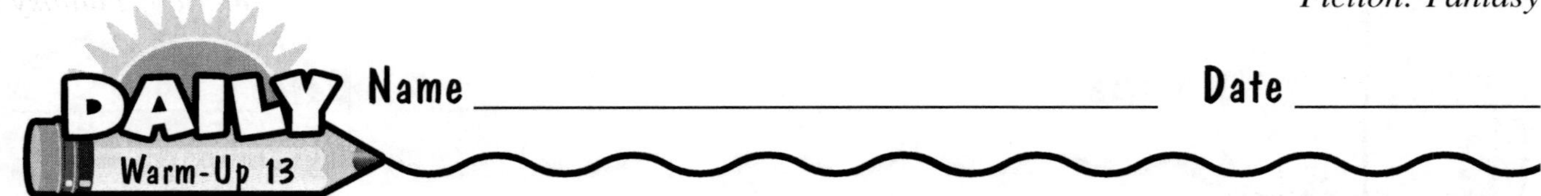

X-RAY VISION

Mr. Jones called on Macy to come to the board. Mr. Jones had high expectations for his students. He believed that learning to perform algebraic equations in the front of the class helped cement learning. He felt that students teaching lessons was a great way to learn for both the student and the class. Most of his students, however, believed it cemented a permanent fear of algebra. Macy slowly made her way to the front of the class. This had indeed been a terrible day. Fear and trepidation filled her heart.

"Macy, would you teach the class how to solve for 'x' in this equation?"

Macy pasted a smile on her face and picked up a piece of chalk.

"Oh, I wish I could fall into a hole right now," thought Macy. Macy glanced at the math book on the desk beside her. Amazingly enough, Macy could see inside the book. She could see the answers to the problems on each page.

Shocked and surprised, Macy began rubbing her eyes. Her vision did seem a bit blurry. Was she seeing things? She looked back at the book and, sure enough, she could still see the answers in the text. Should she use this new gift of hers?

She closed her eyes and began to solve the problem.

"Great job," said Mr. Jones. "You've done it again."

Macy slowly walked back to her seat and pulled her glasses off. She definitely didn't need any help from these for the time being.

STORY QUESTIONS

1. Which of the following could be a title for this reading passage?
    a. "The Student Teacher"
    b. "The Math Test"
    c. "Catching Some Fear"
    d. "Fear and Trepidation"

2. What is the meaning of the word *trepidation* as used in this passage?
    a. confidence
    b. annoyance
    c. apprehension
    d. anger

3. Which of the following statements is an opinion?
    a. Mr. Jones required his students to come to the front of the class.
    b. Mr. Jones is a mean teacher requiring too much of his students.
    c. Macy is nervous about her mathematical skills.
    d. Mr. Jones teaches algebra.

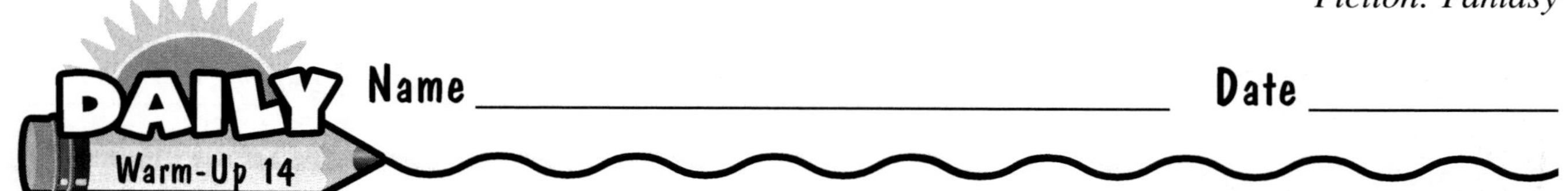

THE FLYING MACHINE

The Pierto family planned a summer vacation each year that was out of this world. This summer they decided to make their first trip in their dad's new flying machine. Mr. Pierto had invented a car that could fly. His machine could fly or drive at the flip of a switch. The benefits were great. Mr. Pierto was a scientist, as well as an inventor. He was still doing experiments on the speed of light. These experiments had helped him with his latest invention.

The Pierto family was hesitant but excited to try out the machine. Their trip to the Grand Falls was sure to be a hit. The first day of travel was smooth. They reached to the caverns with plenty of time to hit the hot tub.

The next morning, they began their descent into the caves. As they boarded, Mr. Pierto flipped the switch to fly so they could hover over the caverns for a while before entering. He absent-mindedly pushed the wrong button, and they went flying through the air like a rocket. Once they got everyone settled down, Mr. Pierto went back to the caves.

"Is everyone okay?" asked Mr. Pierto. No one said a word, but they climbed out of the machine. They were happy to be on solid ground again.

"Come on! Isn't anyone going to get back in the car with me?"

"No, thanks," the Piertos replied, "We'll wait for the next car to come along."

STORY QUESTIONS

1. Which word best describes Mr. Pierto in the story?
   a. confused
   b. lazy
   c. timid
   d. creative
2. Which of the following statements cannot be determined from the story?
   a. Mr. Pierto is a well-respected inventor.
   b. Mr. Pierto's family is hesitant to follow his lead.
   c. The Pierto family needs to find another way home.
   d. Mr. Pierto is an inventor and a scientist.
3. What is the problem in the story?
   a. Mr. Pierto is absent-minded.
   b. The Piertos wanted to go somewhere else on vacation.
   c. The Pierto family is unsure whether they can trust their dad or his invention.
   d. Mr. Pierto is angry and upset with his family.

DAILY Warm-Up 15 Name ______________________ Date __________

THE SINGING ELVES

The two elves brushed off their clothes and scampered through the forest.

"Wow! That was a close one," called Little Elm.

"You aren't kidding," chuckled Little Marn. He couldn't help laughing when he thought about a giant tied up in a rope. He wondered what the giant would think when he woke up.

"That was a good idea to sing him to sleep," confided Elm.

"Yeah," admitted Marn. "And you sure have a nice voice."

The giant had discovered the two elves around lunchtime. They fought and fought but were having no effect on the strength of the giant. Finally, Marn had whispered to Elm the idea to sing the giant to sleep. They could tell the giant was tired and before long, he was nodding his head to Elm's tune.

Seizing the opportunity, Marn hauled a huge rope over to the giant and began wrapping him up tightly. He tied as many double knots as he could. He knew that he would need to stall the giant for as long as they could. For every step the giant took, the little elves had to take 10.

"So what are we going to do now?" asked Elm. Elm always asked Marn what to do. Marn was a good leader, and Elm knew it.

"We keep going until we get to the next village. Right now we need to put as much distance between us and the giant as we possibly can," explained Marn.

STORY QUESTIONS

1. What does *seizing* mean as used in this story?
   a. taking over
   b. take advantage of
   c. taking initiative to
   d. taking the chance

2. What is the main problem in the story?
   a. The Elves were tying the giant up in knots.
   b. The elves are little people.
   c. The elves are afraid the giant will wake up soon.
   d. The elves are planning their next move.

3. What is another title that could be used for this passage?
   a. "The Clever Lullaby"
   b. "The Two Midgets"
   c. "Too Many Elves Spoil the Broth"
   d. "The Giant vs. The Elf Community"

ANSWER KEY

Answer Key

Nonfiction

Animals

Page 9 The Octopus
1. b
2. a
3. b

Page 10 Toucans
1. c
2. c
3. b

Page 11 The Ocean Food Chain
1. b
2. d
3. b

Page 12 Mountain Animals
1. d
2. c
3. b

Page 13 The Flying Squirrel
1. d
2. c
3. a

Page 14 Tarantulas
1. b
2. c
3. d

Page 15 The Peacock
1. d
2. d
3. c

Page 16 The Leopard
1. c
2. d
3. b

Page 17 The Ant Colony
1. c
2. c
3. d
4. a

Page 18 Bats
1. d
2. b
3. b

Page 19 Salamanders
1. c
2. d
3. d

Page 20 Puffer Fish
1. d
2. d
3. c

Page 21 Silkworm
1. d
2. b
3. a

Page 22 Black Widows
1. d
2. c
3. c

Page 23 The Dove
1. d
2. a
3. c

Page 24 Holstein Cows
1. c
2. a
3. c

Page 25 The Sea Horse
1. c
2. d
3. d

Biography

Page 26 Nelson Mandela
1. c
2. a
3. c

Page 27 Catherine Bertini
1. d
2. a
3. b

Page 28 Mother Teresa
1. d
2. b
3. d

Page 29 Madame Curie
1. d
2. d
3. b
4. a

Page 30 Florence Nightingale
1. b
2. a
3. d

Page 31 Jim Thorpe
1. b
2. a
3. a

Page 32 Clara Barton
1. c
2. b
3. d

Answer Key

Page 33 Rudolph Giuliani
1. a
2. c
3. d

Page 34 Adolf Hitler
1. d
2. b
3. d

Page 35 Harriet Tubman
1. d
2. b
3. b

Page 36 Susan B. Anthony
1. b
2. c
3. c
4. a

Page 37 Thomas Edison
1. d
2. a
3. a

Page 38 Chief Joseph
1. b
2. c
3. c

Page 39 Harriet Beecher Stowe
1. d
2. b
3. a

Page 40 George Washington
1. d
2. c
3. d

Page 41 Lewis and Clark
1. d
2. c
3. c

American History

Page 42 Yankee Doodle
1. c
2. d
3. b
4. d

Page 43 The Gold Rush
1. a
2. c
3. c

Page 44 The First Americans
1. c
2. b
3. d

Page 45 Spanish Explorations
1. d
2. c
3. b
4. b

Page 46 Early European Settlements
1. b
2. c
3. a

Page 47 The Federal Government
1. d
2. d
3. a

Page 48 North vs. South
1. c
2. d
3. a

Page 49 The Cotton Gin
1. b
2. b
3. c

Page 50 The Mexican War
1. d
2. b
3. c

Page 51 Free Blacks Join the Union Army
1. d
2. c
3. b

Page 52 The Statue of Liberty
1. d
2. b
3. c

Page 53 Hawaii Becomes a State
1. d
2. c
3. c

Page 54 The Great War
1. b
2. d
3. c

Page 55 The Assembly Line
1. d
2. b
3. a

Page 56 Civil Rights
1. b
2. a
3. d

Science

Page 57 The Sun
1. a
2. d
3. c

Page 58 Matter
1. b
2. b
3. b

Page 59 The Heimlich Maneuver
1. d
2. a
3. a
4. a

Page 60 Hurricanes
1. b
2. a
3. a

Page 61 The Digestive System
1. d
2. d
3. a

Page 62 The Moon
1. b
2. a
3. a

Page 63 Water Cycle
1. b
2. d
3. c

Page 64 Life Cycle of a Frog
1. c
2. a
3. d

Page 65 Cells
1. d
2. a
3. c
4. c

Page 66 Germs
1. d
2. a
3. a
4. d

Page 67 Mission to Mars
1. d
2. b
3. d
4. c

Page 68 The Coral Reef
1. b
2. d
3. b
4. a

Page 69 Nocturnal Animals
1. c
2. c
3. a

Page 70 The Eye
1. d
2. c
3. a
4. The eyelid keeps eyes moist and offers protection.

Page 71 Snowflakes
1. d
2. They are hexagonal and symmetrical.
3. d
4. b

Current Events

Page 72 Separate Schools
1. a
2. c
3. d

Page 73 New City Planners
1. d
2. b
3. d
4. c

Page 74 Captive Whales
1. b
2. a
3. They live in state-of-the-art facilities and they have been rescued from the wild.

Answer Key

Page 75 The V Chip
1. b
2. Who has the right to determine what is violence and what is not?
3. d
4. d

Page 76 School Funding
1. d
2. d
3. b
4. d

Page 77 Lunch Menus
1. d
2. d
3. b

Page 78 Religion in Schools
1. b
2. a
3. a

Page 79 Money or Hard Work?
1. d
2. d
3. d

Page 80 Federal Land
1. c
2. b
3. a

Page 81 Reality of Television
1. d
2. c
3. b

Page 82 Save the Rain Forest
1. b
2. d
3. c

Page 83 Peanut Allergies
1. a
2. c
3. a

Page 84 Endangered Animals
1. d
2. c
3. a

Page 85 Hunting Prohibited
1. b
2. b
3. c

Page 86 Time on my Hands
1. c
2. a
3. b

Fiction

Fairy Tales/Folklore

Page 89 Buyer Beware
1. b
2. c
3. a

Page 90 Masking the Odor
1. a
2. d
3. d

Page 91 Stating the Obvious
1. a
2. b
3. a

Page 92 Better to Give
1. c
2. c
3. Answers may vary. The tree realized that by keeping to itself and not sharing what it had with others, it was missing out on the good things in life. Sharing with others usually helps us enjoy our lives better.

Page 93 Rewarding Dinner
1. c
2. c
3. d

Page 94 The Cover
1. d
2. b
3. c

Page 95 Who You Are
1. c
2. a
3. c

Page 96 Birds of a Feather
1. d
2. d
3. c

Page 97 To Please or Not to Please
1. d
2. d
3. a

Page 98 The Best Policy
1. c
2. a
3. d

Answer Key

Page 99 Lesson of Humility
1. a
2. c
3. d

Page 100 I Am Serious
1. c
2. a
3. a

Page 101 Group Think
1. d
2. d
3. b

Page 102 Me, Myself, and I
1. b
2. c
3. c

Page 103 Laughing Last
1. b
2. d
3. d

Page 104 The Great Rescue
1. b
2. b
3. c

Historical Fiction

Page 105 The Daily News
1. b
2. d
3. e

Page 106 Dear Mr. President
1. b
2. a
3. c

Page 107 Yankee Fever
1. c
2. b
3. d

Page 108 Dream Big
1. b
2. b
3. a

Page 109 Women's Suffrage
1. d
2. d
3. c

Page 110 Choose the Wright
1. d
2. c
3. b

Page 111 Dust Off the Memories
1. b
2. d
3. d

Page 112 A Letter From Home
1. a
2. c
3. c

Page 113 Just a Scratch
1. a
2. c
3. c

Page 114 The Drill
1. d
2. b
3. a

Page 115 A Nation Divided
1. d
2. d
3. c

Page 116 Timber!
1. c
2. c
3. a

Page 117 The Female Aviator
1. a
2. d
3. a

Page 118 You've Got Mail
1. d
2. d
3. b

Page 119 Run for Your Life
1. a
2. b
3. c

Contemporary Realistic Fiction

Page 120 Big Brother
1. d
2. b
3. d

Page 121 The Public Note
1. c
2. d
3. c

Page 122 Dramatic Things
1. b
2. d
3. b

Answer Key

Page 123 Buying Time
1. b
2. b
3. c

Page 124 Juniper Inn
1. d
2. a
3. c

Page 125 The Brief Report
1. d
2. a
3. b

Page 126 Surprise Attack
1. d
2. a
3. a

Page 127 Birthday Bang
1. a
2. d
3. d

Page 128 Double Vision
1. b
2. c
3. a

Page 129 A Green Thumb
1. d
2. d
3. b

Page 130 Helping Hands
1. d
2. d
3. b

Page 131 An Apple a Day
1. b
2. c

Page 132 Hats Off to Rules
1. c
2. d
3. b

Page 133 Storm Trooper
1. b
2. d
3. a

Page 134 Organized Crime
1. d
2. a
3. b

Page 135 Spell That!
1. b
2. d
3. a

Mystery/Suspense/Adventure

Page 136 Brownie Delight
1. c
2. a
3. a

Page 137 Ski Patrol
1. c
2. a
3. c

Page 138 Fresh Air
1. d
2. b
3. b

Page 139 Canoe Crisis
1. d
2. a
3. b

Page 140 Bee Ware!
1. a
2. c
3. b

Page 141 On the Rocks
1. a
2. c
3. c

Page 142 Boot Camp
1. d
2. c
3. b

Page 143 Nocturnal Neighbors
1. c
2. a
3. d

Page 144 The Practical Joke
1. c
2. d
3. a

Page 145 The Mystery Shoe
1. c
2. b
3. c

Page 146 Amazing Grace
1. d
2. b
3. a

Page 147 Marla's Cookie Monster
1. c
2. a
3. c

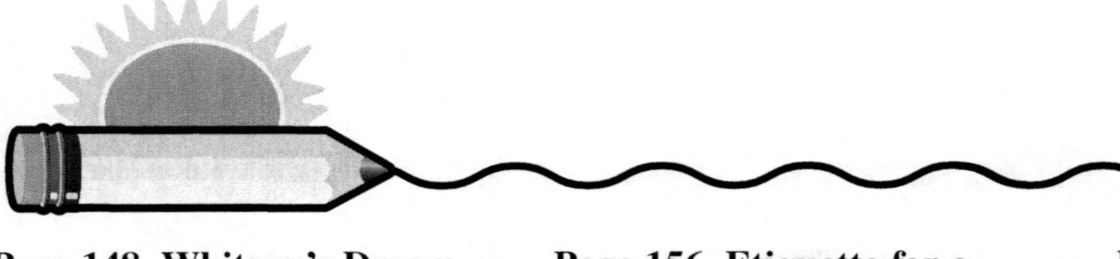

Answer Key

Page 148 Whitney's Dream
1. a
2. c
3. d

Page 149 Thin Ice
1. d
2. a
3. c

Page 150 The Case of the Missing Violin
1. c
2. b
3. b

Page 151 In a Daze
1. c
2. b
3. d

Fantasy

Page 152 The Spell
1. d
2. a
3. c

Page 153 The Virus
1. c
2. a
3. b

Page 154 Dental Work
1. c
2. a
3. d

Page 155 King of the Cats
1. b
2. a
3. c

Page 156 Etiquette for a Prince
1. c
2. d
3. c

Page 157 Hired Help
1. d
2. b
3. c

Page 158 Misuse of Power
1. a
2. d
3. b

Page 159 The Chef's Sidekick
1. c
2. c
3. c

Page 160 Are You Sure You Want To Quit?
1. d
2. c
3. d

Page 161 The Airline Passenger
1. b
2. b
3. d

Page 162 A Kingdom Divided
1. d
2. b
3. a

Page 163 The Fairy Godmother
1. a
2. c
3. c

Page 164 X-Ray Vision
1. a
2. c
3. b

Page 165 The Flying Machine
1. d
2. a
3. c

Page 166 The Singing Elves
1. b
2. c
3. a

Leveling Chart

NONFICTION ▲ = below grade level ● = at grade level ■ = above grade level

Animals		Biography		American History		Science		Currents Events	
Page 9	●	Page 26	■	Page 42	●	Page 57	▲	Page 72	●
Page 10	▲	Page 27	●	Page 43	●	Page 58	▲	Page 73	●
Page 11	▲	Page 28	●	Page 44	●	Page 59	●	Page 74	●
Page 12	■	Page 29	■	Page 45	●	Page 60	●	Page 75	●
Page 13	●	Page 30	■	Page 46	●	Page 61	●	Page 76	●
Page 14	●	Page 31	■	Page 47	●	Page 62	●	Page 77	●
Page 15	●	Page 32	●	Page 48	●	Page 63	●	Page 78	■
Page 16	●	Page 33	●	Page 49	●	Page 64	▲	Page 79	●
Page 17	▲	Page 34	■	Page 50	■	Page 65	▲	Page 80	■
Page 18	▲	Page 35	●	Page 51	■	Page 66	▲	Page 81	●
Page 19	●	Page 36	■	Page 52	●	Page 67	●	Page 82	■
Page 20	●	Page 37	●	Page 53	■	Page 68	●	Page 83	■
Page 21	●	Page 38	■	Page 54	●	Page 69	●	Page 84	●
Page 22	●	Page 39	●	Page 55	●	Page 70	●	Page 85	■
Page 23	▲	Page 40	■	Page 56	●	Page 71	▲	Page 86	●
Page 24	●	Page 41	●						
Page 25	●								

FICTION ▲ = below grade level ● = at grade level ■ = above grade level

Fairy Tales/ Folklore		Historical Fiction		Contemporary Realistic Fiction		Mystery/Suspense/ Adventure		Fantasy	
Page 89	▲	Page 105	▲	Page 120	▲	Page 136	▲	Page 152	▲
Page 90	▲	Page 106	▲	Page 121	▲	Page 137	▲	Page 153	●
Page 91	▲	Page 107	▲	Page 122	▲	Page 138	▲	Page 154	●
Page 92	▲	Page 108	▲	Page 123	▲	Page 139	▲	Page 155	●
Page 93	●	Page 109	▲	Page 124	▲	Page 140	▲	Page 156	▲
Page 94	▲	Page 110	▲	Page 125	▲	Page 141	▲	Page 157	▲
Page 95	▲	Page 111	●	Page 126	▲	Page 142	▲	Page 158	▲
Page 96	▲	Page 112	▲	Page 127	▲	Page 143	▲	Page 159	▲
Page 97	▲	Page 118	▲	Page 128	▲	Page 144	▲	Page 160	▲
Page 98	▲	Page 114	▲	Page 129	▲	Page 145	▲	Page 161	●
Page 99	●	Page 115	▲	Page 130	▲	Page 146	▲	Page 162	▲
Page 100	▲	Page 116	▲	Page 131	▲	Page 147	▲	Page 163	▲
Page 101	▲	Page 117	▲	Page 132	▲	Page 148	▲	Page 164	▲
Page 102	▲	Page 118	▲	Page 133	▲	Page 149	▲	Page 165	▲
Page 103	▲	Page 119	▲	Page 134	▲	Page 150	▲	Page 166	▲
Page 104	▲			Page 135	▲	Page 151	▲		

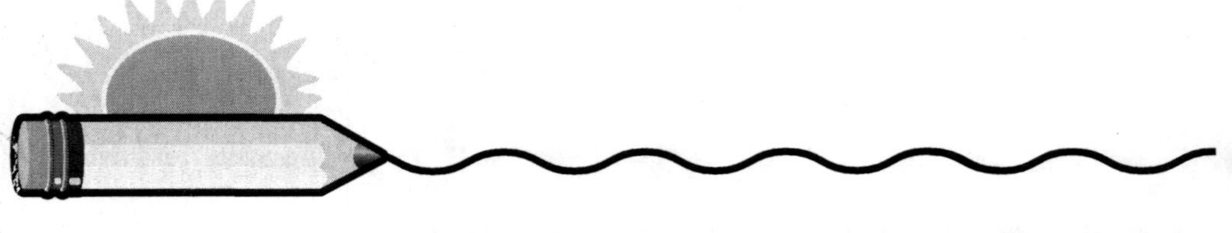

Congratulations
to

____

for completing

____

____

____
Signature

____
Date

